C000115354

## Opting Out of Cong

This book provides a candidate entry explanation for partisan polarization in the U.S. Congress. Danielle M. Thomsen draws on a wide array of data to show that ideological moderates are less likely to run for and remain in Congress than those at the extremes. The book introduces a party fit argument for why moderates have opted out of congressional politics. It suggests that the personal and career benefits of congressional service have diminished for liberal Republicans and conservative Democrats as the parties have drifted apart. Although the political center has long been deemed a coveted position in the legislature, it is now a lonely and lowly place to be. *Opting Out of Congress* argues that partisan polarization is unlikely to diminish if ideological moderates do not run for office. Reformers who seek to restore bipartisanship in Congress must consider how to encourage moderates to launch congressional candidacies.

Danielle M. Thomsen is an assistant professor of political science at Syracuse University. Her research has been published in the *Journal of Politics, Legislative Studies Quarterly,* and *Political Research Quarterly,* and it has been featured in the *New York Times,* the *Washington Post,* and other media outlets. In 2015, she received the E.E. Schattschneider Award for the best dissertation in American politics. She has received financial support from the National Science Foundation, the American Association of University Women, and the Dirksen Congressional Center.

# Opting Out of Congress

*Partisan Polarization and the Decline of Moderate Candidates*

**DANIELLE M. THOMSEN**

*Syracuse University*

CAMBRIDGE
UNIVERSITY PRESS

# CAMBRIDGE
## UNIVERSITY PRESS

University Printing House, Cambridge CB2 8BS, United Kingdom

One Liberty Plaza, 20th Floor, New York, NY 10006, USA

477 Williamstown Road, Port Melbourne, VIC 3207, Australia

314-321, 3rd Floor, Plot 3, Splendor Forum, Jasola District Centre, New Delhi-110025, India

79 Anson Road, #06-04/06, Singapore 079906

Cambridge University Press is part of the University of Cambridge.

It furthers the University's mission by disseminating knowledge in the pursuit of education, learning and research at the highest international levels of excellence.

www.cambridge.org
Information on this title: www.cambridge.org/9781316635032
DOI: 10.1017/9781316872055

© Danielle M. Thomsen 2017

First published 2017
First paperback edition 2017

*A catalogue record for this publication is available from the British Library*

ISBN 978-1-107-18367-4 Hardback
ISBN 978-1-316-63503-2 Paperback

# Contents

# Figures

# Tables

# Acknowledgments

I am deeply indebted to those who helped make this book happen. I am especially grateful for the direction I received from my dissertation committee members. Suzanne Mettler advised my project and provided invaluable guidance during graduate school and as I was completing the book. Her confidence in and support of me have been unwavering, and I feel fortunate to have been shaped and molded by a scholar with such a broad view of American politics. Peter Enns devoted countless hours to my day-to-day research obstacles, and he taught me many larger lessons about social science in the process. Mary Katzenstein has guided me on both research and teaching fronts over the past several years, and she continues to be an enormously influential mentor and role model.

I spent one year of graduate school at Duke University, and I returned afterward as a postdoctoral fellow at the Political Institutions and Public Choice Program (PIPC). John Aldrich and Dave Rohde gave me the time, resources, and support that I needed to write this book. John has an enthusiasm and energy that is unmatched, and he has been an inspiration to me since my first day at PIPC. Dave gave me crucial advice at multiple stages of this project, and I hope the parallels between this book and his work shine through brightly. In addition, this manuscript benefited greatly from a book workshop that PIPC generously hosted. Nick Carnes, Frances Lee, Sean Theriault, John, and Dave took valuable time out of their schedules to read and comment on the entire manuscript. Their suggestions were instrumental in the development of the book, and I am grateful for the guidance each of them has given me since the workshop as well.

xiv                        *Acknowledgments*

I also thank other faculty members at Cornell and Duke who helped me at many points and to participants at department seminars at both universities for their valuable comments on my research. Chris Anderson provided feedback on my dissertation, and Chris Way gave detailed comments on various parts of the project. Bryce Corrigan saved the day with methodological tips on many occasions and continues to do so. I greatly appreciated various conversations with Richard Bensel, Steve Coate, Michael Jones-Correa, Adam Levine, Theodore Lowi, Kevin Morrison, David Patel, Elizabeth Sanders, Sidney Tarrow, and Jessica Weeks during my time at Cornell. At Duke, Bill Keech provided thoughtful suggestions on my research and supported my academic development along the way. Mat McCubbins and Georg Vanberg were particularly helpful at several moments. I also had useful and enjoyable discussions with Tom Carsey, Jason Roberts, and Jim Stimson at UNC.

I have accumulated more debts since joining the faculty at Syracuse University. I cannot express enough gratitude for the time, flexibility, and institutional support I have received from the Maxwell School of Citizenship and Public Affairs, which allowed me to complete the manuscript. I am thankful to my colleagues for sharing their thoughts and suggestions with me as well. I have had helpful conversations about the project and the publishing process with Keith Bybee, Elizabeth Cohen, Chris Faricy, Tom Keck, Audie Klotz, and Dan McDowell. Shana Gadarian and Spencer Piston provided support, advice, and encouragement on many occasions, and they gave insightful comments on the direction and development of the manuscript. I also thank the undergraduates at SU who eagerly discussed the book with me.

Many people provided substantial feedback on various parts of the manuscript. These include Jack Collens, Larry Evans, Jeff Harden, Cherie Maestas, Dan Magleby, Seth Masket, Michael McDonald, Tracy Osborn, Kira Sanbonmatsu, Shauna Shames, John Sides, Michele Swers, Chris Warshaw, and Jason Windett. I received exceptional comments on the project from participants at the Han-Jyun Hou Conference at Binghamton University. Rotem Ben-Shachar helped with several last-minute proofreading requests. Timur Ohloff carefully combed through the entire manuscript. Three anonymous reviewers gave incredibly constructive and thoughtful comments. Patrick McGraw improved the manuscript greatly at the final stage. I am incredibly grateful to Robert Dreesen, the Senior Editor at Cambridge University Press, for his support of the project, and to Robert Judkins and Brianda Reyes at Cambridge as well.

This book would not have been possible without the labors of many other individuals who generously shared their data with me. I am most grateful to Adam Bonica, who not only allowed me to use his data from the outset but also provided helpful responses to my many questions. Chris Tausanovitch and Chris Warshaw were willing to share their district-level ideology estimates very early on as well. Gary Jacobson shared his comprehensive data on congressional elections. I also thank John Evans and John Swain for sharing their retirement data and for their useful follow-ups at various points. The Center for Responsive Politics provided extensive data on newly elected members, and I am grateful to Doug Weber for his assistance. Finally, the Center for American Women and Politics has been invaluable to gender and politics scholars, and Kira Sanbonmatsu has been especially helpful in discussing and sharing these data with me.

My research has received financial support from the National Science Foundation, the Dirksen Congressional Center, the American Association of University Women, and the John L. Senior Chair of American Institutions at Cornell University. I also thank the *Journal of Politics* and *Legislative Studies Quarterly* for allowing me to reprint material from articles published there. In addition, I am sincerely grateful to the former members of Congress, party officials, and staff members who were willing to be interviewed. They took time away from their very busy schedules to share their experiences and insights, and I gained an enormous amount of knowledge and perspective through these conversations. My deepest thanks to them all. Sharon Witiw at the U.S. Association of Former Members of Congress (FMC) was instrumental in connecting me to these members, and I greatly appreciate all of her help as well.

I would also like to acknowledge the friends who made my life better as I worked on this project. I had many good laughs with Rotem Ben-Shachar, Sheila Bridges, Aileen Cardona, Scott Clifford, Molly Demarest, Michael Dichio, Mark Dudley, Melanie Freeze, Mariana Giusti, Jason Hecht, Julianna Koch, Tobias Konitzer, Tim Ryan, Bailey Sanders, Sheryl Ann Simpson, Simon Weschle, and Martha Wilfahrt. I am additionally grateful to Joe Kunkel and Tomasz Inglot, who inspired me to pursue this path many moons ago. Mike Miller has been a mentor and friend since Government 111, more than a decade ago. At Syracuse, I always look forward to women's dinners, and I am thankful to my friends here for their encouragement and support in the home stretch. Mohammad Nikkhah Mojdehi makes my days joyful and warm, and I am grateful for his big heart and unwavering optimism. I feel truly lucky that our paths have crossed.

Finally, I want to thank those who know me the best and have seen me through it all. My parents have been a constant source of love and support. I am deeply grateful for the example they set and for their endless guidance and strength. My sister is my best friend, and I am thankful for the lessons she has taught me, the wisdom she has shared, and the adventures we have had together. This book is dedicated to my family.

# Introduction

The sharp rise in partisan polarization in the United States Congress has been one of the most prominent topics of academic debate for the past decade. The ideological gulf between the Republican and Democratic parties has widened in almost every election since the 1970s. Members of Congress are now first and foremost partisans who adhere to the party line, and the distance between the two parties is at a record high (e.g., McCarty, Poole, and Rosenthal 2006). The absence of moderates from congressional office today is particularly striking from a historical perspective, because just 40 years ago more than half of members of Congress were at the ideological center. The hollowing out of the political center has had a deleterious impact on the policymaking process, and the lack of compromise and negotiation has impeded legislative action on a variety of pressing issues, including immigration, criminal justice reform, and paid employment leave.

Equally troubling as the increase in polarization is the nature of contemporary partisan conflict. The divides on roll-call votes reveal only part of the story. There is another dimension of political conflict that is related to, but distinct from, ideological polarization. This is what Lee (2009) calls partisan bickering and what Theriault (2013) refers to as partisan warfare. Theriault (2013, 11) writes, "The warfare dimension taps into the strategies that go beyond defeating your opponents to humiliating them, go beyond questioning your opponents' judgment to questioning their motives, and go beyond fighting the good legislative fight to destroying the institution and the legislative process." The gravity of the current situation stems from the huge ideological disparity between the parties coupled with the partisan warfare that pervades the congressional environment. One of the more visible effects of the political brinksmanship in Washington occurred in 2011 when the debacle over the debt ceiling resulted in the first-ever downgrade of the U.S. credit rating by Standard & Poor's.

Unsurprisingly, very few Americans are satisfied with the current state of congressional politics. Although voters have long been known to hate Congress but love their own congressman (Fenno 1978), congressional approval ratings have plummeted in recent years. The number of Americans who approved of Congress's job performance sank to a record low of 9 percent in 2013. Thirty years ago, these ratings were three to four times higher than they are today. Gallup has tracked public evaluations of Congress since 1974, and prior to 2008, congressional approval had fallen below 20 percent only twice, in 1979 and 1992 (Riffkin 2014). Now around 80 percent of Americans consistently disapprove of congressional performance. Furthermore, in 2013, the top reason that Americans gave for their disapproval was partisan bickering and gridlock (28 percent); another 21 percent cited Congress's failure to get anything done, and 11 percent said that Congress puts politics ahead of the country (Saad 2013). Notably, these figures are low among both Republicans and Democrats, whereas historically those who support the majority party have had a much more favorable opinion of Congress (Riffkin 2014). In short, the public is not happy with Congress, it is not happy with the partisanship and gridlock in Washington, and the unhappiness is distributed across Republicans as well as Democrats.

Those who bemoan the hyperpartisanship in Congress have not sat by quietly. Three culprits are widely believed to be contributing to partisan polarization: gerrymandering, big money in politics, and primary election systems. Many of the recent policy reforms have attempted to address these issues head on, although they have been largely ineffective to date and polarization has continued to grow unabated. The basic logic of the gerrymandering hypothesis is that districts have become increasingly safe, electoral competition has declined, and only conservative Republicans and liberal Democrats can win in conservative and liberal districts. However, the academic consensus is that gerrymandering matters anywhere from a little bit to not at all (McCarty et al. 2006, 2009; Carson et al. 2007; Theriault 2008; Abramowitz 2010; see Barber and McCarty 2015 for a review). First, Senate and at-large congressional districts have experienced rising polarization without redistricting. Moreover, McCarty et al. (2009) find that polarization is due to the differences in how Republicans and Democrats represent moderate districts, rather than an increase in the number of extreme partisan districts.

Removing big money from politics also does not appear to have a diminishing effect on legislative polarization. Studies of state legislatures show either no relationship between public election funding and legislative polarization or that the public financing of candidates actually leads to more, not less, polarization. For example, Masket and Miller (2014) demonstrate that state legislators who accept full public funding of their campaigns are no more or less extreme than their traditionally funded colleagues. Hall (2015), on the other hand, finds a positive relationship between public funding and state legislative polarization: states with public election funding have higher, not lower, levels of polarization. Yet what both analyses demonstrate is that public funding does not produce *less* polarized political systems. Thus, as Masket and Miller (2015) write, "Reformers looking to curb polarization via campaign finance reform should consider looking at ideas other than public funding."

Some of the most surprising findings concern the impact of partisan primaries on polarization. The logic is again compelling: primary voters favor ideologically pure candidates and pull candidates toward the extremes. The party primary argument has been so powerful that almost all who seek congressional reform advocate changes to the primary system (e.g., Bipartisan Policy Center 2014), yet scholars have simultaneously struggled to find direct linkages between primaries and polarization. For one, the evidence that extremists fare better in primaries is mixed (Brady et al. 2007; Hirano et al. 2010; Hall and Snyder 2015). In addition, Hirano et al. (2010) show that the introduction of primary elections, the level of primary turnout, and the threat of primary competition are not associated with partisan polarization in roll-call voting. Differences in primary rules also seem to provide few answers. Closed primaries, or those in which only party members can vote, do not produce more extreme candidates than open primaries (McGhee et al. 2014; Rogowski and Langella 2014; but see Gerber and Morton 1998). Sides and Vavreck (2013) attribute these collective dead ends to the fact that primary voters look similar on many measures to other voters within their party (see also Geer 1988; Norrander 1989). They conclude, "Polarization does not seem to emanate from voters at any stage of the electoral process" (Sides and Vavreck 2013, 11).

Additional evidence on the limited impact of primaries on polarization comes from recent reforms. Most notably, the implementation of the "top-two primary" in California in 2012 was predicted to increase voter turnout and thereby diminish the effect of extreme voters on candidate selection. The top-two primary was widely expected to help moderate candidates, although subsequent analyses suggest that this goal was perhaps too optimistic. Moderates fared no better under the top-two primary than they would have in closed primaries (Ahler, Citrin, and Lenz 2016), and if anything, California lawmakers took more extreme positions after the adoption of the top-two primary (Kousser, Phillips, and Shor 2017). In sum, there is little indication that any of the recent policy reforms have resulted in the election of more moderate candidates.

This book seeks to point reformers in a different direction and shift the discussion to the ideological makeup of the candidate pool. Indeed, one reason these policies have been less successful than anticipated is that moderates have opted out of congressional politics. The chapters that follow describe why they have done so and why the gulf between the parties is unlikely to diminish on its own. The emphasis on candidate supply reconciles the puzzle of how polarization has continued to increase despite the enactment of recent reforms: in order for a moderate to be elected, there must be a moderate candidate for voters to choose. Regardless of who draws congressional districts, who funds congressional candidates, or who votes in congressional elections, if the only individuals who run for congressional office come from the ideological extremes, it is difficult to see how polarization will fade any time soon. Those who seek to counteract partisan polarization must consider how to encourage ideological moderates to run for Congress, and reformers could aid in this endeavor by recruiting and supporting moderate candidates. At the very least, if we are serious about bridging the gap between the parties, the absence of moderates from the pool of congressional candidates needs to be part of the conversation.

# I

# The Choices Have Changed

In 2012, longtime Republican Senator Olympia Snowe announced her retirement from congressional office. She had served for more than three decades in both the U.S. House and Senate. During her tenure in Congress, Snowe was the face of the ideological center. She was no stranger to casting the swing vote, and she deviated from the party line on many occasions and on the most controversial issues, including abortion, gay rights, and health care. Yet the very attributes that made Olympia Snowe such a respected, admired, and even iconic legislator, the very qualities that would eventually set her apart from almost all her colleagues, would also be the reason she called it quits. Snowe would have sailed to reelection, but in her retirement announcement, she expressed a different concern over how productive another term would be. She blamed hyperpartisanship and the "my way or the highway" ideologies in Congress as the singular reason for her exit from office. The prognosis for bipartisanship is even bleaker when we look at the traditional pathway to congressional office. Not only are ideological moderates leaving Congress, but state legislators like Olympia Snowe who are in the pipeline to higher office now overwhelmingly decide to pass on a congressional career.

The central argument of this book is that moderates are opting out of the congressional candidate pool, further exacerbating the ideological gulf between the parties in Congress. Liberal Republicans and conservative Democrats are outsiders in both parties, and the personal and professional benefits of congressional service are too low for them to run. Just a few decades ago, those in the ideological middle comprised half of the House chamber, and they were highly influential voting blocs. Sizeable numbers of Democrats were conservative on social and economic

5

issues, and they sided with the Republicans in their support for tax cuts and defense spending. Liberal Republicans were a prominent wing of the GOP, and they united with the Democrats on environmental regulation, labor protection, and social welfare policy. Moderates had a say in the policymaking process, and their votes were often the deciding factor in whether legislation would pass or fail. But for liberal Republicans and conservative Democrats today, the value of congressional office has diminished as they have become more at odds with the rest of their party delegation. It is increasingly difficult for moderates to achieve their policy goals and advance within the party or chamber, and they have fewer like-minded colleagues to work and interact with in office. Although the political center has long been deemed a coveted position in the legislature, it is now a lonely and lowly place to be.

The consequence is that partisan polarization in Congress has become self-reinforcing. The vanishing of moderates first began because of a variety of geographical and partisan changes that occurred in the American electorate. Some moderates lost their reelection bids; others retired from office. As both parties became more homogeneous and their centers of gravity shifted toward the extremes, the nature of legislative service changed for those in the ideological middle. Their political leverage waned with the passage of each election cycle, and congressional service became less and less rewarding, as well as less pleasant, for liberal Republicans and conservative Democrats. In short, the rise in polarization and the hollowing out of the political center has discouraged ideological moderates from running for and remaining in Congress. These many, many individual decisions to abstain from congressional politics have important implications for the persistence of partisan polarization, the nature of congressional representation, and the quality of American democracy.

Candidate emergence has received only minimal attention from polarization scholars, but it is crucial for understanding the makeup of those who are ultimately elected. The micro-level decision to run influences the choices that are available to voters and determines who is eligible to win. This book introduces the concept of party fit to explain why moderates are not putting their hats into the ring. Party fit is the idea that ideological conformity with the party influences the value of running for and serving in political office. Legislators' degree of party fit matters for their ability to shape the policy agenda, succeed within the chamber, and forge bonds with fellow members of their party. Although the reelection goal captures part of what members want (e.g., Downs 1957; Mayhew 1974), the argument here is that there is more to being a member of Congress than winning elections. Legislators are members of a party team who are expected to promote the party agenda and tear down the other side (Lee 2009). Party fit matters for whether candidates want to be on the team.

The chapters explore two processes at the candidate level that are shaping aggregate patterns of party change: the decision to run for higher office among state legislators in the congressional pipeline and the decision to run for reelection among members of Congress. First, I find that moderate state legislators are less likely to run for Congress than conservative Republicans and liberal Democrats. In addition, the probability of running for Congress soars among extreme state legislators who face open seats, and because the vast majority of newly elected members enter through open seats, these individuals are a propelling force behind changes in polarization. Second, I find that moderate members of Congress are less likely to seek reelection than their conservative Republican and liberal Democratic counterparts. The liberal Republicans and conservative Democrats of yesteryear who worked across the aisle on social and economic issues alike are opting out of congressional politics, and conservative Republicans and liberal Democrats have taken their place. The entrance of ideologues into the candidate pool, particularly in races where they are most likely to win, and the exit of moderates from the candidate pool have exacerbated partisan polarization in Congress.

The conclusions provide important insights into our understanding of representation in the contemporary context. In the mid-twentieth century, the two parties were diverse coalitions of legislators, representation was highly localized, and members of Congress were best described as ambassadors of their district. Legislators focused on where they, rather than their party, stood on issues and how they, rather than their party, voted on policies. Members engaged in a variety of activities to build name recognition among their constituents: they took positions, claimed credit, and brought home the bacon (Fenno 1973; Mayhew 1974). But that model of representation has become increasingly outdated. Partisan attachments in the electorate have grown stronger, fewer and fewer voters cross party lines, and the incumbency advantage has declined markedly (Bartels 2000; Abramowitz and Webster 2015; Jacobson 2015). It now sounds more plausible to say that no theoretical treatment of Congress that *does not* posit parties as analytic units will go very far. The model of representation that currently characterizes American politics is very much a partisan one.

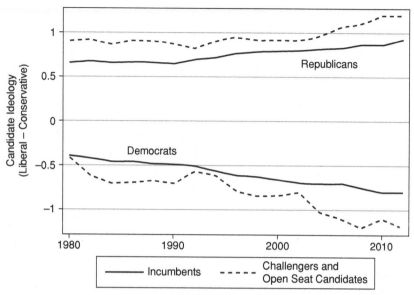

FIGURE 1.1. Mean ideology of U.S. House candidates, 1980–2012
*Source:* Campaign finance scores; Database on Ideology, Money in Politics, and
Elections (Bonica 2014).

## Patterns of Candidate Emergence over Time

Recent data advances allow us to examine how the ideology of congressional candidates has changed between 1980 and 2012. Bonica (2014) uses campaign contribution patterns to estimate campaign finance scores (CFscores) for a wide range of political actors, including members of Congress, state legislators, interest groups, and individual donors. Importantly, these estimates are available for winning and losing candidates, and they provide a more complete picture of the supply of congressional candidates during this 30-year stretch.[1] Figure 1.1 shows the average CFscores of candidates who ran for the U.S. House between 1980 and 2012, broken down into incumbents and nonincumbents. All candidates have increasingly come from the extremes, and the candidates who ran in 2012 were significantly more polarized than those who ran in 1980.

---

[1]  The Bonica (2014) measures are discussed in greater detail in Chapter 2. The CFscores are measures of the preferences of candidates' donors, rather than direct measures of politicians' beliefs. For the sake of simplicity, I refer to these measures as ideology, but they are more accurately understood as a proxy for candidate ideology. Nevertheless, they are the only available proxy, and they are also a very good one, for the ideology of congressional winners as well as losers during this time period.

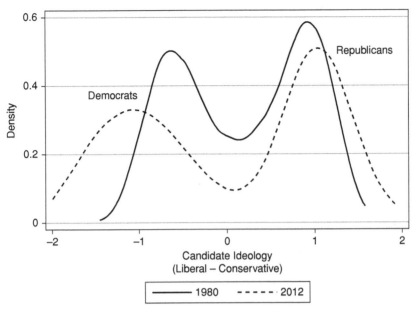

FIGURE 1.2. Ideological distributions of U.S. House candidates, 1980 vs. 2012.
*Source:* CFscores (Bonica 2014).

In fact, for both Republicans and Democrats, the ideological distance between those who ran in 1980 and 2012 is much greater than the distance between incumbents and nonincumbents in most years. In addition, nonincumbent candidates are further apart ideologically than incumbents in every election cycle, which is consistent with the evidence that replacements are responsible for much of the rise in polarization (Theriault 2006). The abstention of moderates from congressional politics has contributed to what Bafumi and Herron (2010) call "leapfrog representation." Member replacement patterns today consist of extremists taking the place of extremists, and moderates are left with a dearth of representation in Congress.

Similarly, Figure 1.2 displays the ideological distributions of candidates who ran in 1980 and those who ran in 2012. The distribution is bimodal for both years, and we see clear ideological differences between Republican and Democratic candidates (see also Ansolabehere, Snyder, and Stewart 2001). But it is also evident that the candidate distributions have changed dramatically over time. The political center has been hollowed out over the last three decades. Republican candidates come increasingly from the conservative end of the spectrum, and Democratic

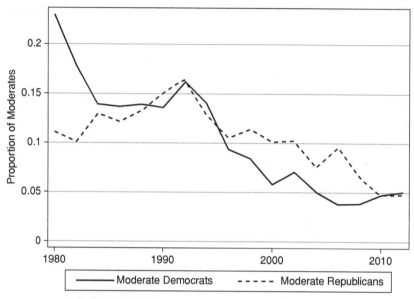

FIGURE 1.3. Ideological moderates as a proportion of U.S. House candidates, 1980–2012
*Source:* CFscores (Bonica 2014).

candidates come increasingly from the liberal end. Very few candidates are staking out the ideological middle.

Another way to examine these trends is to show how the proportion of moderates in the candidate pool changed during this time. Figure 1.3 shows the percentage of liberal Republican candidates in the Republican candidate pool and the percentage of conservative Democratic candidates in the Democratic candidate pool from 1980 to 2012. These are Republican candidates who resemble Olympia Snowe, the veteran moderate from Maine who retired in 2012, and Democratic candidates who resemble John Tanner, a longtime representative from Tennessee and founder of the moderate Blue Dog Coalition, who retired in 2010. The Blue Dog Coalition was created in 1995 by legislators who felt they had been "choked blue" by their colleagues from the left. Like moderate Republicans, Blue Dogs are often at odds with their party on both social and economic issues. In recent years, they have defected from the Democratic Party on key votes such as the Affordable Care Act, the economic stimulus package, and cap and trade legislation (Beckel 2010). Although moderate Democrats like Tanner constituted more than 20 percent of Democratic candidates in 1980, they made up only 5 percent of the Democratic pool in 2012. Similarly, although moderate Republicans never were as large a percentage of the GOP pool, the trend is also one of decline. Moderate Republicans like Snowe constituted 11 percent of the Republican pool in 1980 and a high of 16 percent of the pool in 1990, but their numbers had dwindled to 5 percent by 2012 as well.

It is not the case, either, that no moderates are available to run for Congress. In fact, sizeable numbers of liberal Republicans and conservative Democrats hold state legislative office, which has long been considered the pipeline to congressional office (e.g., Jacobson and Kernell 1983). Between 2000 and 2010, nearly 20 percent of Republican state legislators were at least as moderate as Snowe, and nearly 30 percent of Democratic state legislators were at least as moderate as Tanner.[2] In other words, not only do ideological moderates exist, but more importantly, ideologically moderate *high-quality potential candidates* exist. Data limitations hinder us from comparing the proportion of moderate state legislators in the pre-polarized era with the proportion of moderate state legislators today, but what is most significant is that a substantial number of moderates are serving, currently, in state legislative office. However, they are simply not putting their hats into the congressional ring.

The choices on congressional ballots have changed slowly but steadily over the past three decades. Liberal Republicans and conservative Democrats have in large part opted out of congressional politics. To be sure, Fiorina, Abrams, and Pope (2006) introduced this idea more than a decade ago, although they did not fully explore it empirically. Their concern was instead whether the American public has polarized, and they used this hypothetical scenario to illustrate how we could have a polarized Congress and not have a polarized electorate. But Fiorina et al. (2006) were right to suggest that if the only candidates who run for office come from the ideological extremes, the only candidates who will be elected to office will therefore come from the extremes.

## The Rise – and Persistence – of Partisan Polarization in Congress

Scholars have focused on two main types of explanations for the increase in partisan polarization in Congress. The first set of explanations highlights geographical and partisan shifts in the electorate. For one, Southern constituencies became less homogeneously conservative following the passage of the Voting Rights Act, which enfranchised many African

---

[2] These figures come from the state legislator data that are used in Chapters 4 and 5.

American voters who supported the Democratic Party (Rohde 1991; Aldrich 1995, 2011). Both parties gradually lost their moderate factions, with conservative whites in the South abandoning the Democrats and liberals in the Northeast leaving the Republicans. In addition to the realignment of the South, ideological changes have occurred across the United States. The electoral bases of the two parties shifted from being diverse to more uniform (Stonecash, Brewer, and Mariani 2003; Fleisher and Bond 2004). Voters are now better sorted along party lines, and they increasingly match their partisanship with their ideology (Hetherington 2001; Levendusky 2009). And despite the dispute over mass polarization, most agree that party activists and the politically engaged public have become more extreme in their political preferences (e.g., Layman and Carsey 2002; Fiorina et al. 2006; Theriault 2008; Abramowitz 2010; Layman et al. 2010; Pew Research Center 2014; see Hetherington 2009 for a review).

The second set of explanations instead highlights changes that have occurred within Congress. Increased levels of party homogeneity supplied the House leadership with more tools to foster party discipline and advance the party's agenda (Rohde 1991; Aldrich 1995, 2011; Aldrich and Rohde 2001). Newly empowered party leaders assumed greater responsibility in allocating committee assignments, setting the legislative agenda, and structuring debate on the floor (Cox and McCubbins 2005; Sinclair 2006). In fact, party leaders in the House are now more extreme than the median member of their party (Heberlig, Hetherington, and Larson 2006; Jessee and Malhotra 2010), and they seek to move the policy agenda closer to their own preferences (Cox and McCubbins 1993; Roberts and Smith 2003). Majority party leaders also draw extensively on legislative procedure to exert their will, and the resulting polarization on procedural issues has further exacerbated the ideological warfare between the two parties (Sinclair 2006; Theriault 2008).

The party fit argument is not an account of why partisan polarization started, but rather one of how it has persisted and increased over time. As Rohde (2016) notes, the forces behind polarization have likely not been equally consequential throughout its development. The opting out of moderates from the candidate pool pertains to how polarization has deepened and intensified. Liberal Republicans and conservative Democrats used to benefit professionally and personally from legislative service, but as these shifts in the electorate and within Congress took hold, both parties experienced dramatic internal transformations. Over the course of several election cycles, ideological moderates went from being a sizeable voting bloc to being complete partisan outsiders. As a high-level staffer for a former moderate member of Congress described, "You're seeing the party drift further and further in a direction that is finally just anathema to you. It's like being an immigrant in a foreign land that you didn't choose to move to. Why do that?" (22 January 2013). The vanishing of moderates has altered the value of congressional service for those in office, and it has altered how potential candidates perceive the congressional environment.

The ideological middle has long held a prominent place in the Congress literature, but scholars have devoted little attention to how the experience of the median legislator varies under different circumstances (see Rubin 2013 for an exception). In the polarized scenario, the median is expected to be a less coveted position than the conventional wisdom would suggest. When members have a cadre of like-minded colleagues, they can band together on policy issues and provide each other with moral support. But when legislators are isolated from the caucus in an increasingly small and weak minority, the experience of serving in Congress can instead be alienating and unpleasant. In the contemporary Congress, moderates struggle to influence the policy agenda and advance within the party. They also face growing pressure from leaders and rank-and-file members to toe the party line, and they have fewer moderate colleagues to collaborate and commiserate with in office. In the words of many former moderate members of Congress whom I spoke with, the job has become "frustrating," "unsatisfying," and "corrosive" for those in the ideological center. Leading theories of legislative organization suggest that being in the middle is desirable, but in practice, it is not easy, either politically or socially, to be in this position. For liberal Republicans and conservative Democrats, the benefits of serving in Congress have diminished as the parties drifted further and further apart.

## Electoral and Nonelectoral Considerations

The main theoretical question of this book is why some individuals run for office and others do not. The emphasis on party fit and the value of the office departs from the view that ambitious politicians are motivated, above all else, by winning elections. In what Fiorina (2009) dubbed the "master theory" of electoral competition, Downs (1957, 28) asserted that politicians "formulate policies in order to win elections, rather than win elections to formulate policies." Mayhew (1974) perhaps best summarized this view of legislators as "single-minded seekers of reelection."

Although electoral goals take us part of the way, the argument here is that they do not take us the whole way. The contribution of party fit is to demonstrate that the value of political office varies across ambitious politicians. If candidates care only about holding office for its own sake, then there is little explanatory power in examining differential benefits across legislators. But if legislators also value the office for the policies they can pursue, the ability to advance in the legislature, and the quality of life they will have in office, then differences in nonelectoral benefits across individuals can be an important explanation for who does and does not run for Congress.

To be sure, others have advocated a broader understanding of legislator goals that goes beyond election and reelection. Fenno (1973) laid the groundwork by emphasizing, in conjunction with the reelection goal, the importance of good public policy and influence within the chamber. Legislators are also motivated by the desire to achieve or maintain majority status (Rohde and Aldrich 2010), and they must work together, as teams, to cultivate a favorable party image and tear down the other party (Lee 2009). Majority status is valuable because it has implications for members' ability to achieve other goals. One former member of Congress who spent most, but not all, of his time in the minority remarked, "The ability to influence the outcome of legislation in the minority is effectively zero. It's not 0.001; it's zero. The real Holy Grail is to be the majority. And for good reason, most people want to affect outcomes. They want to be legislators, not orators" (18 January 2013). Rohde and Aldrich (2010) suggest that majority status has become increasingly important as the parties have polarized and as the policy agendas of the parties have diverged.

The party fit argument both builds on and extends these insights. The electoral connection is clearly important, but Downs, Mayhew, and Fenno were writing at a different time and in a different context. Forty years ago, political parties were ideologically heterogeneous groups of legislators. Members were in large part responsible for their own electoral fortunes, and local interests prevailed over partisan interests. But there is a growing disconnect between the contemporary political landscape and the one that Downs and Mayhew had in mind. Today, the two parties in Congress are deeply divided ideologically. The political climate is intensely partisan, and voters draw primarily on the party label when evaluating and selecting candidates. The Republican and Democratic parties have developed strong campaign arms that aid in fundraising, organizing, and messaging (Herrnson 2004). In light of this disconnect, Hacker and Pierson (2014) have advocated a corrective vision, what they call a "policy-focused political science." They write, "In the policy-focused approach, pride of place is given not to elections but to policies – to the exercise of government authority for particular purposes. In place of the 'electoral connection,' the policy-focused perspective stresses the *policy connection* that promotes and sustains coalitions of partisan politicians and organized interests" (Hacker and Pierson 2014, 644). They turn the Downsian view on its head and suggest that "powerful actors often seek to win elections to formulate policies."

This book similarly stresses the increasing relevance of nonelectoral forces in the contemporary political context. In the pre-polarized era, a wider ideological array of members could reap party and policy goods, so the effect of party fit on the decision to run for office was more constrained. Even Fenno (1973), despite his attention to policy and career goals, would have overlooked the impact of party fit. At that time, member ideology was not as closely tied to the ability to influence public policy and advance within the chamber. Legislators worked within and across party lines to pursue their policy goals; committee chair positions and leadership positions were decided in large part by seniority; and legislators traveled and socialized with members from across the spectrum. But as the parties drifted apart, the benefits of the office became more intertwined with member ideology, and the value of serving became more variable across ambitious politicians. Legislator ideology now has clear consequences for who does and does not receive party, policy, and personal rewards. Ideological nonconformists are thus much worse off than conformists, and they are also worse off than they used to be.

The focus of this book is on the increasing importance of party fit in the decision to run for office as well as the diminishing value of congressional office for those in the ideological middle. Although electoral concerns are also likely to discourage moderates from seeking congressional office, the verdict is still out on whether and how much candidate ideology matters for election outcomes. Studies have shown that moderates do slightly worse in the primary (Brady et al. 2007; Hall and Snyder 2015) but slightly better in the general election (Erikson and Wright 2000; Ansolabehere et al. 2001; Canes-Wrone et al. 2002; Hall and Snyder 2015). Others find no relationship between candidate ideology and primary election victory (Hirano et al. 2010). Hall and Snyder (2015) even suggest that the advantage moderates have in the general election cancels out the disadvantage they face in primaries. They conclude,

"Candidates who are ideologically extreme do not have an electoral advantage over those who are ideologically moderate" (Hall and Snyder 2015, 3).

The caveat, of course, is that these analyses are of candidates who actually run. It is impossible to examine the relationship between ideology and electoral outcomes for noncandidates. The weak relationship between ideology and outcomes may reflect what potential candidates and former members of Congress already knew: that they would have lost if they had run. Indeed, Masket (2009) provides a rich account of how political insiders influence primary nominations by directing their resources to ideologically extreme candidates. Sniderman and Stiglitz (2012) similarly show that candidates receive a reputational premium if they take a position that is consistent with the policy outlook of their party, and very liberal Republicans and very conservative Democrats would likely have a hard time winning a primary today.

It is also possible that – accurately or inaccurately – moderates believe they will not win and therefore do not run. In fact, a group of prominent scholars and political practitioners recently convened on National Public Radio's Diane Rehm Show to discuss the polarizing effect of partisan primaries on congressional politics. Midway through the show they turned to the phones for questions and comments. The first call came from a woman who is currently a local elected official in Missouri. She holds a nonpartisan office and is "not shy" about the fact that she is a moderate Republican. Her constituents frequently ask her what she plans to do next. She said, "I tell them, very frankly, that I can't go any higher. I would just be crucified in a primary, and I understand that." She added, "There are a lot of people like me that are local officials, that are very moderate, but are very limited in how far they can go."

The main point here, however, is that there is more to being a member of Congress than winning elections. And there is more to the decision to run for office than an expectation of winning. Although the ability to secure election and reelection is an important factor in the calculus of candidacy, it is not the only factor. As Olympia Snowe's account suggests, the broader political and partisan context also shapes the decision to seek elected office, and the opting out of moderates from congressional politics cannot be explained by electoral factors alone. In the pre-polarized era, we could cover more ground without distinguishing between electoral and nonelectoral considerations, but the nature of congressional service has changed dramatically over the past few decades. The policy, party, and personal rewards that legislators receive are now closely intertwined with their ideology. For moderates today, the benefits of serving in Congress simply do not outweigh the huge costs of running.

Today, we would miss a lot about congressional representation if we collapsed electoral and nonelectoral goals. The candidate-centered electoral process that flourished during the mid-twentieth century gave members more incentive to be individually responsible to their districts rather than collectively responsible to the party. It made political sense for members to pursue narrowly targeted and particularistic legislation because voters appreciated these benefits and they rewarded members at the ballot box. But as the incumbency advantage declined and partisan loyalties in the electorate solidified, the party teamsmanship model that Mayhew (1974) so compellingly argued against has now taken center stage in Congress. In the contemporary era, the party sets the policy agenda, allocates committee assignments, doles out campaign funds, and structures the political process. Members certainly want to be reelected, but if they are going to do so, it will be as members of a political party that stands for a specific set of policies.

The goal of this book is not to dismiss the impact of electoral considerations but rather to highlight the role of nonelectoral factors in patterns of candidate entry and suggest that nonelectoral considerations have only continued to grow in importance as partisan polarization has increased. The analyses that follow address the traditional view that electoral concerns are central in the decision to run for office but also demonstrate that this view, on its own, falls short in the contemporary political environment. A broader view of candidate emergence provides insight into why liberal Republicans and conservative Democrats are not emerging as candidates in what would be relatively favorable districts. A broader view of candidate emergence also helps us to make sense of why popular moderate incumbents have opted to retire from congressional politics. And finally, a broader view of candidate emergence sheds new light on why partisan polarization continues to persist despite high levels of voter dissatisfaction with Congress and the adoption of various policy reforms.

In sum, differences in the value of the office across individuals need to be taken into account in contemporary models of political representation. Skewed patterns of candidate emergence can be an autonomous driver of party and institutional change that is independent of the will of voters. While ideological and geographical shifts in the electorate set partisan polarization in motion, the theoretical argument here offers an additional explanation for how Congress can drift further from the preferences of the public than we would expect from electoral forces alone. Even if voters wanted to elect relatively moderate candidates, serving in Congress may be so unfulfilling that electable moderate candidates will pass on the opportunity to run. The experiential aspect of being a legislator thus has profound implications for the ideological makeup of Congress as an institution and the quality of political representation in the United States.

### Asymmetric Polarization

Although both parties have shifted away from the center, a growing number of academics have also argued that polarization is "asymmetric" and that important differences exist between the two parties (e.g., Hacker and Pierson 2005, 2014, 2015; McCarty et al. 2006; Carmines 2011; Mann and Ornstein 2012; Skocpol and Williamson 2012; Grossman and Hopkins 2015, 2016). They suggest that the Republican Party has charged sharply to the right while the Democrat Party has moved only modestly to the left and that Republicans bear a greater responsibility for the dysfunction in Washington. This view of the GOP as an "insurgent outlier" is aptly summarized by Mann and Ornstein (2012, 103):

The Republican Party has become ideologically extreme; contemptuous of the inherited social and economic policy regime; scornful of compromise; unpersuaded by conventional understanding of facts, evidence, and science; and dismissive of the legitimacy of its political opposition, all but declaring war on the government. The Democratic Party, while no paragon of civic virtue, is more ideologically centered and diverse, protective of the government's role as it developed over the course of the last century, open to incremental changes in policy fashioned through bargaining with the Republicans, and less disposed to or adept at take-no-prisoners conflict between the parties.

Scholars are not alone in their unease about the contemporary Republican Party. A number of prominent politicians have expressed discontent with the current direction of their party. Olympia Snowe's recent book bemoans the rightward shift of the party, and other middle-of-the-road Republicans such as Christine Todd Whitman, Lincoln Chafee, and Bob Dole have openly criticized the GOP's kowtowing to the far-right faction of the party. Mike Lofgren, a veteran Republican congressional staffer who retired in 2011 after nearly 30 years of service, put it this way: "Both parties are not rotten in quite the same way. The Democrats have their share of machine politicians, careerists, corporate bagmen, egomaniacs and kooks. Nothing, however, quite matches the modern GOP. The crackpot outliers of two decades ago have become the vital center today.... The Congressional directory now reads like a case-book of lunacy" (Lofgren 2011). Equally significant is that voters from across the partisan spectrum share these concerns about the intransi-gence on the Republican side. A 2013 Gallup poll showed that Republi-cans, Democrats, and Independents alike voice the same criticism of the GOP. When asked what they dislike most about the Republican Party, 26 percent of Republicans, 22 percent of Democrats, and 17 percent of Independents say the Republican Party is "too inflexible" or "unwilling to compromise." By comparison, only 12 percent of Republicans, 6 per-cent of Democrats, and 7 percent of Independents say the same about the Democratic Party (Saad 2013).

A key point of the study of asymmetric polarization is that the two parties are neither mirror images of each other nor equivalent collections of politicians (Hacker and Pierson 2014). Recent work by Grossman and Hopkins (2015, 2016) details several differences between the parties. They argue that the Republican Party is the agent of an ideological move-ment whose supporters prize doctrinal purity, whereas the Democratic Party is a looser coalition of social groups that seek government action. Freeman (1986) identified similar asymmetries in her comparison of con-vention delegates and suggested that the Democratic Party is an alliance of various subgroups and the Republican Party is united by an adherence to a common conservative identity. As a result, ideological orthodoxy is not imposed on Democratic and Republican politicians in the same way. As Grossman and Hopkins (2015, 133) write, "A party primarily united by ideology will always remain particularly vulnerable to charges from within its ranks that elected leaders... have strayed from principle and must be forced back into line. Democratic politicians face their own share of problems in governing... but they are comparatively free from pressure to exhibit unyielding fidelity to party doctrine."

The bulk of the attention in this book is on the absence of moder-ates from congressional office and the shift of both parties away from the ideological center. Yet party asymmetries with respect to ideologi-cal purity are likely to have implications for the value of the office across officeholders and for the party, policy, and personal benefits that ideolog-ical nonconformists receive in office. If ideological purity is prized more within the Republican Party, Republican nonconformists may experience greater levels of both formal and informal pressure than their Democratic counterparts. Thus, while the general focus here is on the decline of ideo-logical moderates in the contemporary political era, partisan asymmetries in patterns of candidate emergence are addressed as well. Furthermore, the broader goal is to better understand the rise in partisan polarization in Congress, and if one party is more to blame for this phenomenon, it is important to consider any relevant differences between the two parties.

## Data Sources

The empirical chapters draw on a wide variety of quantitative and qualitative data to examine variation in the decision to run for and remain in congressional office. Incumbent ideology is measured with Poole and Rosenthal's (2007) widely used DW-NOMINATE scores, but we cannot study the full range of congressional candidates, particularly losers, with roll-call data. A large portion of the book is therefore based on Bonica's (2014) CFscores referenced above. The CFscores are discussed in more detail in the next chapter. Bonica utilizes campaign finance records from 1980 to 2012 to place a wide array of political actors on a common ideological scale. It should be noted that neither DW-NOMINATE scores nor CFscores are direct measures of candidate ideology. The term ideology is used for the sake of simplicity, but these data are better understood as proxies for candidate ideology. They do not measure the actual beliefs of politicians; DW-NOMINATE scores measure the voting behavior of members, and CFscores measure patterns of campaign contributions from donors. Despite their limitations, however, they are the best available proxies for the ideology of incumbents and congressional candidates during this 30-year period, and they are invaluable for an analysis of candidate supply.

Bonica's (2014) estimates of state legislators are crucial as well, because they allow us to compare high-quality potential candidates who could have run for Congress and did with high-quality potential candidates who could have run for Congress but did not. On top of the fact that state legislators are in the pipeline to congressional office, the Bonica state legislator data are particularly advantageous for the purposes here. First, candidate ideology is on a common scale, so we can readily make comparisons across individuals as well as levels of office; second, due to the size of the dataset, there is ample variation across a host of key political and electoral variables such as seat type and district partisanship; and third, the data are pooled over time and span multiple election cycles. Bonica's data are used throughout much of the book, but I incorporate Shor and McCarty's (2011) estimates of state legislator ideology (NP scores) as well. Shor and McCarty's measures are instead generated from voting patterns and state legislator responses to a national survey of policy preferences.

I also draw on survey data of state legislators that were collected for the Candidate Emergence Study (CES) (Stone and Maisel 2003; Stone, Maisel, and Maestas 2004; Maestas et al. 2006). The CES data provide the most detailed and comprehensive information on how state legislators view the congressional environment. Perhaps the most useful attribute of these data is that they allow us to address the role of both electoral and nonelectoral factors in state legislators' attraction to higher office. Although the actual decision to run for Congress is the ultimate variable of interest, the CES data provide a unique opportunity to analyze the attitudes and beliefs of those who are among the most likely to run for and be elected to congressional office. The survey data complement the behavioral data that are used in the majority of the book.

In addition, I conducted 22 interviews with former members of Congress, congressional staff members, and party elites involved in congressional campaigns and elections.[3] I interviewed a total of 18 former members of Congress, 12 Republicans and 6 Democrats. The U.S. Association of Former Members of Congress (FMC) connected me with members of their organization, and I selected individuals based on their DW-NOMINATE scores. All of them were ideological moderates in their party, though the extent to which they deviated from the party line varied.[4] Most of the members belonged to at least one of the moderate groups in Congress, such as the Tuesday Group and the Republican Main Street Partnership on the Republican side or the Blue Dog Coalition and the New Democrat Coalition on the Democratic side. They represented a range of geographical areas, but many of the Republicans came from the Northeast and many of the Democrats came from the South due to historical patterns of partisan alignment. Some of the former MCs also referred me to members of their staff and individuals who held high-level party positions during various election cycles. The interviews enhance

---

[3] The individuals will remain anonymous. Throughout the book, I note the specific date of the interview, and in most cases I provide a general description of the member's ideology and level of seniority. Additional details about how the individuals were selected and how the interviews were conducted are provided in Appendix A.

[4] The research design of selecting moderates is somewhat limiting. Additional interviews from the mainstream and extreme factions of the parties would permit better insight into how the experience of serving in Congress is shaped by ideological conformity. I ultimately traded breadth for depth because my primary concern is the diminishing value of congressional office among moderates, but the quantitative data allow me to examine patterns of candidate entry across the ideological spectrum.

our understanding of the kinds of experiences that ideological moderates had during their tenure in office, and they reveal how the experiences of moderates changed as the parties grew more and more polarized.

Finally, I rely on estimates of voter ideology across districts to examine the impact of electoral forces. It is difficult to determine whether candidates fail to emerge because of electoral or nonelectoral considerations, but we can nevertheless leverage variation across districts to see whether different types of candidates emerge in different types of districts. I use Tausanovitch and Warshaw's (2013) measures of district ideology and the ideology of Republican and Democratic partisans across districts. These data provide a unique opportunity to compare patterns of candidate entry in congressional districts that would be more and less favorable to liberal Republicans and conservative Democrats.

These various data sources and the strengths and weaknesses of each are listed in Table 1.1. The purpose of utilizing such a wide range of data and measures is to provide a more comprehensive test of the party fit argument. DW-NOMINATE scores are used to examine incumbents; CFscores are used to examine winning and losing congressional candidates as well as state legislators in the pipeline to Congress (and supplemented with NP scores); the CES data are used to examine the attitudes and beliefs of state legislators; and the interviews are used to examine the changing nature of congressional service during this time. The goal is to weave together a variety of high-quality datasets to assess the argument from several angles and vantage points. The use of multiple measures helps to overcome the problems that arise when relying on a single method, dataset, or approach. Importantly, they all lead us to the same conclusion – that moderates have opted out of congressional politics – and the findings increase our confidence in the party fit argument. The data relied on throughout the book are complementary, and together, they tell a richer story about patterns of candidate emergence in the contemporary context.

## Outline of the Book

Chapter 2 introduces the concept of party fit and discusses how ideological conformity with the party influences the value of the office and the calculus of candidacy. It provides the theoretical framework for why moderates have opted out of the congressional candidate pool in the contemporary context. The qualitative data are a central part of the chapter,

TABLE 1.1. *Details of data sources*

| Data | Use | Strengths | Weaknesses |
|---|---|---|---|
| DW-NOMINATE scores for members of Congress (Poole and Rosenthal) | – Analyze the decision to retire among U.S. House members | – Roll-call voting behavior is the standard measure of legislator ideology<br>– Extend over a long time period | – Not available for nonincumbents<br>– Not available for the pool of likely congressional candidates |
| CFscores for congressional candidates and state legislators (Bonica) | – Analyze changes in the ideology of U.S. House candidates over time<br>– Analyze the decision to run for the U.S. House among state legislators | – Available for incumbents and nonincumbents<br>– Common ideology scale allows comparisons across levels of office and measurement of party fit concept<br>– Ample variation across key political and electoral variables<br>– Span multiple election cycles | – Are a proxy for ideology and do not measure the stated beliefs of politicians |
| NP scores for state legislators (Shor and McCarty) | – Analyze the decision to run for the U.S. House among state legislators | – Generated from different data than CFscores<br>– Ample variation across key political and electoral variables<br>– Span multiple election cycles | – Unable to make comparisons across levels of office or measure the concept of party fit |
| CES survey of state legislators (Maisel, Stone, and Maestas) | – Analyze the attitudes of state legislators and their attraction to the U.S. House | – Complement the behavioral data<br>– Most comprehensive data on the stated attitudes, beliefs, and ideology of state legislators<br>– Allow analysis of electoral and nonelectoral factors | – Very few run for Congress<br>– Districts are anonymous so cannot similarly account for political and electoral variables<br>– Data from a single year in the 1990s |
| Estimates of congressional district ideology and partisans within congressional districts (Tausanovitch and Warshaw) | – Analyze variation in candidate entry across different types of congressional districts | – Gain leverage on whether the profiles of congressional candidates vary across districts and in districts with different types of partisans | – Cannot determine whether candidates perceive districts and district partisans in this way<br>– Not on the same scale as the candidate estimates, so cannot directly assess distance from partisans |
| Interviews with more than 20 former members of Congress, their staff, and party elites | – Analyze the experiences that moderate members had in office | – Provide a richer understanding of how the value of the office changed for moderates over time | – Cannot examine changes in the value of the office for nonmoderates during this time |

and the interviews illustrate how the ability of moderates to influence policy, advance within the chamber, and forge bonds with their co-partisans diminished as the parties drifted apart. I also address how patterns of candidate emergence contribute to aggregate party change over time and how the abstention of moderates from congressional politics has contributed to partisan polarization. Chapter 2 concludes by examining electoral considerations. I use Tausanovitch and Warshaw's (2013) estimates of partisan ideology across districts to analyze whether a higher proportion of moderate candidates run in districts where they would be more likely to win. The data reveal little variation in candidate entry across different types of districts that would be more and less favorable to moderate candidates, and this variation has only continued to decrease over time. In addition, I look at victory rates across different groups of candidates and show that moderates do not fare dramatically worse than either conformists or ideologues.

Chapters 3 through 5 are based on two datasets of state legislators. State legislators are particularly important for the "how" of polarization because they constitute the pool of high-quality potential congressional candidates. State legislative office is the main pipeline to congressional office (Jacobson and Kernell 1983), and former state legislators are a large percentage of the sitting members of Congress (50 percent; National Conference of State Legislators 2013). Chapter 3 draws on survey data from legislators that were collected for the CES to examine the perceptions of state legislators (Maestas et al. 2006). The analyses demonstrate that moderates are less likely to be attracted to a congressional career, less likely to think they can win, and less likely to value a seat in the U.S. House than those at the extremes. These differences are largely restricted to the Republican side, but the results also reflect distinctions between the two parties and the time period in which the survey was conducted.

In Chapter 4, the party fit argument is taken one step forward to the decision to run for Congress. I draw on Bonica's (2014) CFscores to examine the decision to run for the U.S. House among state legislators from 2000 to 2010. Again, the state legislator data are critical because they allow us to compare the potential runners with the actual runners. This chapter first shows that a sizeable number of liberal Republicans and conservative Democrats hold state legislative office. As noted above, nearly 30 percent of Democratic state legislators and 20 percent of Republican state legislators are at least as moderate as John Tanner (D-TN) and Olympia Snowe (R-ME). The main finding is that the probability of running for Congress varies dramatically across state legislators, and moderates are much less likely to seek higher office than those at the extremes. State legislators who resemble ideologues such as Paul Ryan (R-WI) and Nancy Pelosi (D-CA) are 20 times more likely to run for a House seat than those who resemble moderates such as Olympia Snowe and John Tanner. These findings hold even after controlling for seat type, district partisanship, legislator experience, and a variety of factors that also shape the decision to run for office.

Chapter 5 examines the driving forces behind polarization in greater detail, focusing on open seats and asymmetric polarization. Open seat candidates have a far greater probability of being elected than do challengers. As Gaddie and Bullock (2000, 1) write, "Open seats, not the defeat of incumbents, are the portal through which most legislators enter Congress." Compared to the relatively few candidates who defeat incumbents, open seat winners have the largest influence on the party's ideological course, and they are a key factor in whether and how much the ideological gulf between the parties widens or diminishes. This chapter shows that across state legislators, the probability of seeking congressional office increases when the seat is open, though the likelihood of running soars among conservative Republicans and liberal Democrats. Chapter 5 also illuminates an additional mechanism for asymmetric polarization, as candidate entry on the Republican side differs from that on the Democratic side. In this chapter, I draw on both CFscores and Shor and McCarty's (2011) estimates of state legislator ideology. I find that moderate Democratic and Republican state legislators have both opted out of congressional elections, but conservative Republicans are more likely to run for Congress than liberal Democrats. The findings are crucial for understanding the action of polarization and the specific forces that are driving partisan polarization and asymmetric polarization.

Chapter 6 extends the party fit framework to the decision to seek reelection and explores how disparities in legislator retention also matter for changes in polarization. I use Poole and Rosenthal's (2007) DW-NOMINATE scores to analyze the decision to retire among members of Congress from 1982 to 2010. I find that liberal Republican and conservative Democratic members of Congress are more likely to leave congressional office than ideological conformists during this time period as well. This relationship is especially apparent in the polarized era, when it became increasingly difficult for moderates to achieve their goals in office. If members no longer receive the party, policy, and personal benefits of congressional office, they have fewer reasons to stay there. While the exit of moderates only exacerbates the disparity between the parties, it is easy to see why the sacrifice of public service is greater for some than it is for others.

Chapter 7 addresses a consequence of the party fit argument for contemporary patterns of female representation. At the national legislative level, the United States is ranked 99th worldwide, with women comprising 19 percent of the House of Representatives (Inter-parliamentary Union 2016). Less attention, however, has been paid to the growing partisan gap among women in Congress: the number of Democratic women has increased dramatically since the 1980s while the number of Republican women has stagnated. Women now make up one-third of the Democratic Party but only 9 percent of the GOP. In other words, to the extent that we are concerned about the dearth of women in Congress, the problem is by and large a Republican one and it is tied to the rise in polarization. The chapter illustrates how these patterns of candidate entry have also shaped the partisan gap among women in office. First, conservative men outnumber conservative women in state legislative office more than five to one, and these Republicans are the most likely to seek higher office. Furthermore, the Republican women in Congress in the 1980s and 1990s were in the moderate wing of the party, and they were disproportionately affected by the rightward shift of the GOP. The hollowing out of the political center has hindered the advancement of Republican women in Congress, and it has stalled women's representation more generally.

The final chapter discusses the implications of these trends for partisan polarization in Congress. The prognosis is not good, and polarization is likely to persist in the years ahead. However, the findings enhance our understanding of the mechanisms of polarization and leave us with lessons for the future. The focus on the supply of congressional candidates also reconciles the puzzle of how polarization has continued to increase with the recent null findings around the gerrymandering, public election funding, and party primary hypotheses. Previous policy reforms have yielded less than fruitful outcomes, and the argument here sheds light on why these reforms have been less successful than expected. This book suggests that the congressional candidate pool is a more promising place to start.

# 2

# Party Fit and the Calculus of Candidacy

New York Republican Amory "Amo" Houghton was elected to the U.S. House of Representatives in 1986. He served in Congress for 18 years, and he was one of upstate New York's most respected representatives during his tenure. In six of his eight reelection bids, Houghton received more than 70 percent of the vote. Houghton sat on the prestigious Ways and Means Committee and he was unabashedly moderate in his political views. Houghton was one of the most vocal pro-choice Republicans in Congress, and he supported environmental protection, civil rights, funding for the arts, and an occasional tax increase. In a 2000 interview, Houghton said, "I don't have this venomous hate for the blue team, if the Republicans are the red team" (McIntyre 2000). Maryland Democrat Beverly Byron felt the same. She was elected in 1978 and went on to have a 14-year career in the House. She was the first woman to chair an Armed Services Subcommittee and she was a staunch defender of military and defense spending. Byron often broke ranks with the Democrats and sided with the Reagan and Bush administrations. She was once asked about the portraits of Reagan in her office and replied, "I've got pictures of Jimmy Carter in the other room" (Jenkins 1990). In a recent interview, Byron said she considers herself to be a middle-of-the-road Democrat, but she counted liberals and conservatives among her closest friends in Congress (Rodgers 2012).

When Beverly Byron and Amo Houghton were in Congress, moderates achieved enough of their goals as legislators to make congressional service worthwhile. They likely frustrated some of their colleagues even then, but the partisan borders within Congress were much blurrier than they are today. As the boundaries of the parties solidified, the nature of congressional service changed dramatically, and it worsened for those in the ideological middle. This chapter introduces the concept of party fit to shed light on why moderates have opted out of the candidate pool. Two main points are advanced here. First, the value of the office varies across individuals depending on their ideological conformity with the party – what I call their party fit. Second, the impact of party fit on the decision to run for office has continued to grow as the parties have polarized ideologically. In the contemporary context, it is increasingly difficult for liberal Republicans and conservative Democrats to achieve their policy, party, and personal goals, and the value of congressional service has diminished for moderates as a result. The outsider status of ideological moderates has weighed more heavily on the decision to run for Congress as the parties have drifted further apart.

We know little about how the likelihood of running for office varies across those of different ideological stripes, yet the decision to seek congressional office shapes the supply of political candidates and determines who is eligible to win. In fact, the entry of new members and the exit of incumbents entirely charts the ideological trajectories of the parties in Congress. To understand the mechanisms that are driving partisan polarization, we need to look at the choices that voters are given when they go to the polls. And to understand the choices that voters are given when they go to the polls, we need to consider why some individuals run for office and others do not.

### Political Parties and Candidate Emergence

Political parties were never intended to figure prominently in American politics. The Constitution makes no mention of parties, and the Framers sought to prevent any single group from having undue influence and power. This institutional framework laid the foundation for candidate-centered campaigns and elections, although the relative strength of political parties has waxed and waned over time. The golden age of parties in the United States was the late nineteenth and early twentieth centuries, when parties controlled nominations, organized and mobilized voters, and transmitted campaign rhetoric (see Carson and Roberts 2013). The parties were, as Sorauf (1980, 447) notes, "the medium through which the campaign was waged."

The glory days of political parties would not last, and the party organizations experienced a gradual decline between the early 1900s and the mid-twentieth century. By the 1960s, attention had shifted to the growing importance of interest groups, political consultants, and political action committees (Sorouf 1980). Party control over congressional nominations had weakened (Jacobson 2013). Political scientists emphasized the candidate-centered nature of American politics and devoted most of their attention to the rise of the incumbency advantage, which left little room for parties to shape campaigns and elections. In the candidate-centered era, primary voters, rather than party bosses, determined who would receive the party nomination. The party was deemed a remnant of the past.

A growing number of scholars have recently argued, however, that parties play a larger role in recruiting and nominating candidates than the conventional wisdom suggests (e.g., Cohen et al. 2008; Masket 2009; Dominguez 2011). Key party actors organize well in advance of primaries to select or recruit candidates to receive the party's nomination, and they ensure that their preferred candidates are provided with the necessary resources to win the primary and that their undesired candidates do not receive such assistance. Across a variety of offices, party leaders attempt to influence the slate of candidates by encouraging some individuals to run for office and discouraging others (Masket 2009). Such appeals are important because they can increase interest in running and intent to run (Broockman 2014), and party recruitment is positively associated with the decision to run (Lawless and Fox 2010; see Broockman 2014 for a review). Cohen et al. (2008) focus specifically on presidential elections, which have typically been viewed as well beyond the realm of party influence, and they similarly find that party elites winnow the field by building coalitions around a single candidate.

Although partisan actors affect the nomination process in significant ways, candidates still bear the bulk of the responsibility for their campaigns (Kazee 1994). Individuals file their own paperwork to become candidates, and for the most part, they raise their own money, devise their own strategies, and direct their own campaign operations. As Herrnson (2004, 35) notes, "[Parties] serve more as vehicles that self-recruited candidates use to advance their careers than as organizations that can make or break those careers. Party recruitment has been largely replaced by a process referred to as candidate emergence." A recruiter for one of the national parties said, "It is a major decision to run for Congress . . . People have got to be willing to take a chance, to go out and raise the money, and devote a year of their life to running" (1 March 2013). A different national party recruiter echoed this point: "The truth is, most recruiting for Congress is self-recruiting. You are interested in politics, you are engaged with your party, and you decide to run. It's not because somebody told you about it; it's a motivation you have" (22 March 2013).

Candidates also bear the personal and professional costs associated with a congressional bid. And these costs are not trivial. For one, because most potential congressional candidates have reached some degree of success in their private lives, they may incur financial losses by putting their careers aside or on hold. Members of Congress certainly earn more than most Americans, but the salary is probably less than many of them made before they held office and less than they will make when they leave. Second, if they are lucky enough to be elected, when the grueling campaign season ends, most will have a grueling travel schedule between Washington and their districts. Third, candidates and elected officials are under constant scrutiny, and their private lives are opened up to the public. In the words of one former member, "People forget that you pay a big price to run for Congress. It's nice to say, 'You make $170,000 and blah, blah, blah.' But the opportunity costs are huge. It's not just financial. It's a big personal cost, not only to your family but to yourself, your reputation" (28 February 2013). In sum, it is the individual who must decide whether or not to throw her hat into the ring; it is the candidate who bears the costs for making that decision; and it is the candidate who is responsible for the outcome of the election.

## Party Fit and the Calculus of Candidacy

Although parties have become more influential in congressional elections (Herrnson 1986, 2004, 2010), the candidate-centered structure of the nomination process has compelled political scientists to focus on the ambitious office seeker, the so-called "self-starter" (see La Raja 2010 for a rich review). Ambition theory was stated first by Schlesinger (1966) and then transformed into a formal "calculus of candidacy" by Rohde (1979). An ambitious politician desires a long career in elected office, and whether she stays in one office ("static ambition" in the original formulation by Schlesinger), seeks to advance up the informal hierarchy of offices ("progressive ambition"), or even withdraws from politics entirely ("discrete ambition") is contingent on the configuration of benefits, costs, and risks that the ambitious politician faces. The expected utility of running for an office can be reduced to the probability of winning the seat times the benefit of holding the office minus the costs of running for it, expressed formally as $E(U) = p(B) - C$.[1] An individual is more likely to run for office as the probability of winning $(p)$ increases, the benefits of the office $(B)$ increase, and the costs of running $(C)$ decrease.

Of the three components of the calculus of candidacy, electoral concerns have been paramount in studies of political ambition. Scholars have explored a wide range of factors that influence candidates' likelihood of victory, such as the local and national political climate, previous electoral margins, district partisanship, and favorability of economic conditions (e.g., Rohde 1979; Bond, Covington, and Fleisher 1985; Jacobson 1989). The presence of an incumbent has perhaps the largest effect on a candidate's electoral prospects, particularly for quality candidates (Jacobson 2013; see also Banks and Kiewiet 1989). The overwhelming emphasis on electoral success is perhaps best represented by Mayhew's (1974) classic argument that legislators are "single-minded seekers of reelection." In describing the importance of the electoral incentive, Mayhew (1974, 16) writes that winning "has to be the proximate goal of everyone, the goal that must be achieved over and over if other ends are to be entertained."

The "other ends" are the subject of this book. Nonelectoral ends warrant our attention because they are an important, and an increasingly important, part of the candidate emergence process. The theoretical framework developed here focuses on how the partisan environment matters for the value of political office. I seek to introduce a new variable – what I call party fit – into studies of candidate entry. Party fit is the ideological congruence between a candidate and the party to which she would belong upon election or reelection.

The core argument is that the value of the office differs across individuals depending on their degree of party fit. Political parties have policy reputations that give meaning to their label and distinguish them from their opponent (Snyder and Ting 2002; Grynaviski 2010; Aldrich and Freeze 2011; Sniderman and Stiglitz 2012). The value of the office is greater when the party stands for policies that the legislator or potential legislator prefers. This variation in the benefits of holding office helps to explain why some individuals seek elected office and others do not. Individuals are more likely to select into electoral contests if they are a good ideological fit for the party, while those who are not will instead abstain.

---

[1]  A long line of research has used this conceptual framework (e.g., Schlesinger 1966; Black 1972; Rohde 1979; Aldrich 1980; Jacobson and Kernell 1983; Brace 1984; Abramson, Aldrich, and Rohde 1987; Maestas et al. 2006).

There are three reasons why ideological conformity with the party affects the value of an office. First, party fit influences whether legislators can achieve their policy goals. A national party recruiter spoke at length about the policy goals of candidates: "The ability to get something done is always a question for people that want to serve in public office. Can they be effective? Can they make a difference?" (22 March 2013). One former member of Congress said, "Those in office want to affect outcomes. They want to be legislators, not orators." Ideological nonconformists are less likely to shape the legislative agenda (Cox and McCubbins 2005), and they will be uncomfortable voting in favor of a policy agenda if they do not share these beliefs themselves. Furthermore, legislators face intense pressure to support the party's agenda, and those who defect can be punished for their actions and denied party rewards (Sinclair 2006; Theriault 2008; Pearson 2015).

Second, party fit influences the degree to which legislators can advance within the legislature or party. Party rewards are allocated to members who are of assistance to the team, and working with the party results in more, and oftentimes better, private goods (Lee 2009). Party loyalists are more likely to receive desirable committee posts (Rohde and Shepsle 1973; Smith and Ray 1983; Cox and McCubbins 1993; Sinclair 1995; Pearson 2015), and House leaders are closer to the party median than would occur by chance (Jessee and Malhotra 2010). The selection of leaders who resemble the median helps ensure that party agents execute the wishes of the caucus as a whole (Kiewiet and McCubbins 1991; Rohde 1991; Cox and McCubbins 1993). Those weighing a congressional run will consider how their ideology will affect their ability to move up the career ladder. It will likely be difficult for nonconformists to persuade their fellow partisans to entrust them with the party's agenda.[2]

Third, party fit influences the day-to-day experiences that legislators have in office. Ideological conformists by definition have more like-minded colleagues around them than do nonconformists, and this matters for the sense of camaraderie that members have with others. One former member likened the House floor to "a school cafeteria; you sit in the same place, with people that are ideologically aligned with you" (28 February 2013). Another member casually referred to those who shared his viewpoints as his "friends" (2 April 2013). A high-level staffer also

---

[2] Party fit may be more or less salient for candidate emergence depending on the particular historical context. For example, when party leaders had less power over the legislative agenda, we might expect party fit to have mattered less in this context. The benefits of party membership could have at least been higher for ideological nonconformists than they are today. This is discussed in more detail later.

highlighted how the personal and professional aspects of congressional service are intertwined: "This is a very human game – the kinds of people you're hanging around with, the way they approach the world, the way they see issues, and the way they see colleagues on the other side of the aisle" (22 January 2013). Although the bonds that members create can and do cross ideological lines, the congressional environment can also be isolating and hostile for those who do not share the worldview of their co-partisans.

Scholars have yet to fully explore how the partisan environment matters for the decision to run for office. Snyder and Ting (2002, 91) are among the few to suggest that "the costs [of party membership] will be different for different types of candidates." They show formally that these costs are lower for candidates whose ideologies are close to the preferences of the party than for those whose ideologies are further from the preferences of the party. As a result, parties effectively screen out candidates whose preferences are not sufficiently close to the party platform (Snyder and Ting 2002). The party fit argument builds on Snyder and Ting's (2002) insights but emphasizes the policy, party, and personal benefits of the office. Party fit also differs in that the magnitude of the effect can change over time and across contexts. Members from across the spectrum may have an easier time pursuing their policy goals in some congresses but not others; ideology may influence party rewards at some points but not others; and personal relationships and friendships may cut across ideological lines in some sessions but not others.

In sum, the main argument is that ideological conformity with the party influences the value of the office. Party fit differs from previous discussions of nonelectoral goals in that the benefits of the office are explicitly tied to members' ideological leanings. The expectation applies to incumbents considering a reelection bid and potential candidates who are considering running for office. Of course, the political situations of incumbents and nonincumbents differ markedly, and the likelihood that an incumbent seeks reelection will be much higher than the likelihood of a potential candidate running. Yet both constitute the pool of potential candidates for the next election cycle, and both are relevant to how the supply of congressional candidates has contributed to recent partisan changes in Congress.

## Party Fit in the Contemporary Context

The earliest research on legislator goals gave little attention to the benefits of congressional office because these benefits were understood to be constant across members (e.g., Downs 1957; Mayhew 1974). What differed across legislators were their reelection chances, which is why Mayhew (1974) focused on members' efforts to advertise their activities, claim credit, and take positions on issues. Fenno (1973) was among the first to suggest that the benefits of the office were not constant across members even at that time. He argued that, in addition to reelection, members also care about public policy and influence in the chamber.[3] Rohde and Aldrich (2010) added majority status as another factor that shapes the value of holding office, and increasingly so as the policy agendas of the parties have split (see also Maestas and Stewart 2012). In general, though, the value of holding office was thought of as relatively constrained across members, with majority party members and party leaders gaining more benefits from congressional office than their counterparts. This conception of the benefits of the office made sense when partisan attachments in the electorate and within Congress were weaker and members' ability to reap policy, party, and personal rewards in office was not as closely tied to their ideology.

The effect of party fit on candidate emergence is increasingly relevant in the current context because the value of congressional office is more variable across individuals. In the pre-polarized era, we could go further, though still not the whole way, toward understanding legislator behavior without paying as much attention to nonelectoral factors. Indeed, part of the reason both Mayhew and Fenno overlooked the relationship between member ideology and either electoral or nonelectoral goals was the smaller impact of ideology in the electoral and legislative environment at that time. Members across the ideological spectrum could shape the legislative agenda, advance in the party hierarchy, and forge alliances with their colleagues. However, the Congress of yesterday is a far cry from the Congress of today. As the parties drifted apart, the variance in the benefits of holding office increased across members. Now, in the midst of rising polarization, ideological conformists are much more likely to receive policy, party, and personal benefits than ideological deviants, regardless of how much electoral support they had in the last election or expect to have in the next one.

Today, candidates can also more easily assess their party fit because the parties' policy reputations are clearer and more distinct. In the mid-twentieth century, legislators with a wide array of preferences were united

---

[3] Though in Fenno's (1973) account, member ideology was not linked to members' ability to receive policy and party goods.

under a single party label that was murky and muddled. Voters rewarded incumbents, rather than political parties, at the ballot box. As Jacobson (2015) details, from the 1950s through the early 1980s, the incumbency advantage rose in parallel with a decline in party loyalty and a rise in split-ticket voting. Since then, it has fallen in concurrence with a sharp increase in party loyalty and straight-ticket voting for offices at all levels. Abramowitz and Webster (2015) find that from 1960 to 1980, Republican House candidates won just under 60 percent of the districts where Republican presidential candidates did well. By 2012, party-line voting was so strong that Republicans had "won a remarkable 95 percent of contests in Republican-leaning districts while Democrats won 93 percent of contests in Democratic-leaning districts" (Abramowitz and Webster 2015, 19).

In the contemporary era, members of Congress are part of a team that has a clear policy agenda, and the benefits of the office are distributed based on their adherence to this agenda. The central hypothesis is that, in the current polarized context, the value of congressional office is too low for liberal Republicans and conservative Democrats to run. It has become increasingly difficult for ideological moderates to influence the policy agenda, advance within the party, and forge bonds with their co-partisans.

### Diminished Policy Impact

In a 2013 article in the *National Review*, former moderate Republican Steve LaTourette discussed the policy impact of moderates in Congress: "It's a question of numbers. If you think that the [conservative] Republican Study Committee has 150 members out of 233 and the [moderate] Tuesday Group's sitting at 36, 40 – well, the math doesn't work in their favor" (Strong 2013). Former moderate Democrat and founder of the Blue Dog Coalition John Tanner similarly lamented, "The Blue Dogs could play a critical role if they could get a critical mass" (Kane 2014). Indeed, the moderates I interviewed described how their bargaining position changed as polarization increased. In the words of one moderate Republican who held office in the 1990s, "The moderates used to mean something. They were oftentimes the difference on whether legislation would pass or fail" (14 January 2013). Another explained, "We would appoint a delegation to see the Speaker, Majority Leader, or Whip, and say I've got 40 votes in my pocket that are no unless you bend the policy. We were a force to be reckoned with. If we didn't go with them, they didn't have a majority. We could influence policy on a daily basis" (2 April 2013).

A moderate Democrat who was in office during this time agreed, "[I was part of] a group of about 35 or 40 members that were pretty significant. If President Clinton had us on his side, then we were going to sustain the veto and he could effectively rule with less than a majority in Congress. That was an era of moderate fiscal Democrats having influence. That group of Democrats was the linchpin in Clinton being able to govern" (18 January 2013). A high-level staffer of a former representative similarly noted, "You matter to the extent that your votes matter. The whip paid attention to moderates not because he liked moderates but because he knew we controlled a bloc of votes. If we'd get [the votes], he wouldn't run over us" (22 January 2013).

Many members said that the influence of moderates in the 1990s was rooted in their numbers. One staffer explained, "The moderates were courted by the White House, by outside interest groups, and by party leaders. Swing votes are what matter, so as long as you're a swing vote, people are going to be after you" (22 January 2013). In this case, having people "be after you" is a good thing. A moderate Republican who served in Congress for nearly 25 years described how, during the Reagan years, those who were in a "small hardy band of moderates" were courted by the Administration. After he got invited to "yet another" function at the White House, he recalled a conservative Republican colleague saying, jokingly, "I support the Administration all the time and eat cold pizza in my office, and you're down at the White House eating high on the hog." This member elaborated on the treatment that was given to partisan nonconformists:

We were paid more attention to. My feeling is that if you're entirely predictable, then you're ignored and taken for granted – either he's going to be with us or he'll never be with us. For those who don't always agree with the party, they're the ones that are paid the most attention. During the Clinton years, there were steak dinners. [Laughs] My wife and I had a wonderful time, socially, at the Clinton White House. I was frequently, not the majority of the time, but frequently in the camp of those who were following the wishes of the Clinton administration in terms of legislation. It wasn't because we wanted invitations to have lunch, it's because we supported a higher minimum wage, environmental issues, a whole bunch of things. (14 January 2013)

The moderates of yesterday were able to put pressure on the party leadership and wield some control over the legislative agenda, and they had an impact on policy because they could show their votes. A member of the Tuesday Group recounted the following story of how they used their leverage to influence reproductive health care. He said that every year in the appropriations process, when domestic family planning came up, conservative members always had an amendment that required parental consent for birth control. Every year this member would bring an amendment to the floor to strike the parental consent clause, and he would win because the Democrats voted for it as well as the moderate Republicans. The conservatives "got tired of getting their butts ripped on this one," so one year they went to the whip and asked him to make sure that this member's amendment was not made in order. He explained that in order to offer an amendment, members have to go to the Rules Committee the day before the debate, present their amendment, and ask the committee for permission to make it in order. He was always granted this opportunity, but that year he found out that the Rules Committee was not going to make his amendment in order.

The day before the family planning vote, the Foreign Operations Appropriations bill was up for a vote. The bill was controversial; no Democrats were going to vote for it, and virtually every Republican had to be present to vote. At the Tuesday Group meeting, the member told his colleagues that the whip had given the Rules Committee quiet orders to make his amendment on parental consent out of order. He said that he needed everybody in the Tuesday Group to vote no on the Foreign Operations bill that afternoon. When the vote came that day, this member was at the floor early and he had his thumb down. They had fifteen minutes to complete the vote. He said "his friends" were walking in and putting their voting cards in the machine. As requested, they were pushing the red button for no. The whip and his team were completely taken by surprise by the red votes on the board. When the whip's staff saw this member with his thumb down, the whip ran up to the member. He described the exchange that unfolded:

[The whip] literally grabbed me by the tie and said, "You can't take this bill down just because you're mad about your amendment for tomorrow." Now there are about three minutes left in this vote. I said, "Look at the vote, it's going down. I think what you mean to say to me is that what I am doing is not very nice." "Well it's not very nice!" I said, "What you're doing to me on this family planning thing is not very nice either." The whip replied, "Alright, I will not tell the Rules Committee not to make your amendment in order." Now there's like a minute left. I said, "Nah, you've got to tell me that they will make it in order." He agreed, "Okay, your amendment will be made in order." Now there's about 30 seconds left. I said, "You have to tell me one more thing." "What's that?!" "You have to tell me that I'm pretty." "Alright, you're pretty!" I put my thumb up, everyone switched their votes, and the bill passed. The next day, my amendment was in order, and we won. (2 April 2013)

Yet much of this policy work was done quietly and behind the scenes. One Republican remarked, "We did a lot more to keep things off the floor and to adjust them before they came on the floor" (23 January 2013). The Republican whip at the time used to ask prominent moderate members how this group would respond to various pieces of legislation: "He would quiz me, 'If we did this, what would your people think?' That's what he'd say, 'your people.' He wasn't trying to get information to change his mind, but he would get intelligence to guide his decisions. He would gauge the degree of my response – either 'all hell would break loose' or 'well, you're going to get opposition'" (14 January 2013).

However, as the makeup of the parties changed, so too did the experiences of moderates. Their waning numbers made it increasingly difficult for them to shape the legislative agenda. The formal membership of the Tuesday Group has not declined in the same way the Blue Dogs' membership has, but its ideological center has moved to the right. Even Representative Charlie Dent (R-PA), the current co-chair of the Tuesday Group, has said that its members are "a little more conservative today" than when he first joined. Political scientist Alan Abramowitz puts it more directly: the current members of the Tuesday Group may be "stylistically more moderate" in terms of language and presentation, "but their voting records say otherwise" (quoted in Zwick 2011). For the moderates of yesterday, this new crop of members made less than desirable allies. One high-level staffer whom I interviewed highlighted these internal divisions: "Every single time we talk, [the former member] will say, 'Boy, did I leave at the right time. If we had stayed, we wouldn't have been able to work the way we did because there wouldn't have been anyone to work with. The fierceness is getting more and more, and it would be very hard'" (22 January 2013).

Forging bipartisan policy coalitions also became harder as the parties drifted apart. When asked how his congressional career evolved, a former moderate Republican stated, "Early on, it was easier to be moderate than it was when the party became more conservative and more Southern. Through H.W. Bush and the Clinton era, being a moderate was a pretty cool thing because you could make deals with the other side. But during the [George W.] Bush administration, people got dug in on both sides and it made it really hard" (23 January 2013). This member noted, "You can't go across the aisle like you used to to get things done. People come here to get things done. They came to help their community, get things fixed in their community, get things built, and create a better quality of life. You can't do that now. It does change the reward for all the sacrifices you make to be there" (23 January 2013).

### Decline in Party Rewards

Obtaining a leadership position or even a desirable committee assignment became increasingly difficult for moderates as well. One moderate Republican remarked, "[If you were a moderate] you couldn't get elected to any position of conference leadership. I did run once, but someone else won. After that I never ran for leadership." I asked this member if she thought she was not able to get a leadership position because of her ideology. She replied, "That was my conclusion" (23 January 2013). Those in the Tuesday Group did try to get an edge into leadership, but "they gave us positions of no power, name only... We knew that we could not stand for leadership in any capacity" (24 January 2013). In his memoir, *Seeking Bipartisanship*, former moderate Republican Ray LaHood (OH) wrote that he was the "case study for how leaders punish wayward members." LaHood was one of only three newly elected House members who refused to sign the Contract with America. This decision closed the door to any leadership position, resulted in his temporary removal from presiding over the House, and left him "an odd man out" in the party (LaHood 2015, 23).

Party loyalty is also an influential factor in the distribution of committee assignments (Pearson 2015). One moderate Republican put it very simply: "There is no question that committee assignments were allocated in such a way" (7 February 2013). Another member elaborated, "If you dare deviate too much from the party line, at least within the GOP circles, you pay a penalty in some cases. The next time comes around and you want a better committee assignment, you're given little attention. I never had a chance of getting Ways and Means, Energy and Commerce, or Appropriations because I deviated too much from the party position." With respect to whether his ideology was a factor in why he received his particular committee assignment, he replied, "No question about it. For most people, their voting record determines how they're treated in terms of requested committee assignments. Freshmen are interviewed by the committee chair, and if the chair discovers that you believe in climate change, you don't have a chance of getting on that committee" (14 January 2013).

Many of the moderate Republicans had stories about how they were denied committee positions or demoted to lower-tier committees. One member explained how, in not granting her request, the leadership even purported to be acting in the member's best interest: "When I wanted to get on Appropriations, [the leadership told me,] 'We don't want to put you on the spot, because you'd have to vote on some of those issues and your constituency wouldn't like it. You can't be the renegade on Appropriations; you have to cooperate. And you don't want to do that; it would be terrible.'" She then added, "It was all phony, but nevertheless" (22 January 2013). Another moderate recalled how, after he expressed interest in being a subcommittee chair, Speaker Gingrich told him, "Sure, you can." Then Gingrich rescinded the offer because, this member was told, "Grover Norquist doesn't want this" (14 March 2013). The Speaker never gave the member an explanation, but he suspected it was because he was too moderate.

Another member who served on the Transportation Committee for over a decade gave this account: "When we lost the majority in 2006, [the ranking member] determined that my future wasn't on the Railroad Subcommittee, it was on the Coast Guard Subcommittee, which was not a very good post. I objected, and he said, 'Well, it's your labor votes. We can't have you do that.' I went to [the Speaker] and he said he'd talk to [the ranking member]. He did, and it didn't make any difference." The member concluded, "They can't kill you, but what they can do is indicate, well, you're done. You're not going to be in charge of railroads anymore" (28 February 2013). The fates of a handful of other moderate Republicans were even worse. One high-level staffer explained that after 1995, when party leaders changed committee assignments from being based on seniority to being leadership driven, a number of members who would have received chair positions under seniority were passed over "because they were viewed as not sufficiently reliable" (22 January 2013).

The experience of one former member who sat on the Appropriations Committee provides a rich illustration of how the allocation of committee assignments has changed in recent years. He recalled that in the late 1980s and 1990s, the leadership was less concerned with the member's ideology: "[With respect to the Appropriations Committee,] they just wanted somebody who was respected, hardworking, conscientious; there was no litmus test. More and more, there's a litmus test. On both sides. [Then] it was just politics, it was who was better organized and who could make the best case." I asked this member whether he was ever subjected to an ideological litmus test. "There was one test," he said.

I was a subcommittee chairman on Appropriations. When there was an election, I was of course reelected [as subcommittee chair]. The leadership had given more power to the Steering Committee so the Steering Committee had more control over who got what positions. I remember going in there one time. I had to interview with them as a subcommittee chair on Appropriations. They interviewed the full committee chairman and the subcommittee chairmen on Appropriations because Appropriations was so powerful and so important. The Steering Committee votes on who gets these chairmanships. They make a recommendation to the conference, and the conference basically ratifies it. So when I went before the Steering Committee, one specific member really grilled me about spending, really came after me. It was the first time that my Republican credentials were questioned, and she didn't really have the votes to stop me. But she made it very clear. I didn't know whether she was doing her own bidding or someone else's bidding, but in any event, I got it. (23 January 2013)

This member suggested that the ideological makeup of the Steering Committee in the 1990s, then the Committee on Committees, might have mattered for committee assignments then as well. He said, "I knew when I went to Washington [that I wanted to be on Appropriations] so I had a plan and I followed the plan and it worked." But, the member noted, "If I had tried this maybe ten years later, I might have had a problem because more of the decisions were made by Southern conservative members. When I went through, there were more Eastern, Midwestern, and Northern representatives [on the Committee on Committees], so it was easier for me to line up support" (23 January 2013).

It should be noted that not all members are concerned with advancing to leadership, at least not to the same degree. One of the moderate Democrats echoed the comments of her Republican counterparts, and she too believed she did not play a role in leadership because of her unwillingness to vote in lockstep with the party. She continued, "But that wasn't exactly what I was interested in" (22 January 2013). Similarly, a moderate Republican member who entered Congress at a later stage in life said, "I didn't have any place to go; I wasn't looking for a leadership position . . . I'd had my career in business. I wasn't going for any brass ring. I didn't want to be head of any committee; I didn't want to be the Speaker of the House. I just wanted to do what I could for the district and for the country" (14 March 2013). Yet policy and leadership goals are intertwined to some degree, and the higher members move up in the party or chamber, the more of an impact they are likely to have on policy outcomes.

## A Hostile Congressional Environment
In addition to their diminished policy impact and stature in the chamber, a third factor made congressional service increasingly difficult for those in

the middle. Many of these members, particularly moderate Republicans, spoke at length about how the job itself became "frustrating," "unsatisfying," and "increasingly confrontational" (14 January 2013; 25 January 2013). A moderate Democrat who retired added that it was "no longer as much fun" (25 January 2013). One Republican groaned, "Everything was a fight," and likened his experiences to "those clown things you punch" (22 January 2013). These day-to-day struggles did wear on members: "Every day going in and being the odd man out ... It's grueling; it's exhausting; it's corrosive" (22 January 2013). Another said, "It's not fun anymore. Your job is not supposed to be fun like going to an amusement park, but it should be pleasant. Members are saying it's not pleasant anymore. Legislators now have such intense feelings. You're viewed like a heretic by people who have a different point of view than you. That's not very good, not very healthy for the republic" (14 January 2013). The political environment was becoming more hostile, and the daily interactions between members reflected the heightened level of partisanship in Congress. The experiences of moderate Republicans and Democrats differed the most in terms of intraparty conflict.

Most of the moderate Republicans gave several examples of negative interactions they had with their conservative colleagues. One member described his experience at a weekly party conference meeting: "The leadership would go over the schedule for the week; the whip would say this is what we're going to do. It's sort of a cheerleading session, chin up the troops, keep them psyched up to follow the party line. Then they always have an open forum, and invariably it was people on the right who spoke at those. Occasionally a moderate would get up. I remember standing up there and advocating an increase in the minimum wage and I was booed. By my own conference" (14 January 2013). A former staffer to a moderate Republican explained how the tension between moderates and ideologues surfaced in both formal and informal settings:

There was one time a [conservative] Republican member asked [the moderate] in an elevator how he would react to some particular environmental thing. Our view was going to matter. [The conservative] was a California member, so [the moderate] said, "What does Henry Waxman think of it?" He didn't say, "I will do whatever Waxman [a liberal Democrat from California] wants." He just wanted to get a sense of how controversial this was. Probably wasn't the most politic thing to say, but not outrageous. That member refused to talk to [the moderate] for at least three months, maybe longer, because he had asked the view of a Democrat. (22 January 2013)

One reason this exchange was not very "politic" was that this member was not engaging in partisan team play. Members typically turn to their co-partisans for additional information on a policy issue (Kingdon 1981). The shared interests of partisans bring members closer together and distance them from the opposition (Lee 2009). As this anecdote reveals, members who step outside of the party boundaries face consequences for doing so.

Another moderate Republican gave a particularly disturbing account of how her colleagues helped to mount a primary challenge against her:

A congressman and a prominent party leader came up into my district to help a former congressman who was running against me in the primary. They helped him raise money to defeat me, and they brought the Club for Growth. I defeated them and the Club for Growth. The second time they came up, I went to [the leader] personally and said, "This has got to stop. I am a sitting congresswoman. You have no business coming into my district trying to defeat me. You may not agree with me, but helping my opponent raise money, that's outrageous."

She then took the issue up at a conference meeting. She stood up in front of her colleagues and said, "I want to say that I am running for Congress. I sit with you here, and people in this conference are helping my opponent raise money." Then "[the leader] perked up and said this must not be done and so on. His last words were, 'Well, you may not agree with her politics, and she may be a moderate, but there ain't nobody in this group that doesn't like [her].'" The member paused and added, "Think about this; you are standing up in a crowd of more than 200 people. But I had to do that. I thought you should understand how hard that is" (7 February 2013).

Trying to unseat a co-partisan is especially egregious, but most of the Republicans had stories about how conservative members took jabs at them. In fact, the party rarely employs formal sanctions, and most altercations between members take place on the sidelines – in the elevators, at committee hearings, and during conference meetings. As one moderate noted, "I never had any threats, but ridicule, yes" (14 March 2013). Another moderate recalled this exchange at a committee meeting: "There was a [freshman] representative who was holier than thou. He'd look at me with such disdain, like you're part of the problem, you're the reason they sent me here. This guy was implying that I was just a bleeding heart" (23 January 2013). Another moderate described a similarly negative confrontation: "I was in the elevator that you take up to the House floor, and a fellow member from Texas said, 'So you're a self-identified moderate, middle-of-the-road guy, right?' I said yes. He said, 'There's only two things in the middle of the road: yellow lines and dead skunks'" (28 February 2013).

As above, these types of interactions did not seem to affect all moderates equally. One former member said, "At a Republican meeting, [the whip] ridiculed me as being soft. [He said,] 'Is this the type of representative we want to have, who will not stand up for those things we all believe in?' And he went on this way. There were some people who couldn't stand that. But it didn't bother me." This member even went on to claim, "Serving in Congress was the most wonderful experience I'd ever had in my life" (14 March 2013). Yet the general evaluations of the party were not very rosy. As one moderate Republican said, "Things are not good, not good at all for Republicans, and especially not good for moderates" (7 February 2013).[4]

Most moderate Republicans agreed that intraparty retribution usually came from members rather than the leadership. In the words of one member, "The party leaders are different. Every single person has a vote, and leaders need every single one to vote for them. It's not so much top leadership. They know you need diversity within the conference, quite frankly" (23 January 2013). This is in part because their replacements would likely be worse for the party. Once a moderate was accused of not being conservative enough, and he reminded the leadership, "If you don't have me, you're going to get a Democrat, not a conservative Republican." He then added, "They got a Democrat when I left" (14 January 2013). Another moderate said, "Newt Gingrich, to his credit, recognized that without people like me, they're not the majority. There aren't enough people like him to win enough seats to give the Republicans the majority. He suffered our presence because he realized that without us, he's not the Speaker of the House" (28 February 2013).

---

[4] Some members also discussed how other moderates were treated, and the various accounts were occasionally inconsistent. For example, one moderate described her own experiences as follows: "Some of [my co-partisans] genuinely liked me and respected what I was doing, but they were all nice to me. Nobody was ever nasty." However, this member came up in another interview and was described as being shunned. Conversely, one member suggested that two of the other moderates I spoke with were not ridiculed, but those members themselves gave several examples of the negative interactions they had with partisan colleagues. In general, I opted to discuss the member's own portrayal of events.

Majority party status is a key consideration for leaders and members alike (Lee 2009; Rohde and Aldrich 2010). One moderate Democrat who spent most, but not all, of his time in the minority speculated that the size of the caucus might also matter for how different factions of the party are treated: "Part of it is when there are 265 Democrats, you can alienate a certain number of people. But when the number is smaller and you have more tension in terms of trying to retake the majority, you need everyone. You can't piss an individual person off at all" (18 January 2013). The degree of ridicule may vary based on the size of the caucus, but moderate Republicans reported negative interactions with their colleagues when they were in either the majority or the minority. And even though much of the bullying came from rank-and-file members, as one member noted, "The top leadership condoned it" (7 February 2013).

### Party Asymmetries

The effect of party fit may differ for Republicans and Democrats due to the distinct characters of the parties. Grossman and Hopkins (2015, 2016) suggest that ideological orthodoxy is not similarly valued in both parties. They argue that the Republican Party is the agent of an ideological movement whose supporters value doctrinal purity, whereas the Democratic Party is a looser coalition of social groups that seek government action (see also Freeman 1986). Indeed, despite recent attention to factions within the Republican Party, the Democratic Party has remained relatively more ideologically diverse than the GOP (Bonica 2014). The relative heterogeneity within the Democratic caucus may mean that leaders have fewer party sticks at their disposal (Rohde 1991; Aldrich 1995, 2011; Aldrich and Rohde 2001). Pearson (2015) also finds that intraparty groups in the Democratic conference are better able to limit leaders' abilities to exert party discipline than they are in the Republican conference. Due to these differences in structure and organization, Republicans may experience greater levels of formal and informal pressure to conform to party orthodoxy than their Democratic counterparts.

A related point is that the two parties differ with respect to ideological clarity, and politically elite Democrats have a somewhat looser understanding of ideology than politically elite Republicans. Data from a 2006 survey of political experts across congressional districts show that 71 percent of Republican experts identify as conservative or very conservative while only 53 percent of Democratic experts identify as liberal or very liberal. The standard deviation in self-reported ideology is 0.98 for Republican experts and 1.29 for Democratic experts (Stone 2010).

Similarly, the standard deviation in self-reported ideology for Republican and Democratic state legislators in the CES dataset is 0.81 and 1.33, respectively (Maestas et al. 2006). As well, the Democrats who ran for the House from 1980 to 2012 were more diverse than the Republican candidates (Bonica 2014). The standard deviation in candidate ideology was 0.50 for Republicans and 0.62 for Democrats, and the larger ideological spread among Democratic candidates is apparent in all but 3 of the 17 elections during this time. Although the ideologies of both parties have become clearer over the past few decades, what it means to be a Republican seems to be clearer than what it means to be a Democrat.

As noted above, the moderate Democrats I spoke with did not have the same experiences as their Republican counterparts. First, party rewards have not been withheld to the same degree on the Democratic side, particularly in terms of committee assignments. One Democrat stated, "I just had to convince [the Steering Committee] that those were the committees that would benefit my constituents and that I had some understanding of and background in [the issues]. There was certainly no litmus test" (11 February 2013). Another agreed, "I don't feel I was discriminated against by the Democratic caucus in any shape, manner, or form. I was chosen to be on Energy and Commerce in 1994, which was a competitive process. And on Energy and Commerce, I was chosen to be a subcommittee ranking member pretty much continuously. There might have been people who felt discriminated against; I did not, period" (18 January 2013).

To be sure, one of the moderate Democrats believed she did not play a role in leadership because of her unwillingness to toe the party line, but many of the other moderate Democrats I interviewed actually held high-level leadership positions. They experienced limited pressure to change their policy positions, and in some cases, leaders even preemptively excused moderates from voting with the party. One former Democratic member recalled, "I had any number of people in the leadership tell me, 'Don't worry if you have to [vote against the party] because of your district. Do what you have to do.' I never had anybody put pressure on me to vote one way or the other. Never" (11 February 2013).

Democratic leaders would certainly ask moderates to support the party's agenda, but there seemed to be few repercussions for not doing so. As one Democrat said,

I never felt any pressure in the Democratic caucus. Tip O'Neill would come to me on an issue and say, "Can you help me on this?" I would say, "Mr. Speaker, I cannot help you on this." That was the end of the conversation, no pressure.

I could vote my conscience and my district without feeling undue pressure, and that happened to me a number of times under [Speakers] Tip O'Neill, Jim Wright, and Tom Foley. Many times they asked me, and they took my answer as my final decision. I never received any threats about my chairmanship, unlike what my colleagues in the Republican conference experienced. (25 January 2013)

What is more, Pearson (2015) suggests that Blue Dog Democrats were able to support the party because they influenced the legislative process along the way and that the policy influence of majority party Blue Dogs was greater than that of majority party Tuesday Group members. In 2009 and 2010, for example, Speaker Nancy Pelosi negotiated at length with senior Blue Dogs over the Affordable Care Act, and they played an important role in eliminating the public insurance option even though they ultimately voted against the bill (Fabian 2010; Kane 2014).

In addition, moderate Democrats did not express similarly negative interactions with fellow members. One member stated simply, "I never was ridiculed. [Your colleagues] knew you had to go where your persuasion is" (11 February 2013). Another moderate Democrat agreed, "I didn't think there were any obstacles because of my ideology." He elaborated, "There was clearly a debate going on [in the party], but I don't think anyone took it personally in any negative way. It's not life and death. There will be another day; there will be another issue. You're going to be friends with people on the opposite side of that particular issue... People have respect for other members. It's not a little deal that people get elected" (18 January 2013).

But the Democrats have still had to deal with their own internal divisions. One member described the events that unfolded within the Democratic caucus following the 1994 elections:

I can remember it like it's today. The Democratic caucus was meeting in the Ways and Means Committee room. There were 250 odd Democrats in the Congress that ended. It was unprecedented how many people lost in the 1994 cycle. It was one of these group therapy sessions. The purpose was [to talk about] what happened and what we were going to do. Everyone had a few minutes to talk. The room was full. It lasted for hours, four or five hours. Maybe one hundred people spoke, and with heart-wrenching intensity. I remember thinking to myself that this was an absolutely incredible meeting. Of the people there, the clear majority of those who spoke attributed our losses to us not being liberal enough. I was thinking to myself that in the United States of America, there were probably two hundred people that thought the reason the Democrats lost was because we were not liberal enough. Of those two hundred people, one hundred were members of Congress in that room. (18 January 2013)

It is difficult to believe that Democrats were never pressured to support the party, since moderate Republicans as well as moderate Democrats became more loyal over this time period (Roberts and Smith 2003). Indeed, in a 2009 interview with the *Star Tribune*, Blue Dog Democrat Collin Peterson (MN) said, "I go against my party sometimes, and it's not easy. You come under a lot of pressure. Peer pressure and leadership pressure" (Diaz 2009). We should be cautious given the small sample of members interviewed here, and it is possible that pressure has increased within the Democratic ranks in recent years. But Democrats still largely respect the norm of seniority in the allocation of committee assignments, and moderate Democrats appear to have a more cordial relationship with their colleagues and a greater policy impact than moderate Republicans (Pearson 2015; Karol forthcoming). It is also telling that virtually no moderate Democrats who left office have been critical of the party, whereas several prominent moderate Republicans have publicly voiced their concerns over the direction of the GOP. Although moderate Democrats reap fewer benefits and rewards than they used to, ideological nonconformity seems to be tolerated to a greater degree on the Democratic side.

### Direction of Ideological Distance

While those who are too extreme for the party may also be dissuaded from seeking office, party fit is expected to work in different ways depending on the direction of the distance. Neither ideologues nor moderates are probably the most popular members of their party, and there have been public displays of exasperation among party factions in recent years. However, within the framework developed here, the value of the office is nevertheless expected to be greater and the congressional environment is expected to be more attractive to ideologues than it is to moderates. For one, ideologues are less likely to be cross-pressured than those in the middle, because their preferences are much closer to their party's position than that of the opposing party. Moderates often face tradeoffs that ideologues do not between supporting their party and supporting a more desirable policy offered by the other party.

Ideologues are also more likely to receive party rewards. Ideologues in Congress today are much more likely to advance in the party and obtain a leadership position than moderates (Grofman, Koetzle, and McGann 2002; King and Zeckhauser 2002; Heberlig et al. 2006; Harris and Nelson 2008; Jessee and Malhotra 2010). Patterson (1963) noted long ago that leadership choices vary across contexts and that extreme members are more likely to be selected as leaders in highly partisan legislatures.

These members are better able to sharpen interparty divides and engage in "counterpunching" across the aisle (King and Zeckhauser 2002). Pearson (2015) also finds that Republican leaders were willing to discipline moderates, but they rewarded recalcitrant conservatives. In an analysis of the 104th and 105th Congresses, she shows that members of the Tuesday Group had fewer resolutions considered on the floor, and fewer of their amendments were made in order. Tea Party Republicans, in contrast, had more of their amendments considered in the 112th Congress (Pearson 2015, 170). Pearson (2015, 173) suggests that life was more uncomfortable in the GOP for moderate dissenters than conservative dissenters, but in both parties, moderates have been on the losing end of the distribution of party benefits.

In addition, if prospective candidates consider the anticipated direction of the party, it is clear that the extreme ends of both parties have prevailed in recent years. While just 10 to 20 percent of Republican representatives belonged to the conservative Republican Study Committee in the 1980s, nearly 70 percent of Republicans in the current Congress are members (Mann and Ornstein 2012). On the Democratic side, the Congressional Progressive Caucus also experienced a "remarkable reversal of political fortune" in recent years (Brodey 2015). The number of members has grown steadily since its founding in 1991, and the CPC now boasts around 70 members, the largest share of the full Democratic caucus it has ever had (Brodey 2015). Liberal Democrats and conservative Republicans have seen their numbers soar over the past several election cycles, and many more legislators now share the ideological worldview of ideologues than that of moderates. In contrast, future prospects look more and more dismal for moderates, as neither party is likely to move toward the center any time soon. Ideologues might expect the future value of congressional office to increase, while moderates might expect the future value to be even lower than it currently is. In fact, for those who consider their party's future location, it is possible that the value of the office may even be higher for ideologues than for conformists, though I have no strong expectations due to the measurement issues that will be discussed below.

Although ideological extremity is not expected to have a negative effect on the probability of running for Congress, the value of the office is likely to decrease among extreme ideological outliers. For example, in Shames' (2017) study of political ambition among law, policy, and business students, one MPP student at Harvard said, "Another reason I wouldn't run is I'm too much on the left. I find that the current left is too centrist, and I just wouldn't feel comfortable with that. People who fit more comfortably within those spheres are more likely to run; I mean, you don't see hardcore environmentalists or libertarians running in a serious way."

We can think about party fit in multiple ways, and party fit may operate differently depending on the context. In the contemporary polarized era, distance from the party in the extreme direction does not have the same implications for the value of congressional office as distance in the moderate direction. It is more difficult for moderates to achieve their goals in office, and moderates and ideologues do not face the same disadvantages in their pursuit of policy and party benefits. The experience of serving in office is also likely to be more fulfilling, as well as more pleasant, for ideologues as their ranks grow. My focus is on the declining value of congressional office among moderates for two reasons. First, the opting out of moderates from the candidate pool has huge implications for polarization over the long term. Moderates kept the parties anchored at the center, and the middle has dissolved with their departure. Moreover, ideologues must value congressional office because we know that replacement processes are responsible for much of the increase in polarization (e.g., Fleisher and Bond 2004; Roberts and Smith 2003; Theriault 2006; Carmines 2011). The other reason for the focus on moderates is theoretical, as this depiction of those in the center is somewhat inconsistent with leading theories of legislative organization. The latter point is discussed below.

### The Best Seat in the House

In Krehbiel's (1991, 1993) classic work on legislative organization, the median legislator in the chamber occupies perhaps the most coveted position in the House. In this model, policy outcomes reflect the preferences of the floor median, and this legislator wields an enormous amount of power and influence over the policy agenda. It is therefore puzzling if those who would have the most legislative clout choose not to run or if those who have the most legislative clout choose to retire. Slim congressional majorities should have further enhanced the power of moderates. Indeed, a former Republican senator described how the institutional environment was especially favorable for moderates when he was first elected:

With a 50–50 Senate, we [five moderate Republicans] were the swing votes. If we vote for the Democrats, the Democrats win; if we vote for the Republicans, the Republicans win. This was our moment in history. We could've been the most powerful five people in the country because of a fluke of numbers, going from utterly powerless to ultimate power. Nothing passes without our agreeing to it. Come see us on every piece of legislation; we'll decide if it passes. We missed our opportunity.

I asked the senator why he thought that happened. "That's the million-dollar question. We couldn't band together on the key vote of the first Bush presidency, which was the tax cuts. [Vice-President] Cheney got on [the moderates]. They peeled away [and supported the party]." The former moderate senator also attributed this loyalty to the party's control of rewards and to "frankly, lack of backbone. [Members think,] 'I don't want to buck 45 other people in the party. I want to go along and get along.' You don't want to get kicked out of the club. You're going to need the party behind you when you run for reelection. There's peer pressure. It's a mix" (8 March 2013).

It should be evident that the party fit framework instead starts with the notion that party leaders set the policy agenda (e.g., Rohde 1991; Aldrich 1995, 2011; Cox and McCubbins 1993, 2005; Aldrich and Rohde 2001; Sinclair 1995, 2006). In this case, increased ideological distance from the leadership results in a decreased impact on the policy agenda, and the best policy seat in the House is where the leadership is. But regardless of who sets the policy agenda, the value of the office may still be lower for moderates depending on the configuration of preferences in the legislature. Consider two distributions of legislators; one is unimodal and the other is bimodal. The floor median is the same, and those to the left and right of the median are Democrats and Republicans, respectively. Yet the benefits of the office differ for the median legislator in each case. In the unimodal case, there are many legislators in close proximity to the median. But in the bimodal case, there are few centrists and they are outsiders in their party. Without numerical leverage, legislators in the middle experience pressure from their colleagues at the extremes. As fewer moderates choose to join or remain in this environment, the number of centrists diminishes further. The severity of the pressure on those who remain increases because fewer moderates are available to target and more ideologues are available to pressure them.

In general, little attention has been paid to how the situation of the median legislator varies under different circumstances. Rubin's (2013) recent work is a notable exception. She argues that legislators located at the floor median require "the scaffolding of an intraparty organization to secure pivotal status." Potentially pivotal members can more fully exercise their authority over party leaders and other party factions when they manage to stay together and coordinate their defection. The ability to mount a successful challenge also depends on the willingness of the other party to collaborate. Rubin (2013, 110) writes, "A legislator is pivotal only if she can threaten to leave, and a legislator can only threaten to leave if she can credibly work with the other party." Such a threat has likely become less credible as the parties have drifted apart and as leaders have increasingly pursued internal strategies. One aide to a Blue Dog Democrat remarked, "The GOP leadership has adopted a Republicans-only approach to passing all bills; they have the strategy of getting 218 votes with Republican votes. We have no opportunity for input; it's a Republicans-only process" (quoted in Pearson 2015, 50). As partisanship increased in the Republican-controlled congresses in the 1990s and early 2000s, Blue Dogs replaced their outsider tactics with insider ones, and they were fairly well integrated into the Democratic Party when the Democrats regained the majority in 2006 (Pearson 2015).

The broader point is that the experience of the median legislator changes across contexts. In a polarized environment, the median is expected to be less desirable than some theories would suggest. And it is easy to understand why in light of the differences in the benefits of the office across individuals. As the moderates' party organizations have withered away, legislators located at the floor median can neither credibly threaten to work with an increasingly distant and insular opposition party nor muster sufficient numbers to influence the direction of their own party. Moderates also face growing hostility from leaders and rank-and-file members, and they have fewer like-minded colleagues and friends to work with in office. Prominent theories of legislative organization suggest that being pivotal is desirable, but in practice, it is often difficult, both politically and socially, to be in this position. Furthermore, the fact that we do not see moderate candidates seeking congressional office and we do see moderate incumbents leaving congressional office provides at least some indication that the floor median is no longer the best seat in the House.

### The Causal Argument: How Party Fit Exacerbates Polarization

Party fit can be a stabilizing force in party politics, as parties remain stable when they attract like-minded candidates to run for office. However, when parties begin to change course due to some other factor or set of factors, candidate self-selection processes can be a mechanism of change as well. As noted in the previous chapter, party fit is not an account of why the parties in Congress started to diverge, and we must rely on other explanations for the origins of polarization. The most developed explanation highlights partisan and geographical shifts in the electoral coalitions of the two parties (see Jacobson 2000). Some would pinpoint the origins of polarization as the passage of the Voting Rights Act of 1965 and the electoral realignments that ensued (Rohde 1991; Aldrich 1995, 2011; Aldrich and Rohde 2001). Following the rise in elite partisanship (Hetherington 2001; Smidt forthcoming), the persistence in polarization has also been attributed to the clearer sorting of voters into the two parties (Hetherington 2001; Levendusky 2009), polarization of the engaged public (Abramowitz and Saunders 2008; Abramowitz 2010), and increasing extremism among party activists (Layman and Carsey 2002; Fiorina et al. 2006; Theriault 2008; Layman et al. 2010).

As these changes took hold, the party coalitions in Congress evolved as well. Although incumbents who seek reelection win at rates over 90 percent, the turnover that occurs between congresses is sizeable enough to affect the party's course. From 1980 to 2012, an average of 14 percent of the House membership, or roughly 60 members, changed with each legislative session (Manning and Peterson 2013). During this time, the number of first-term representatives ranged from a high of 109 members, or 25 percent of the House, in the 103rd Congress (1993–4) to a low of 30 members, or 7 percent of the House, in the 101st Congress (1989–90) (Manning and Peterson 2013). Through the entrance of new members and the exit of incumbents, party caucuses shift slowly but steadily with each election cycle. Thus, although party fit can be a force for stability, the concept of party fit is very much a dynamic one.

As the interviews suggested, what it meant to be a Republican or a Democrat in the 1980s is very different from what it means to be a Republican or Democrat today. Conservative Southern Democrats and liberal Northeastern Republicans were influential wings of their parties throughout much of the late twentieth century (Polsby 2004; Kabaservice 2012). One of the older moderate Republicans whom I interviewed echoed this point. He said, "I'm not a conservative; don't call me a conservative. I'm a Republican. The conservatives have taken over my party. My heroes were Dewey, Eisenhower, Rockefeller, people like that. They represented the party" (14 March 2013). For moderates, the benefits of holding congressional office decreased as the party moved away from them. Because the hollowing out of the center occurred over many elections, it is difficult to know when a tipping point may have been reached and when the value of the office became too low for moderates to run. However, the issue of timing will be addressed in more detail in the concluding chapter.

## Concepts and Measurement

### *The Concept of Party Fit*

Party fit is the ideological congruence between a candidate and the party to which she would belong upon election or reelection. The better a candidate fits with her party, the more policy, party, and personal benefits she derives from the office (see also Aldrich and Thomsen forthcoming). The natural measure of party fit is simply the difference between the ideal point of the individual and that of her party in the legislature. To measure party fit empirically, we therefore need to establish how to measure candidate ideology and how to measure party ideology. The candidate ideology measures are straightforward, in large part because of data availability, but the question of how to measure the ideology of the party is trickier.

Party ideology is defined here as the ideology of the party leadership. Ideological congruence with the leadership is a good indication of whether an individual will receive the policy, party, and personal benefits of the office.[5] For one, party leaders greatly influence the legislative agenda, and they pursue an agenda that is in line with their preferences (e.g., Rohde 1991; Cox and McCubbins 2005; Sinclair 2006). The majority party leadership decides the content of the policy items that will be considered as well as how policies will be considered for debate. For both the majority and minority parties, the leadership represents the policy outlook of the party on various issues (Evans and Oleszek 1999; Grynaviski 2010). In addition, party leaders provide the clearest signal of which legislators are able to advance up the party hierarchy, as they themselves obtained an influential position in the chamber. The leadership is responsible for allocating goods and rewards to party members (Aldrich et al. 2015; Pearson 2015), and these private party goods help legislators to further their individual goals (Fenno 1973). In the words of one member, "When you do things for the... leadership it is like putting money in the bank" (Ripley 1967 quoted in Lee 2009, 14).

Party ideology could be defined in a variety of ways, such as the ideology of the median legislator in the party, the most recently elected cohort of candidates, or the most vocal legislators in the party. It is also possible that potential candidates consider the anticipated direction of the party.[6]

---

[5] I follow Jessee and Malhotra's (2010, 372) definition of party leaders, which includes elected party leaders, Speakers, and whips, as well as conference chairs and vice-chairs, conference secretaries, policy and research committee chairs, and campaign committee chairs.

[6] These are all different measures of the same concept of party fit.

Given that incoming candidates have emerged from the extremes (Theriault 2006; Bafumi and Herron 2010), moderates will likely see their legislative clout continue to decline in the coming years, while ideologues will see theirs increase. In this case, expected party ideology would be a more extreme estimate than that of current party ideology, although the anticipated location of the party is difficult to measure. Party fit can be conceptualized in several ways, but distance from the leadership is closely tied to the benefits of the office and it provides a clear and consistent location from which to measure party fit.

The extent to which the party's ideological course is predicted to change, as well as the direction of this change, reflects the location of the leadership relative to the caucus. Currently, Democratic and Republican leaders in the House are to the left and right of their party medians, respectively (Harris and Nelson 2008; Heberlig et al. 2006; Jessee and Malhotra 2010; King and Zeckhauser 2002). As such, the candidates who are more likely to run are pulling the parties away from the center and toward the poles, and the moderate incumbents who are more likely to retire are hastening these shifts. However, if leaders were at the median of their party, the argument would predict ideological persistence. If leaders were more moderate than the party medians, we would expect party convergence.[7] In addition, the rate of party change depends on whether party fit works in different ways depending on the direction of distance. As discussed above, it is likely that the current congressional environment is more attractive to ideologues than it is to moderates. The value of congressional office may even be higher for ideologues than for conformists if they consider the party's future location in their assessment of party fit. The prediction of party change here, and more specifically of increased polarization, is a reflection of both measurement and context: party fit is measured as distance from the leadership, party leaders are currently more polarized than the caucus, and distance is expected to work in different ways depending on the direction. In order to predict dynamics of party change at any particular point in time, we need to have a solid understanding of the context as well.

---

[7] The party leadership changes over time as well, in part due to shifts in the makeup of the caucus (Rohde 1991; Aldrich and Rohde 2001). Why party leaders change over time is beyond the scope of this book. What is important is that the makeup of leaders is almost certainly exogenous to the pool of potential candidates who have never run for Congress. In addition, leader turnover is relatively rare, so the retirement of members is also not likely to have a huge impact on the makeup of leaders.

## The Concept of a Candidacy

"Running for Congress" is also surprisingly difficult to measure. A political candidacy consists of many stages. For example, prospective candidates must gauge support from party leaders and activists, file to become candidates, and announce their candidacy to the media and public. They may ultimately appear on the primary and possibly the general election ballot, but not all who file the requisite paperwork to become candidates are listed on the ballot. Some drop out before the election for personal, professional, or financial reasons. The main question, then, is what counts as a political candidacy.

We might even want to think of office seeking as a spectrum, with having political ambition at one end and appearing on the primary or general election ballot at the other. The pool of ambitious individuals is dramatically winnowed at the appearing on the ballot end of the spectrum. Indeed, perhaps one reason scholars of candidate emergence have focused on political ambition is that being on the ballot is such a rare event. While political ambition is a necessary condition for running for office, it is certainly not a sufficient one. Not only are expressing a desire to run for office and running for office very different acts, but also they have very different implications for the makeup of our legislative institutions.

The answer to what counts as a candidacy depends on what, specifically, we are trying to explain. If the decision to run is of ultimate interest, filing the paperwork and publicly declaring a candidacy are probably sufficient. If the media report on an individual's withdrawal from the race before the primary, this provides additional validation of a candidacy. However, if the actual pool of choices that voters face is of ultimate interest, then the criteria for a candidacy are steeper. Only those who remain in the contest through the primary election are relevant. Of course, all of these operationalizations of a political candidacy have drawbacks. If only the on-ballot candidates are included, this might exclude some who were, for example, persuaded to wait until a different cycle but were viable contenders up to that point. If we include all who filed, this sample might consist of too wide a range of individuals, such as those who have no available record of a candidacy because they changed their minds very early on or legislators who ended up retiring for whatever reason but had intended to seek reelection at the time of the filing deadline. These individuals probably should not be counted as candidates.

The theoretical concern of this book involves the calculus of candidacy, and the empirical concern of this book involves the choices that voters have when they go to the polls. The two are clearly intertwined, but the slight distinction presents a conundrum in terms of the appropriate sample of candidates to use. The former would be better served by a broader definition of "candidate," and the latter would only be served by the narrowest definition. Scholars have paid little attention to who counts as a candidate, but perhaps the single most defining feature of a candidate is that she is voted on by an electorate. Thus, this definition of a candidate – being on the primary ballot – will be used here. It is the calculus of being put to a vote that has greater consequences for the individual as well as the actual composition of Congress.

### Measuring Candidate Ideology

The lack of available data has long hindered the study of candidate ideology. Poole and Rosenthal (2007) constructed DW-NOMINATE scores to examine the ideology of members of Congress, but there were no measures that placed all congressional candidates, winners as well as losers, on a common ideological scale. Ansolabehere et al. (2001) developed the first solution to this problem by comparing the policy positions of candidates running in races where both candidates had a roll-call voting record. The analysis extended from 1874 to 1996, and they supplemented these data with responses to Project Vote Smart's National Political Awareness Test (NPAT). Others have done snapshot analyses of candidate ideology that are similar to the NPAT (e.g., Fiorina 1974; Erikson and Wright 1989), and more recently, Burden (2004) conducted the Candidate Ideology Survey (CIS), which asked all major party candidates running in 2000 to place themselves on a left–right scale. However, these datasets also have limitations. The snapshot measures do not allow comparisons over time, and although Ansolabehere et al. (2001) are able to overcome this problem, a large portion of their data do not include candidates who were never elected to office.

A new dataset developed by Bonica (2014) allows us to address these concerns. Bonica utilizes campaign finance records from 1980 to 2012 to construct ideology scores for the vast majority of congressional candidates, winners and losers, incumbents and nonincumbents, who ran during this time.[8] (See Bonica 2013, 2014 for a full discussion of the data.) These data are particularly useful and valuable here on top of the

---

[8] Of the full sample of those who appeared on the ballot from 1980 to 2012, 73 percent of the primary candidates (17,681 out of 24,228) and 92 percent of the general election candidates (12,518 out of 13,547) have Bonica ideology scores. The Bonica dataset includes candidates who filed with the Federal Election Commission. Candidates who

basic fact that they are the only available measures of the ideological positions of congressional winners and losers over time. First, candidate ideology is placed on a common scale so we can compare across individuals as well as state and federal institutions; second, the dataset includes thousands of candidates and there is ample variation across a host of key political and electoral variables; and third, the data span a sufficiently long time period to allow for historical analyses.

Legislator ideology is most commonly measured with roll-call votes, and Poole and Rosenthal's DW-NOMINATE scores are the gold standard in the Congress literature. Bonica's CFscores are more accurately described as a measure of the revealed preferences of candidates' donors. Bonica (2013, 2014) has conducted a series of analyses to establish the validity of the scores, and he has demonstrated that they are highly correlated with other measures of ideology. CFscores are correlated with DW-NOMINATE scores at 0.93, and within-party correlations are strong for both the House and Senate.[9] The CFscores are also robust to changes in incumbency status. Bonica estimates two distinct ideal points for when the candidate ran as an incumbent and as a nonincumbent, and nonincumbent CFscores are correlated with incumbent CFscores at 0.96. The relationship between nonincumbent CFscores and future DW-NOMINATE scores is no weaker than it is for incumbent CFscores (Bonica 2014, 371–2). Furthermore, with respect to the classification of votes, CFscores perform nearly as well as DW-NOMINATE scores, which provides especially compelling evidence of the validity of CFscores. As Bonica (2014, 371) notes, "Whereas DW-NOMINATE scores condition directly on roll-call data, the CFscores do not. Thus, the predictions made by the CFscores are not merely made out of sample; they are taken from an entirely different type of data."[10]

do not exceed the $5,000 threshold of campaign fundraising are not required to file. Those who are excluded are thus more likely to be long-shot candidates, but it is not clear that they are more likely to be extremists. Even so, these excluded candidates composed only 7 percent of primary winners and 0.03 percent of general election winners, so they are highly unlikely to have an influence on policy outcomes.

[9] Within-party correlations are 0.6 for House and Senate Democrats and 0.7 for House and Senate Republicans.

[10] Bonica (2014) suggests that contribution records may even offer a more complete measure of candidate ideology than does legislative voting. Contributors can consider a wide array of factors beyond voting behavior, such as policy goals, endorsements, and cultural values. Yet more generally, Bonica's goal is not to replicate DW-NOMINATE scores as closely as possible. He writes, "The two measures should be viewed as complementary. One is a measure of ideological voting while the other is a measure of ideological giving. As such, each provides a validity check on the other" (Bonica 2014, 372).

One potential pitfall of the CFscores is that they could be depicting both ideology and valence. A "liberal" or "conservative" score could be partially capturing the fact that candidates are low quality and not getting mainstream donors. This is unlikely to be a huge concern in the analyses here, however. Partisan polarization in Congress is not driven by long-shot candidates; it is driven by quality candidates who win. The empirical analyses in this book focus on high-quality potential candidates because I am interested in the decision to run among those who are most likely to be elected to Congress. State legislators have long been understood to be quality candidates (Jacobson and Kernell 1983), and members of Congress who seek reelection are among the most highly qualified candidates possible. Another potential pitfall involves making comparisons between state legislators and members of Congress with similar ideology scores, as state legislators and members of Congress deal with different sets of policy issues. Yet this is also unlikely to be a grave problem given the ideological consistency in elite preferences and the fact that CFscores do not change much at all before and after candidates are elected to office. More generally, the benefits of using the Bonica data far outweigh the tradeoffs, and they are the best available metric for my purposes. Despite the limitations of the data, the CFscores provide a unique opportunity to examine the impact of candidate supply on polarization.

## Electoral Considerations and Candidate Emergence

The party fit argument highlights the importance of the value of the office for the calculus of candidacy, but a long line of scholarship has shown that electoral considerations are central to the decision to run. Thus, although congressional districts have become more homogeneous and voters are better sorted, we might still expect to see variation across districts in the types of candidates who run. A larger number of moderate Republicans may run in liberal districts, and a larger number of moderate Democrats may run in conservative districts. Similarly, there may be fewer moderate Republicans (Democrats) running in the most conservative (liberal) districts. In addition, we might see variation depending on how conservative or liberal party activists are. Liberal Republicans and conservative Democrats may be more likely to run in districts with a more liberal Republican base and a more conservative Democratic base, respectively, and they may be less likely to run in districts with more conservative Republican partisans and more liberal Democratic partisans. As

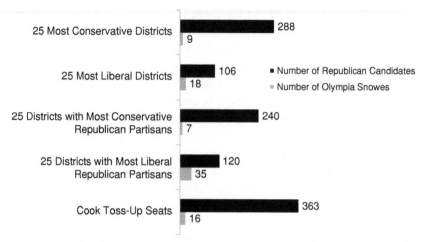

FIGURE 2.1. Republican candidates across congressional districts, 2000–2012
*Sources:* Bonica (2014); Tausanovitch and Warshaw (2013).

well, moderates may be more likely to run in toss-up seats because they may attract the most support in the general election and expect primary voters to vote strategically.

I examine these various logics with respect to the candidate pool in the 2000–2012 cycles. I use Bonica's (2014) candidate estimates, Tausanovitch and Warshaw's (2013) estimates of congressional district ideology and the ideology of Republican and Democratic partisans in each district, and the Cook Political Report's list of toss-up seats during this period. Figure 2.1 shows the number of Republican candidates who ran for Congress between 2000 and 2012 and were at least as moderate as Olympia Snowe, the former legislator from Maine. A greater proportion of Snowes ran in liberal districts and in districts with liberal Republican partisans. Candidates like Snowe constituted 29 percent of candidates in districts with the most liberal Republican partisans and 17 percent of candidates in the most liberal districts, compared to 3 percent of candidates in districts with the most conservative Republican partisans and 3 percent of candidates in the most conservative districts. Moderates such as Snowe also constituted 4 percent of candidates in the nearly 200 races that the Cook Political Report rated as toss-up during this time.

Yet we must also keep in mind that these figures span seven election cycles. The more general takeaway is that very few Olympia Snowes are running for Congress, regardless of the makeup of the district, the makeup of party activists, or the closeness of the race. Of the 3,961 Republicans

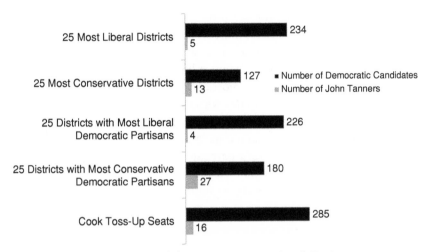

FIGURE 2.2. Democratic candidates across congressional districts, 2000–2012
*Sources:* Bonica (2014); Tausanovitch and Warshaw (2013).

who ran between 2000 and 2012, only 228, or 6 percent, were at least as moderate as Snowe. In short, individuals such as Olympia Snowe are no longer putting their hats into the ring, and it matters relatively little whether the district is more or less conservative, whether party activists are more or less conservative, or whether the seat is a toss-up.[11]

Figure 2.2 presents the breakdown for Democratic congressional candidates. The figure shows the number of Democratic candidates who ran for Congress from 2000 to 2012 and were at least as moderate as John Tanner, a former representative from Tennessee and founding member of the Blue Dog Coalition. The numbers in Figure 2.2 echo those on the Republican side. A larger proportion of candidates like John Tanner ran in conservative districts and in districts with the most conservative Democratic partisans (10 percent and 15 percent, respectively), whereas moderates such as Tanner constituted 2 percent of candidates in the most liberal districts and 2 percent of candidates in districts with the most liberal Democratic partisans. But again, the general pattern is of individuals like John Tanner simply not running anywhere. Of the 3,624 Democrats who ran for Congress from 2000 to 2012, a mere 170, or 5 percent, were at least as moderate as Tanner.

---

[11] Again, it is not the case that moderates are not available to run. Between 2000 and 2010, 18 percent of Republican state legislators were at least as moderate as Snowe and 27 percent of Democratic state legislators were at least as moderate as Tanner. These data are discussed in Chapter 4.

Furthermore, what limited variation there was from 2000 to 2012 has only continued to diminish over time. Of the 669 GOP candidates who ran in 2012 alone, 30 were at least as moderate as Snowe (4 percent); of these 30, 4 came from districts with the most liberal Republican partisans and 1 came from a district with the most conservative Republican partisans. Of the 595 Democratic candidates who ran in 2012, 30 were at least as moderate as Tanner (5 percent); of these 30, 2 came from districts with the most conservative Democratic partisans and 1 came from a district with the most liberal Democratic partisans. It is less clear how well purely electoral-based logics can explain current patterns of candidate entry. At the very least, we would expect to see more variation across congressional districts.

### Could Moderates Win?

A lingering question is whether moderates could win if they ran. This is difficult to analyze empirically given the dearth of moderate candidates (Thomsen 2014), but it is important to consider because it relates to the various motivations of running for office. As noted in the previous chapter, it is not clear whether and how much moderate candidates are penalized by voters (Ansolabehere et al. 2001; Canes-Wrone et al. 2002; Brady et al. 2007; Hirano et al. 2010; Hall and Snyder 2015). As Hall and Snyder (2015, 5) observe, "In most of these analyses, the size of the estimated effect of ideological positioning is small." Furthermore, the impact of primaries on candidate extremism is far from certain (Hirano et al. 2010; Kousser et al. 2017; McGhee et al. 2014; Rogowski and Langella 2014). It is difficult for primary voters to distinguish between same-party candidates, particularly in races where resources are scarce and media coverage is limited (Hirano et al. 2015; Ahler et al. 2016). The lack of moderate candidates, coupled with the limited evidence that moderates fare significantly worse at the ballot box, is consistent with the argument that factors beyond just winning matter for the decision to run.

Nevertheless, we can briefly examine primary victory rates across different types of candidates, as primaries are purported to be the main obstacle to moderate candidate victories. On the Republican side, there were 2,600 candidates who won their primaries between 2000 and 2012. Of the 2,600 GOP primary winners, 1,476 (57 percent) were within 0.25 units of the party leadership, 743 (29 percent) were more than 0.25 units on the ideologue side of the leadership, and 381 (15 percent) were more than 0.25 units on the moderate side of the leadership. As a proportion of the GOP runners, 75 percent of the conformists, 57 percent of the ideologues, and 63 percent of the moderates won their primaries. On the

Democratic side, 2,617 candidates won their primaries between 2000 and 2012. Of the 2,617 winners, 1,101 (42 percent) were within 0.25 units of the party leadership, 1,125 (43 percent) were more than 0.25 units on the ideologue side of the leadership, and 445 (17 percent) were more than 0.25 units on the moderate side of the leadership. As a proportion of the Democratic runners, 81 percent of the conformists, 73 percent of the ideologues, and 68 percent of the moderates won their primaries. Moderate Democrats do win at a slightly lower rate than liberal Democrats, but the differences in victory rates across candidates are not large in either party. While very liberal Republicans and very conservative Democrats are unlikely to win in the current context, it is possible that relatively moderate candidates could.

In fact, although electoral vulnerability was an issue for some of the retiring members whom I interviewed, most were confident they would have won reelection. One member said, "[Losing] wasn't a consideration really. I've never lost an election, and I was pretty sure I'd win the next one" (23 January 2013). We can look to the recent 2016 cycle for additional evidence. Richard Hanna (NY), one of the more moderate Republicans in Congress, retired from office. He won reelection by 20 percentage points in 2012, and the Democrats did not run a candidate in 2014 because he looked so safe. Hanna did have a fairly difficult primary race in 2014 but he still won by seven percentage points. In a recent article in the *Economist*, he said his reasons for leaving are partly personal, but "mostly he is discouraged by how little his centrist voice counts in Congress – not least because his party has moved 'far to the right'" (Economist 2016). Retiring members do, however, tend to downplay their chances of losing, and it is difficult to ascertain how large this looms in the decision to retire. Moderates are likely to face tougher primary or general elections, but the probability of reelection is still high across members. Many of the members I spoke with had represented their districts for over a decade, in some cases two or more, and such assessments are logical given the perks of incumbency. Yet the ability to win is a key component of the decision to run, and whenever possible, I examine and account for electoral considerations in the chapters that follow as well.

## Summary

This chapter advanced two main points. First, the core of the party fit argument is that the value of congressional office differs across individuals depending on their ideological conformity with the party. Second, the impact of party fit on candidate emergence has only continued to grow in importance as the parties have polarized ideologically. In the pre-polarized era, nonelectoral benefits were considered to be constant across members, but as the parties have drifted apart, the value of congressional office has become less constrained and more variable across individuals. Nonelectoral benefits matter more for the calculus of candidacy as members' ability to receive policy, party, and personal rewards has become increasingly tied to their ideological leanings.

While the median legislator has long been prominent in congressional scholarship, contemporary patterns of candidate entry suggest that the ideological center may be less desirable than it used to be. Over the past 30 years, there has been a sharp decline in the number of liberal Republicans and conservative Democrats who throw their hats into the ring. Candidates certainly care about winning, but even if moderates were elected to office today, their policy impact would be limited and they would struggle to move up the career ladder. On top of this, the congressional environment has become an increasingly hostile place for those in the middle, and moderates would have a hard time interacting with colleagues who do not share their worldview. For ideological centrists, the benefits of serving in Congress are too low for them to run. These patterns may be particularly pronounced on the Republican side due to the distinct characters of the parties, but the primary concern here is the opting out of moderates from both parties. The differential value of the office for ideologues and moderates has important implications for theories of candidate emergence as well as the persistence of partisan polarization in Congress.

# 3

# Ideology, Attitudes, and Political Ambition

More than 50 years ago, Schlesinger (1966, 1) wrote, "Ambition lies at the heart of politics. Politics thrive on the hope of preferment and the drive for office." But why do some people have the drive for office and others not have it? In many ways, it is difficult to see why anyone would want to subject herself to a life of politics, especially at the congressional level. In a recent *Atlantic* article posing that exact question, the subtitle read, "How Democratic and Republican officials cajole potential candidates into signing on for constant stress, ceaseless fundraising, and the danger of losing your job every two years." One former state House candidate described the process of running for office as "one of the most awful, humiliating, degrading and physically demanding things anybody can do" (Schoeneman 2014). And indeed, few people choose to run for office at any level. A 2014 Pew Research study showed that about 2 percent of Americans have ever sought local, state, or federal office. Federal-level candidates are a miniscule fraction of all office seekers – about 1 percent of those who run (Ansolabehere 2011).

Virtually no one runs for Congress, but a very small and very elite minority does (Carnes 2013). This chapter examines levels of political ambition across a select group of individuals who are among the best situated to run for Congress: state legislators. As discussed in Chapter 1, state legislators constitute the pool of those who are most likely to run for and be elected to Congress. I draw on survey data on state legislators that were collected for the Candidate Emergence Study (CES) (see Maestas et al. 2006). The analyses show that moderates are less likely to be attracted to a congressional career, less likely to think they can win, and less likely to value a seat in the U.S. House than ideologues. These differences are largely restricted to the Republican side, which reflects important distinctions between the two parties and the time period in which the CES was conducted. The findings shed light on the impact of electoral and nonelectoral factors on political ambition, and they reveal how moderates and ideologues differentially view the value of a congressional career. In short, ideologically moderate state legislators, specifically moderate Republicans at this time, are skeptical of the value of congressional office long before they must decide whether to launch a candidacy.

## The Study of Political Ambition

It is one thing to ask those who have entered the political arena why they chose to do so, but it is quite challenging to predict the determinants of a political candidacy. The difficulty is in part rooted in identifying the noncandidates: those who could have run for office but did not, those who thought about running for office but did not, or those who might have been viable candidates but never considered running. Systematically finding and surveying these individuals is no small feat. We are also confronted with the small-$n$ problem: although there are a large number of elected offices in the United States, very few of those who are eligible to run for office actually do so. This becomes increasingly true at higher levels of office.

Scholars have studied political ambition in a variety of ways. One approach is to analyze the decision to run for elected office (e.g., Rohde 1979; Abramson et al. 1987; Maisel and Stone 2014; Thomsen 2014). The sample is narrowed to a pool of individuals who would be the most likely to run for a particular office. This group constitutes the "candidate eligibility pool." In behavioral research, the eligibility pool often consists of existing officeholders, and the focus is on variation in progressive ambition. Rohde (1979), for example, explored the decision to run for higher office among House members who were presented with an opportunity to run for the U.S. Senate or their state governorship, and Abramson et al. (1987) looked at the decisions of U.S. Senators to run for the presidency. In addition, analyses of the decision to run for office tend to use objective rather than subjective measures of the political opportunity structure and the electoral context, such as the number of higher seats available, district competitiveness, and the partisan makeup of the district. They also typically span a long time period and include multiple election cycles.

Another approach is to explore attitudes and perceptions about running for office among potential candidates (e.g., Stone and Maisel 2003; Lawless and Fox 2005, 2010; Fulton et al. 2006; Maestas et al. 2006; Maisel and Stone 2014). Here the eligibility pool often includes individuals in the traditional pipeline to an office or those who would be viable candidates. The Candidate Emergence Study (CES) and the Citizen Political Ambition Study (CPAS) are two of the best examples of this approach. The CES, which was conducted by Maisel, Stone, and Maestas, surveyed hundreds of state legislators and individuals who were identified by political elites to be potentially strong U.S. House candidates. These data provide the most comprehensive information on the perceptions of those in the congressional eligibility pool. Lawless and Fox (2005, 2010; Lawless 2012, 5) used a similar design for the CPAS, but they instead focused on the potential interest in office seeking that precedes the decision to run. The CPAS included nearly 4,000 people in the professions that produce the most candidates for public office: law, business, education, and political activism. The two waves of this study have offered some of the best insights to date into nascent political ambition.

The CES and CPAS have different strengths. The CES consists of individuals who are for the most part already politically ambitious, as they are either current officeholders or on the radar of political elites. Thus, the CES gives substantial weight to how potential candidates evaluate the various parts of the calculus of candidacy. Many of their analyses pay particular attention to respondents' perceived probability of winning, though they are also interested in the expected costs and benefits of running for office (Fulton et al. 2006; Maestas et al. 2006; Maisel and Stone 2014). In contrast, the CPAS includes many people who have never considered a political career, and it therefore gives less priority to the structural and contextual variables that shape the decision to run.

Yet they share a focus on the beliefs and perceptions of potential candidates. The main variables of interest include respondents' reported attraction to a political career, their stated likelihood of running for office, and whether or not they have considered a political candidacy. Lawless and Fox (2010) devote one chapter in their book to the actual decision to run, and Maisel and Stone (2014) recently wrote an article on the determinants of a congressional candidacy. But in general, the analyses examine variation in attitudes rather than variation in behavior. This is likely due in part to the limited number of individuals who run for office. In the CES data on potential congressional candidates, only 1.9

percent of the sample, or about 20 people, ran for Congress in the election immediately following the survey (Maisel and Stone 2014). Nearly 15 years later, the number of runners had increased to around 85, but this is still a relatively small number of people (Maisel and Stone 2014, 436). Lawless and Fox (2010, 208) had more overall runners in their sample – 9 percent of their eligible candidates ran – because they combined local, state, and federal offices; however, only 4 percent of this 9 percent (roughly 11 individuals) ran for federal office (Lawless and Fox 2010, 50).

Studies of political ambition that draw on primarily behavioral versus primarily attitudinal data are different, but they can be used in complementary ways. The survey data allow us to open up the black box of candidate emergence and understand why and how potential candidates decide whether or not to run for office, but again, the main limitation is that very few of those surveyed will actually run. Behavioral analyses have a larger number of runners because the sample can often be the entire population of cases and the data can be pooled over time. In Rohde's (1979) analysis, there were 111 individuals who ran for higher office, but what makes this figure especially impressive is that they were running for the most elite offices in the country. But the sample also includes 3,040 cases, and the data span more than two decades. More generally, attitudinal and behavioral studies of eligible candidates provide different insights into candidate emergence, and I draw on both types of data to analyze the relationship between ideology and the decision to run for office.

Candidate ideology has yet to be included as a significant variable of interest in political ambition research, at least in the way described here. If there is a conventional wisdom about the impact of ideology on candidate entry, it is rooted in electoral considerations: candidate ideology matters to the extent that it will hinder or enhance her ability to win. For example, those who conform to the partisan makeup of a district face a more favorable political environment and are expected to be more likely to enter a race. Stone and Maisel (2003) indeed demonstrate that a potential candidate's ideological congruence with the district differentially shapes electoral competition in primary and general elections.

This way of thinking about ideology is, however, conceptually and practically distinct from the party fit argument, which suggests that ideological conformity with the party shapes the value of the office itself. Put differently, the conventional wisdom suggests that if candidate ideology matters at all, it is for the perceived probability of winning, whereas the party fit argument suggests that candidate ideology matters for the perceived benefits of the office. The distinction is crucial not only for generating a richer picture of the decision to run for office but also for understanding the mechanisms of partisan polarization and the nature of legislative representation in the contemporary era.

## The Candidate Eligibility Pool

Due to the focus here on the U.S. House of Representatives, the pool of potential candidates used for the CES is the most appropriate. The CES researchers generously made the data publicly available, and I draw on their data on state legislators in this chapter. Again, state legislative office has long been the traditional pathway to congressional office (Jacobson and Kernell 1983), and 51 percent of those who served in Congress between 1999 and 2008 had prior state legislative experience (Carnes 2012).

The CES data are unparalleled in the depth to which they reveal potential candidates' perceptions of the electoral and political environment. First, the data allow an analysis of ideological variation in how state legislators rate their attraction to a House career. CES researchers have used this variable to measure political ambition and respondents' expected utility of running for Congress (Maestas et al. 2006; Maisel and Stone 2014). Second, the CES data enable us to delve into the various parts of the calculus of candidacy and explore how state legislator ideology affects respondents' perceived ability to achieve their electoral and nonelectoral goals. This is helpful because the conventional wisdom and the party fit argument often yield an observationally equivalent outcome. The former predicts that moderates are less likely to run because they think they cannot win; the latter predicts that they are less likely to run because they do not value a seat in the U.S. House. The CES data, unlike the behavioral data that are used in the rest of the book, allow us to distinguish between electoral and nonelectoral factors. To be clear, the argument is not that moderates do not run only because of nonelectoral factors, but rather that nonelectoral considerations are an important and largely untold part of their abstention. Although the relationship between ideology and political ambition has yet to be fully explored, if there were a conventional wisdom, it would be that moderates do not run only because of electoral factors. A broader view of candidate emergence that takes nonelectoral considerations seriously is increasingly necessary to understand why moderates do not run in the contemporary partisan era.

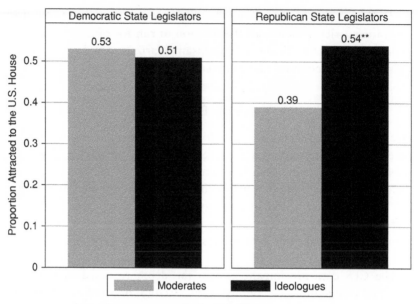

FIGURE 3.1. Attraction to a career in the U.S. House
*Source:* 1998 Wave of the Candidate Emergence Study (Stone and Maisel 2003; Stone et al. 2004; Maestas et al. 2006).
** $p < 0.01$. Statistical significance denotes differences between moderates and ideologues by party.

### Who Wants to Run for Congress?

The central claim in this chapter is that ideologically moderate state legislators are less likely to be attracted to a congressional career than conservative Republicans or liberal Democrats. Figure 3.1 shows the proportion of moderates and ideologues who rate their attraction to a U.S. House seat as somewhat high, high, or extremely high. The measure is intended to capture even the slightest inclination to seek higher office. Ideologues include Democrats who identify as liberal or very liberal and Republicans who identify as conservative or very conservative.[1] Among Democratic state legislators, 51 percent of liberals and 53 percent of moderates are attracted to higher office (the difference is not significant). In contrast, 54 percent of conservative Republicans but only 39 percent of moderate Republicans say their attraction to a House seat is at least somewhat high ($p < 0.01$). Congressional office is less appealing to moderate

---

[1] The same pattern emerges with a broader definition that includes slightly liberal Democrats and slightly conservative Republicans.

Republicans than it is to their conservative co-partisans, but the same difference does not emerge on the Democratic side.

I use logistic regression to further examine the relationship between state legislator ideology and political ambition. There are approximately 550 state legislators in the sample here.[2] As in Maestas et al. (2006), political ambition is measured as respondents' attraction to a U.S. House seat. Again, the dependent variable is coded one if they rate their attraction to a career in the U.S. House as at least somewhat high and zero otherwise, and about half of respondents are at least somewhat attracted to a House seat. The main independent variable of interest is the state legislator's self-reported ideology, which is on a 7-point scale that ranges from very liberal to very conservative. Ideology is coded so that higher values correspond to Republican liberalism and Democratic conservatism.[3]

The model includes a host of variables that account for the various parts of the calculus of candidacy, many of which come directly from Maestas et al. (2006). First, the ability to win is influenced in part by the ideology of voters in the district, which is measured as the distance between the state legislator's ideology and her perceived ideology of voters in the district. The model also includes the state legislator's assessment of winning the nomination, which is an index of whether she rates herself as at least somewhat likely to win the party nomination in the upcoming election, in the next three or four terms, and in the foreseeable future.[4] Those who have been contacted by the party are also expected to be more ambitious. The benefits of the office are measured by their evaluations of the prestige and effectiveness of a career in the U.S. House and the

[2] The data are drawn from the 1998 wave of the CES. The CES survey was mailed to state legislators whose districts overlapped with 200 randomly selected congressional districts in 41 states. The specific states are not identified in the publicly available data. The survey was mailed to 2,714 state legislators, and 874 of them responded, for a response rate of 32.2 percent (see Maestas et al. 2006, 199). Due to missing data, there are 597 respondents in the Maestas et al. (2006) study; the smaller number here is because of the inclusion of ideology. I am not able to use the 2000 wave of the state legislator data because ideology was not included in that survey. Maestas et al. (2006) use only the 1998 wave in their study of state legislators as well.

[3] In addition, I ran the models with respondents' positions on several policy issues that are included in both party platforms. Respondents are coded as nonconformists if they are indifferent to or oppose the position in their party's platform on an issue and conformists if they favor their party's position. The results are the same with the policy and ideology measures, but I focus on ideology due to the emphasis on polarization.

[4] I also interacted the state legislator's ideology with her perceived chance of winning. The interaction is insignificant across models, and the results are virtually identical to those in Table 3.1. The interaction is not of ultimate theoretical interest, so I do not include it here, but the results are provided in Appendix B.

state legislature in which they currently serve. These two evaluations were combined, and the difference between them is a measure of the relative value of a House seat. In terms of costs, those in professionalized state legislatures may perceive the costs of running to be higher, whereas the costs may be lower for those who face term limits. As family costs and campaign costs increase, state legislators are also less likely to want to run.[5] Finally, the perceived costs may be higher for women and older state legislators.

The results are presented in Table 3.1. The variables that seek to capture the components of the calculus of candidacy reflect the expectations outlined above. The perceived ability to win the nomination, the relative value of a House seat, and party recruitment are positively associated with attraction to a congressional career. State legislators are less likely to be attracted to higher office as perceived campaign costs and family costs increase. Female state legislators and those who are older also report lower levels of attraction to a House seat. All of these results conform to those in Maestas et al. (2006).

With respect to ideology, Republican liberalism and Democratic conservatism are negative but do not reach conventional levels of significance in the full model of state legislators in Column 1. However, when we examine the results by party, moderate Republicans are less likely to be attracted to a House seat than their conservative counterparts.[6] The magnitude of the effect is large in comparison to the control variables as well.[7] A standard deviation increase in Republican liberalism results in a 10 percentage point decline in the probability of being attracted to a congressional career. A similar increase in the perceived chance of winning leads to an 11 percentage point rise in state legislators' attraction to a House seat, and the effect of a one-unit increase in the value

---

[5] These measures, as well as the probability of winning, party recruitment, and seat value variables, are taken from Maestas et al. (2006). The family cost index is an average of three responses assessing how much "loss of personal and family privacy," "loss of leisure time," and "separation from family and friends" discourage state legislators from running for the U.S. House. The campaign cost index is an average of two responses assessing the need to raise large amounts of money and enduring negative advertising attacks. Each response is on a four-point scale that ranges from "makes no difference" to "strongly discourage."

[6] The model is not sensitive to the inclusion of the control variables. For Republicans, the relationship between ideology and attraction to a House seat holds with and without the controls. For Democrats, the relationship is insignificant with and without the controls as well.

[7] Predictor variables were standardized to have a mean of zero and a standard deviation of one.

TABLE 3.1. *Attraction to a career in the U.S. House*

|  | All | Republicans | Democrats |
|---|---|---|---|
| Ideological moderate (Republican liberalism; Democratic conservatism) | −0.15 (0.11) | −0.40* (0.18) | −0.06 (0.17) |
| Distance from voters in House district | 0.03 (0.11) | −0.34* (0.17) | 0.26 (0.17) |
| Chance of winning nomination | 0.33** (0.11) | 0.49** (0.17) | 0.25† (0.15) |
| Contacted by political party | 0.37** (0.12) | 0.48* (0.21) | 0.32* (0.16) |
| Relative value of House seat | 0.24* (0.11) | 0.27† (0.15) | 0.27† (0.14) |
| In professionalized state legislature | −0.09 (0.10) | 0.03 (0.16) | −0.14 (0.14) |
| Faces term limits | 0.01 (0.21) | −0.24 (0.33) | 0.21 (0.29) |
| Campaign cost index | −0.27* (0.12) | −0.11 (0.18) | −0.39* (0.16) |
| Family cost index | −0.48** (0.11) | −0.57** (0.17) | −0.40* (0.16) |
| Female | −0.42† (0.25) | −0.61 (0.48) | −0.48 (0.33) |
| Age | −0.91** (0.12) | −0.94** (0.18) | −0.83** (0.16) |
| Constant | 0.07 (0.13) | 0.10 (0.20) | 0.05 (0.18) |
| Number of observations | 577 | 275 | 302 |
| Log likelihood | −309.34 | −132.50 | −168.65 |

*Source:* 1998 Wave of the CES (Maestas et al. 2006).
*Note:* Entries are logistic regression coefficients with standard errors in parentheses. The dependent variable is 1 if the state legislator is attracted to a career in the U.S. House and 0 if not.
** $p < 0.01$, * $p < 0.05$, † $p < 0.10$.

of a House seat and party recruitment is 6 and 11 percentage points, respectively. A standard deviation increase in ideological distance from voters results in a 9 percentage point decrease in the probability of being attracted to a congressional career. Age has the largest impact, with a similar shift decreasing state legislators' ambition by 23 percentage points. Yet it is important to note, too, that a maximum increase in Republican liberalism, from very conservative to slightly liberal, diminishes respondents' attraction to a House seat by 47 percentage points, from 69 to

22 percent. For Republicans, ideology clearly has implications for state legislators' attraction to congressional office.[8]

Among Democrats, the relationship between ideology and attraction to a House seat is not statistically significant, though the null result is not too surprising on the Democratic side for a few reasons. First, the survey was conducted in 1998, and there were key differences between the two parties in Congress. In the 105th Congress (1997–98), the median House Republican had a CFscore of 0.80 and the median Democrat had a score of −0.65. Also, the standard deviation of the GOP in the 105th Congress was 0.27, whereas the Democratic Party had a standard deviation of 0.33. Moderate Democrats were thus a better fit for the party in the late 1990s, and many of the leaders who were setting the agenda and doling out party rewards were more moderate then as well (Heberlig et al. 2006). Furthermore, as discussed in Chapter 2, the two parties seem to differ with respect to ideological purity and clarity. Politically elite Democrats have a relatively broader understanding of ideology than politically elite Republicans, and the standard deviation in self-reported ideology for the Republican and Democratic state legislators here is 0.81 and 1.33, respectively (Maestas et al. 2006). Although party fit is expected to matter more today than it did just a few decades ago, the size of the effect may differ for Republicans and Democrats.

A final observation with respect to the results in Table 3.1 is that it is impossible to measure party fit – the distance between the party and the potential candidate – with the CES data. Left–right ideology is used as a proxy for party fit here, with Republican liberalism and Democratic conservatism representing decreased levels of fit. This proxy of party fit may work better for Republican potential candidates because the congressional GOP had shifted further to the right end of the spectrum, but it may be a more imperfect measure for Democrats because the party had not shifted as far to the left at that time. The above concerns are alleviated in the subsequent chapters because the data are more recent, they

---

[8] I am not able to test whether respondents self-select out of running or are gate-kept out by party leaders, but I expect both mechanisms to be at work. Among very conservative and conservative Republicans, 4.4 percent reported being contacted by the party, versus 1.8 percent of those with more liberal preferences, which conforms to the argument here. In terms of the model, this would lead me to underestimate the effect of ideology as candidate ideology might have an influence on party recruitment but not vice versa, as the ideology of most legislators does not change significantly over time (Poole and Rosenthal 2007).

span a longer period of time, and they enable a more precise measurement of party fit.

## Electoral Motivations and Benefits of the Office

But why are moderates, and specifically moderate Republicans, less likely to be attracted to a congressional career? Is it because they believe they would lose or because they do not value the office? The CES data are also useful because they allow us to examine electoral and nonelectoral considerations. Two variables in the CES dataset capture state legislators' expected chance of winning and the perceived benefits of the office, both of which correspond to higher levels of ambition in the previous analysis and in the Maestas et al. (2006) study. The first is state legislators' perceived likelihood of winning the party nomination, and the second is the relative value of a House seat.[9] This section analyzes these two components of the calculus of candidacy as dependent variables and explores how ideology matters for the perceived probability of winning and the expected benefits of a House seat. The conventional wisdom is that moderates are less likely to believe they can win than ideologues, and the party fit argument is that moderates are less likely to value a U.S. House seat than ideologues.

Figure 3.2 provides a closer look into state legislators' perceptions of the electoral and congressional environment. The bars show the proportion of ideologues and moderates who believe they are likely or extremely likely to win the party nomination and the proportion who rate the policy effectiveness of the U.S. House as high or extremely high.[10] There are three main takeaways in Figure 3.2. First, conservative and very conservative Republicans rate their chance of winning the nomination as higher and view the U.S. House as more effective than those who identify as more moderate ($p < 0.10$ and $p < 0.05$). Second, these patterns do not emerge on the Democratic side. If anything, liberal and very liberal Democrats rate their electoral prospects and the congressional

---

[9] I also used their combined evaluation of winning the primary and the general election. The results are the same, but I focus on the primary because candidates must first obtain support from primary voters.

[10] These measures of electoral and nonelectoral goals are dichotomous here for simplicity, but the coding in Maestas et al. (2006) is used in the full analysis. Ideology is also dichotomized, with the ideologue category composed of liberal and very liberal Democrats and conservative and very conservative Republicans and the moderate category composed of all others.

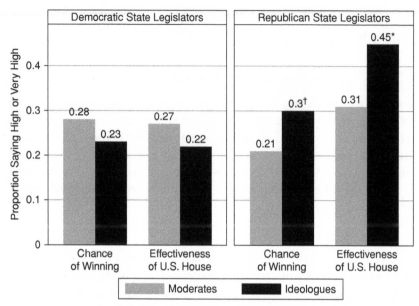

FIGURE 3.2. Perceived chance of victory and effectiveness of the U.S. House
*Source:* 1998 Wave of the Candidate Emergence Study (Maestas et al. 2006).
* $p < 0.05$, † $p < 0.10$. Statistical significance denotes differences between moderates and ideologues by party.

environment as less favorable than those who are more moderate, though these differences are not statistically significant. Third, while all Republicans perceive the U.S. House as more effective than Democrats, Republican ideologues rate the institution far more favorably than any other group of legislators. Nearly half of conservative and very conservative Republican state legislators rate the effectiveness of the U.S. House as high or extremely high.

I also use OLS regression to examine the relationship between legislator ideology, the perceived ability to win, and the value of a House seat. As in Maestas et al. (2006), the chance of winning the primary is scaled as a pseudo-probability that ranges from 0.01 (very unlikely) to 0.99 (very likely). The relative value of a House seat is measured as in Table 3.1 and in Maestas et al. (2006). Ideology is again coded so that higher values correspond to Republican liberalism and Democratic conservatism. The control variables differ slightly due to the change in dependent variables. State legislators who were contacted by the party and those who can raise more money are expected to rate their chance of winning and the value of a House seat higher. Female state legislators, older respondents, and those who face strong incumbents may have more negative assessments of their chance of winning and the value of a House seat. Not all of the controls are expected to have the same effect on both of the dependent variables, however. Stone and Maisel (2003) show that when district partisanship is more favorable, the probability of winning the party nomination is lower, but the value of a House seat may be higher. Conversely, respondents who have served more terms in state legislative office and those in professionalized state legislatures may report a higher chance of winning but a lower seat value, given the costs of leaving the state legislature.

Table 3.2 displays the results for the full sample of state legislators and by party. With respect to the control variables, state legislators who were contacted by the political party and those in professionalized state legislatures believe they are more likely to win the nomination. Similarly, state legislators who can raise more money to fund a campaign and expect to receive support from outside groups assess their chances of victory as higher. Respondents in favorable partisan districts say they are less likely to win the party nomination because the level of primary competition will be higher (Stone and Maisel 2003). Older respondents perceive their chances of victory as lower but assess the value of a House seat as higher. State legislators also rate their probability of winning as lower but the value of the seat as higher when the incumbent is strong. Women and those who have served a greater number of terms in state legislative office are less likely to value a seat in the House.

In terms of the main variable of interest, the full models in Columns (1) and (2) show that moderates are not less likely than their more extreme counterparts to think they can win the nomination, but they are less likely than ideologues to value a seat in the U.S. House. When the results are displayed by party, it is clear that much of the action is on the Republican side. Moderate Republicans perceive their chance of winning the nomination as lower, on average, than do their conservative counterparts. A one-unit increase in liberalism results in a four percentage point decline in the perceived chance of winning the primary. The magnitude of the effect of ideology is also comparable to the additional variables, with age exerting the largest impact on the perceived likelihood of victory. This finding echoes the prevailing narrative about ideological moderates, particularly moderate Republicans, having a hard time gaining support from primary voters. Although it is impossible to examine the victory rates of those who do not run, the CES data suggest that moderate Republicans

TABLE 3.2. *Probability of winning and benefits of the office*

| | All legislators | | Republicans | | Democrats | |
|---|---|---|---|---|---|---|
| | Win nomination | Value of house seat | Win nomination | Value of house seat | Win nomination | Value of house seat |
| Ideological moderate (Republican liberalism; Democratic conservatism) | -0.01 (0.01) | -0.29* (0.11) | -0.04* (0.02) | -0.42** (0.16) | -0.01 (0.02) | 0.18 (0.16) |
| Favorable district partisanship | -0.06* (0.02) | -0.07 (0.23) | -0.07† (0.04) | -0.40 (0.33) | -0.07* (0.03) | 0.28 (0.32) |
| Ability to raise money | 0.04** (0.01) | -0.16 (0.12) | 0.05** (0.02) | -0.17 (0.18) | 0.03† (0.02) | -0.33* (0.17) |
| Contacted by political party | 0.06** (0.01) | -0.04 (0.11) | 0.06** (0.02) | 0.03 (0.16) | 0.06** (0.02) | -0.14 (0.16) |
| Terms in state legislative office | -0.01 (0.01) | -0.47** (0.12) | -0.01 (0.02) | -0.50** (0.16) | -0.01 (0.02) | -0.34* (0.16) |
| In professionalized state legislature | 0.05** (0.01) | -0.10 (0.11) | 0.05** (0.02) | -0.16 (0.16) | 0.04** (0.02) | -0.08 (0.15) |
| Incumbent strength | -0.03** (0.01) | 0.28* (0.11) | -0.01 (0.02) | 0.26 (0.16) | -0.05** (0.02) | 0.25 (0.16) |
| Support from outside groups | 0.02† (0.01) | 0.15 (0.12) | 0.06** (0.02) | 0.07 (0.17) | -0.01 (0.02) | 0.24 (0.16) |
| Female | -0.02 (0.03) | -0.93** (0.27) | 0.02 (0.05) | -0.61 (0.46) | -0.03 (0.04) | -0.44 (0.36) |
| Age | -0.11** (0.01) | 0.29* (0.12) | -0.10** (0.02) | 0.01 (0.16) | -0.10** (0.02) | 0.43** (0.16) |
| Constant | 0.55** (0.02) | -1.08** (0.19) | 0.54** (0.03) | -0.34 (0.25) | 0.56** (0.03) | -1.94** (0.27) |
| Number of observations | 585 | 642 | 266 | 291 | 319 | 351 |
| $R^2$ | 0.27 | 0.08 | 0.32 | 0.10 | 0.28 | 0.06 |

*Source:* 1998 Wave of the CES (Maestas et al. 2006).

*Note:* Entries are OLS regression coefficients with standard errors in parentheses.

perceive their electoral prospects to be worse than do their conservative counterparts.

The party fit argument pertains more specifically to the value of office. The results in Table 3.2 suggest that moderate Republicans also rate the relative value of a House seat as lower, on average, than conservative Republican state legislators. A shift in ideology from very conservative to slightly liberal results in a 2.1 point decline in state legislators' value of a congressional seat, or 11 percent of the range of the 20-point scale. A comparative shift from the minimum to the maximum number of terms in the state legislature leads to a 1.4 point decrease in the value of a seat in the House, or 7 percent of the range of the scale. Although ideology matters for state legislators' perceived ability to win the nomination, ideology also impacts the expected value of a congressional career. Both of these factors shape the calculus of candidacy and the decision to seek higher office. Indeed, potential candidates want to win, but they also want to have an impact if they are elected to office.

Among Democrats, moderates and liberals are again indistinguishable in terms of their perceived chance of winning and expected value of a House seat. Regarding electoral goals, the ideological makeup of party activists was perhaps less salient to Democratic state legislators when the CES was conducted. Layman et al. (2010, 333) show that the percentage of conservative Republican activists increased more than threefold between 1988 and 2000, while the percentage of liberal Democratic activists remained unchanged during this period. Perhaps these sharp ideological changes among GOP activists made ideology particularly relevant to Republican but not to Democratic potential candidates. In terms of the value of congressional office, moderate Democrats were still able to influence policy, advance in the chamber, and forge bonds with like-minded colleagues into the 1990s. As discussed above, the measurement of party fit in this chapter may be less appropriate for Democrats here given the time period of the survey.

## Summary

Traditional factors such as party recruitment, the ability to garner voter support, and the perceived costs of running for office matter in clear ways for political ambition, but scholars have paid less attention to how ideology may also influence the appeal of a political career. This chapter demonstrated that moderate Republican state legislators are less likely to be attracted to a career in the U.S. House than their conservative counterparts. The second section analyzed the various parts of the calculus of candidacy. Moderate Republicans rate their probability of winning the nomination and the value of a House seat as lower than conservative Republicans. Moderate and liberal Democrats are indistinguishable in terms of their attraction to a congressional career, perceived chance of winning, and relative value of a House seat, but this may reflect the differences between the parties as well as the time period in which the CES was conducted.

Again, the argument is not that electoral considerations do not matter, but rather that nonelectoral factors are an increasingly important part of why moderates are opting out of congressional politics. As shown in Chapter 2, the fact that moderates are not running for Congress regardless of seat type, the makeup of the district, or the makeup of party activists suggests that something else is also going on. If candidate entry were only based on the probability of winning, there would at least be more ideological variation across different electoral circumstances. The CES data provide a unique opportunity to look into the perceptions of state legislators, but it would be ideal to test the argument with more recent data and data that spanned a longer time period. Moreover, even among those who are the most likely to run for Congress, very few will ever do so. The remaining chapters take the party fit argument one step forward and turn to the actual decision to run for Congress. By analyzing the ideology of those who seek congressional office, we can more fully understand how contemporary patterns of candidate emergence contribute to partisan polarization.

# 4

# Ideological Moderates Won't Run for Congress

In October 2013, veteran Republican Representative C.W. Bill Young announced he would not seek reelection to Florida's 13th congressional district. National Republican leaders immediately began their quest for a replacement. They reached out to Jack Latvala, a longtime state senator who represented more than two-thirds of the U.S. House district. Latvala had no interest in running for Congress, and he did not even return their call (Huey-Burns and Conroy 2013). That same year, Bill Cole, a rising state senator from West Virginia, received a personal visit from members of the National Republican Campaign Committee. They tried to persuade him to run against vulnerable Democratic Representative Nick Rahall in the state's 3rd district. They gave him the "rock star treatment" and assured him that the seat would be the Republicans' top target in the country (Huey-Burns and Conroy 2013). But their efforts failed to work; like Latvala, Cole had no desire to run for Congress.

*RealClearPolitics* asked Latvala, the Florida state senator, why he passed on the opportunity. He said, "I make an impact on things in Tallahassee on a daily basis. I couldn't make much of an impact in Washington" (Huey-Burns and Conroy 2013). The state senator added, "I don't think I'd have fun in Washington. I know it might be politically incorrect to say that they're beyond help up there, but it certainly doesn't look encouraging." I interviewed a former member of Congress who was a recruiter for the Democratic Party in th 1990s, and he similarly suspected that the dysfunction in Washington is holding individuals back from running for Congress. He speculated that serving in Congress is no longer seen as a wonderful job, "given all the craziness that's going on." He elaborated, "Their friends and neighbors will say, 'Why would you want to do that? These people are nuts. They can't get anything done. Why go up there?'" (1 March 2013). A more recent recruiter for the Republican Party said that the political climate is not a deterrent for all potential candidates, though. When asked if the party has had any problems recruiting candidates because of the hyperpartisanship in Congress, he said, "No, the dysfunction is, by many Republicans, viewed as... more of a motivation that is based on wanting to shape [the current] policies" (22 March 2013).

Regarding the recent influx of ideologues, the former Democratic recruiter noted, "The Republican Party is getting more and more conservative and they are attracting more and more of those types of people to run... Similarly, the Democratic Party is attracting those on the left" (1 March 2013). Yet as one moderate who served in Congress for nearly two decades remarked, "The House of Representatives is supposed to look like America. It's not supposed to look like the most conservative wing of the Republican Party and the most liberal wing of the Democratic Party. Whether they like it or not, some of America isn't bright red or bright blue" (28 February 2013). The quality of political representation is compromised when only a narrow ideological subset of individuals is willing to engage in electoral contests. If promising potential candidates such as Jack Latvala and Bill Cole overwhelmingly opt to forego a congressional bid, this has enormous implications for the nature of representative democracy.

This chapter extends the party fit argument to the decision to run for Congress. I draw on Bonica's (2014) CFscores to examine variation across state legislators in the decision to seek congressional office from 2000 to 2010. Two important findings emerge. First, there is no shortage of moderates who are well situated and well qualified to run for Congress, as a sizeable number of liberal Republicans and conservative Democrats are currently in the pipeline to Congress. Second, moderate state legislators are dramatically less likely to launch a congressional candidacy than those at the extremes. The results hold even after controlling for seat type, district partisanship, legislator experience, and fundraising ability. The argument here is that the benefits of serving in Congress are too low for moderates to run. One of the moderates whom I interviewed put it this way: "If you led a life where you have talent, you can get a job that supports you and your family and be reasonably comfortable, then why would you run for Congress? The answer was always that you do it because the honor of serving and the good that you can do outweighs that cost. For a moderate today, I don't know if they can say that" (28 February 2013). The findings in this chapter suggest that very few moderates can, in fact, say that.

### Ideology of State Legislators in the Congressional Pipeline

The survey data in the previous chapter shed light on the perceptions of state legislators as well as their perceived ability to achieve their electoral and nonelectoral goals. However, we are ultimately interested in how patterns of candidate entry contribute to partisan polarization, and it is crucial to analyze the ideological profile of state legislators who run for Congress and appear on the ballot. Bonica's (2014) data on state legislator ideology enable a comparison of high-quality potential candidates who could have run for Congress and did with high-quality potential candidates who could have run for Congress but did not. The Bonica data are also more recent, and they span multiple election cycles. The dataset includes ideal points for approximately 31,000 state legislators who did and did not run for Congress from 2000 to 2010.[1] The data enable a test of party fit specifically in the polarized era, as partisan polarization had become a defining characteristic of Congress during this time.[2]

Figure 4.1 shows the ideological distribution of state legislators in the sample used here. To put these values into context, the graph provides the ideological locations of various former and current members of Congress, including moderates like Olympia Snowe and John Tanner and conformists like former House Speakers John Boehner and Nancy Pelosi. A few patterns are noteworthy. First, a clear partisan divide exists among state legislators. Republicans cluster toward the right end of the

---

[1] The goal was to restrict the sample to "quality congressional candidates" who do and do not run for Congress (Jacobson and Kernell 1983). Thus, the sample includes state legislative incumbents who make their first run for Congress and state legislative incumbents who run for the state legislature again but could have run for Congress. The sample excludes first-time state legislative candidates who are not yet quality candidates, those who have previously run for the state legislature and lost, and state legislators who seek higher state legislative office.

[2] Bonica's state legislator estimates are available from 1990 to 2010, but I restrict the sample to estimates from 2000 to 2010. The number of state legislative candidates who filed with the FEC was significantly lower prior to 2000, so the number of state legislators in the dataset who could have run for office was unreasonably low. Specifically, there are 8,027 observations in the dataset between 1990 and 1998, compared with 31,030 between 2000 and 2010. According to the National Conference of State Legislatures, there are 7,300 state legislators nationwide in a given election cycle, so the latter figure is a much closer approximation of the eligible pool of state legislators (National Conference of State Legislators 2013).

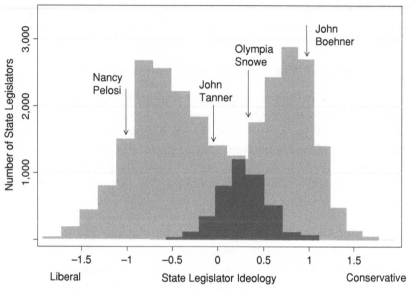

FIGURE 4.1. Ideological distribution of state legislators, 2000–2010
*Source:* State legislator estimates are from Bonica (2014).

distribution, and Democrats cluster toward the left end. However, a substantial amount of partisan overlap also emerges among state legislators. This stands in stark contrast to Congress, where there is no ideological overlap between Republican and Democratic legislators (Poole and Rosenthal 2007).

An important and related point is that plenty of moderates are well situated to run for Congress. Among Republican state legislators, 18 percent have ideology scores that are at least as liberal as Olympia Snowe's. Among Democratic state legislators, 27 percent have scores that are at least as conservative as John Tanner's. Furthermore, state legislators who resemble mainstream liberals and conservatives like Nancy Pelosi and John Boehner, respectively, comprise a relatively small proportion of the pool of state legislators: 24 percent of Republican state legislators are at least as conservative as Boehner and 12 percent of Democratic state legislators are at least as liberal as Pelosi.

Figure 4.2 shows the ideological distribution of state legislators who ran for the U.S. House during this time. We see a clear shift of the distribution away from the center and toward the extremes. Among the 239 Republican runners, only 17 had scores that were as or more liberal than

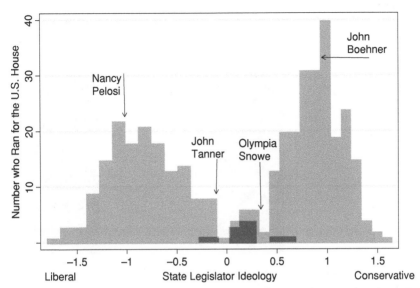

FIGURE 4.2. Ideological distribution of state legislators who ran for the U.S. House, 2000–2010
*Source:* Bonica (2014).

Snowe's (7 percent). Among the 164 Democratic runners, a mere 11 had scores that were as or more conservative than Tanner's (7 percent). The ideological overlap between Republican and Democratic state legislators almost completely vanishes. In addition, state legislators like Boehner and Pelosi are much closer to the median of the ideological distribution of runners. The median ideology scores of Republican runners and nonrunners are 0.90 and 0.72, respectively, and the median ideology scores of Democratic runners and nonrunners are −0.82 and −0.48, respectively. Among state legislators who ran for the House, 41 percent of Republicans were at least as conservative as Boehner and 32 percent of Democrats were at least as liberal as Pelosi.

We can also look at the proportion of ideologues and moderates who launched congressional candidacies. Figure 4.3 shows the proportion of moderate state legislators like Snowe and Tanner who ran for the U.S. House compared with the proportion of conservatives and liberals like Boehner and Pelosi who did so. Republican state legislators like Boehner were significantly more likely to run for Congress than those like Snowe, and Democratic state legislators like Pelosi were significantly more likely to run for Congress than those like Tanner ($p < 0.01$ for both parties).

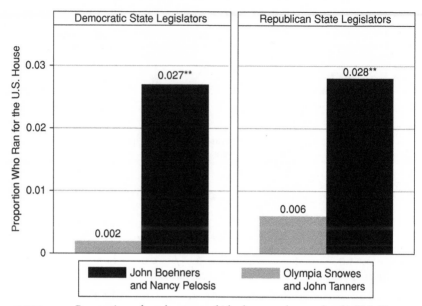

FIGURE 4.3. Proportion of moderates and ideologues who ran for the U.S. House, 2000–2010

*Source:* Bonica (2014).

** $p < 0.01$. Statistical significance denotes differences between moderates and ideologues by party.

Nearly 3 percent of conservative Republican and liberal Democratic state legislators launched congressional candidacies. By comparison, only 0.6 percent of moderate Republican and 0.2 percent of moderate Democratic state legislators did so. In short, virtually no moderate state legislators are choosing to run for Congress in the contemporary partisan era.

To be sure, across state legislators, the proportion of runners for the U.S. House is low. Hardly anyone seeks congressional office. Of the 31,000 state legislators in the sample here, only 403, or 1.3 percent, appeared on party primary ballots. Although it is difficult to determine a baseline probability of running for Congress, Maestas et al. (2006, 200) find that 6 of the 874 state legislators in the CES ran for Congress in the election immediately following their survey (0.7 percent). In their full sample of potential congressional candidates, which included state legislators as well as those who were identified as strong candidates by district informants, 1.9 percent sought congressional office that year (Maisel and Stone 2014, 435). In any single year between 1998 and 2012, the largest percentage of potential candidates who ran for the House was

2 percent (2000 and 2002) and the smallest percentage was 0.8 percent (2008) (Maisel and Stone 2014, 435). In the sample of state legislators here, the high was 1.9 percent (2002) and the low was 1 percent (2006).

It is clear that, across samples, very few individuals make the leap and run for Congress. This is true even among those in the congressional pipeline – individuals who would be the most likely to run as well as win. In fact, one reason it is so important to look at the end stage of the candidate emergence process is that so few people ever decide to launch a political candidacy. We saw in Chapter 3 that almost half of state legislators said they were at least somewhat attracted to a congressional career. What the figures here demonstrate is that even among those who say they are politically ambitious and even among those who say they are likely to run, very few will do so. Perceptions of the electoral environment are important for understanding the mechanisms that shape the decision to run for office, but what matters most for changes in polarization in Congress is the actual makeup of the candidate pool.

## The Decision to Run for Congress

Our main concern is why some high-quality potential candidates run for office and others do not, but it is important to briefly consider whether the pool of congressional candidates with state legislative backgrounds varies by party. If successful Republican candidates are less likely to have previous state legislative experience or if Republican candidates are more likely to be political amateurs, an analysis of state legislators may be less relevant for patterns of polarization in Congress. However, there is little evidence of such partisan differences either among the pool of successful candidates or among the full pool of congressional candidates. The same proportions of Democrats and Republicans in Congress – successful candidates – have previous state legislative experience (51 percent of Democrats and 52 percent of Republicans) (Carnes 2012). Moreover, in the full pool of successful and unsuccessful nonincumbent candidates who ran for Congress from 2000 to 2010, 17 percent of Republicans and 15 percent of Democrats had state legislative backgrounds. Thus, state legislators seem to be an appropriate sample from which to assess the broader implications of party fit for changes in congressional polarization.[3]

---

[3] Chapter 5 more fully examines House candidates with and without state legislative experience and where they fall on the ideological spectrum.

The central claim is that state legislators are less likely to run for Congress as their distance from the party increases. In the contemporary context, ideological moderates are expected to be less likely to pursue a congressional career than those at the extremes. I use logistic regression to analyze the relationship between ideological conformity with the party and the decision to run for office. The dependent variable is coded 1 if the state legislator runs for Congress in a given year and 0 if she runs for the state legislature.[4] A state legislator's party fit is coded so that higher values correspond to increased distance from the party in Congress. An additional benefit of using the Bonica (2014) dataset is that state and federal actors are on a common ideological scale so party fit can be precisely measured. As discussed in Chapter 2, because the party leadership sets the policy agenda and distributes party rewards, I use the mean ideology of the leadership to measure the congressional party, and I follow Jessee and Malhotra's (2010) definition of party leaders.[5]

In other specifications of the model, I include a squared term to test whether the effect of party fit is nonlinear, and I interact party fit with direction of distance to examine whether distance works in different ways for moderates and ideologues. Ideologues may be more likely to run than moderates due to differences in the value of the office for each, though the probability of seeking congressional office is expected to decrease among extreme ideological outliers as well. I also use Shor and McCarty's (2011) estimates of state legislator ideology, and although I cannot measure the concept of party fit directly because there are no available measures for the congressional party, the substantive results are the same. These results will be discussed in the next chapter.

The model includes a host of electoral, partisan, and institutional variables. Seat type is perhaps the single most relevant factor for quality potential candidates considering their first electoral bid, and I control for whether an incumbent was running for reelection in the state

---

[4] Because the dependent variable is the decision to run for Congress, state legislators can be in the dataset multiple times. The results are the same if the data are collapsed by individual, but this is a better test of the argument. In this sample, 403 (1.3 percent) of these decisions were to run for Congress and 30,522 were to run for the state legislature again (239 of the runners were Republicans and 164 were Democrats). I also used rare event logistic regression, and the results are identical. The state legislators represent 49 states; Nebraska is excluded because its legislature is nonpartisan.

[5] I have also measured party fit as distance from the congressional party mean. The results are the same, but I use distance from the party leadership for the reasons noted in Chapter 2.

legislator's congressional district.[6] I calculated the average amount of money individuals raised as state legislators from Bonica's data, as this likely corresponds to their ability to fund a congressional campaign. I control for the number of times individuals sought state legislative office to capture their experience as candidates as well as the gender and party of the legislator. I include the partisan balance of the state legislature, as this may influence the appeal of serving in congressional office (Klarner 2013). The ideology of voters and donors will also likely play a key role in the decision to run for office. To account for these factors, I use Tausanovitch and Warshaw's (2013) measures of the ideology of same-party subconstituencies in the state legislator's congressional district, as well as Bonica's ideology score for the average donor in the congressional district. The models include state and year fixed effects to control for factors such as primary election type, state legislative term limits, and differences in the number of congressional seats across states.

The results are presented in Table 4.1.[7] Of most importance are the coefficients on the party fit variables. Across models, decreasing values of party fit have a negative effect on candidate emergence: the further the state legislator is from the congressional party, the less likely she is to run for Congress.[8] Yet as shown in Columns (2) and (3), the direction of distance also matters for the decision to run. In fact, increasing distance from the party in the ideologue direction is expected to have a *positive* effect on the probability of running, although the relationship is negative

[6] I used Census data to assign state legislative districts (SLDs) to their corresponding congressional district (CD). For SLDs that fall into more than one CD, I used the CD in which the SLD comprised a larger portion of the CD population. Gary Jacobson generously provided the incumbency data. This measure of open seats accounts for whether the seat was open at any time in the election cycle, as the goal is to capture any opportunity in which there was no incumbent. There were 42 special elections that are thus also included in the measure of open seats, but the results remain the same if these are excluded.

[7] I also interacted party fit with the legislator's party. The interaction is not significant; however, if the state legislator's ideology is used instead of the party fit measure, the party × ideology interaction is significant, with moderate Republicans less likely to run than moderate Democrats. This difference is obscured by the measurement of party fit. Because the GOP has moved further to the right than the Democrats have moved to the left, equally moderate legislators have different values of party fit by party. Put differently, moderate Republicans are more distant from their party than moderate Democrats are. The concern in this chapter is with the concept of party fit, but I discuss partisan differences in more detail in the next chapter on asymmetric polarization.

[8] The models are not sensitive to the inclusion of the control variables, and the findings hold with and without the controls. The results are also provided for Republicans and Democrats separately in Appendix C. Partisan differences are discussed in more detail in the next chapter.

TABLE 4.1. *Determinants of running for the U.S. House, 2000–2010*

| | (1) | (2) | (3) |
|---|---|---|---|
| Distance from party in Congress | −1.37** | −2.68** | −3.53** |
| | (0.25) | (0.43) | (1.09) |
| Distance from party × ideologue side | – | 6.12** | 9.46** |
| | | (0.65) | (1.59) |
| Distance from party squared | – | – | 0.87 |
| | | | (1.05) |
| Distance from party squared × ideologue side | – | – | −4.21* |
| | | | (1.76) |
| Ideologue side | – | 0.52** | 0.14 |
| | | (0.18) | (0.25) |
| Open Congressional seat | 2.85** | 2.85** | 2.85** |
| | (0.12) | (0.13) | (0.13) |
| Republican | 0.49** | 1.10** | 1.12** |
| | (0.15) | (0.21) | (0.21) |
| Ideology of same party voters in district (higher = extreme) | −1.03 | −3.89** | −3.88** |
| | (0.54) | (0.62) | (0.63) |
| Ideology of average donor in district (higher = conservative) | −0.48* | −0.70** | −0.69** |
| | (0.24) | (0.24) | (0.25) |
| Log of mean receipts raised as state legislator | 0.28** | 0.31** | 0.31** |
| | (0.08) | (0.08) | (0.08) |
| Number of times run for state legislature | 0.32** | 0.46** | 0.46** |
| | (0.04) | (0.04) | (0.04) |
| Female | −0.03 | −0.26 | −0.26 |
| | (0.13) | (0.14) | (0.14) |
| Democratic control of state legislature | 0.07 | 0.09 | 0.09 |
| | (0.25) | (0.26) | (0.26) |
| Constant | −9.82** | −8.84** | −8.81** |
| | (1.27) | (1.25) | (1.25) |
| Number of observations | 30,925 | 30,925 | 30,925 |
| Log likelihood | −1628.65 | −1486.97 | −1483.57 |
| State and year fixed effects | Yes | Yes | Yes |

*Note:* Entries are logistic regression coefficients with robust standard errors clustered by individual in parentheses. The dependent variable is coded 1 if the incumbent state legislator ran for Congress and 0 if the incumbent state legislator ran for the state legislature again. ** $p < 0.01$, * $p < 0.05$.

among extreme ideological outliers. Again, the empirical focus here is on those in the ideological center due to (a) their theoretical prominence in the literature, (b) their crucial role in minimizing polarization, and (c) the fact that state legislators on the moderate side of the party in Congress comprise the bulk of the observations in the dataset. Nevertheless, both

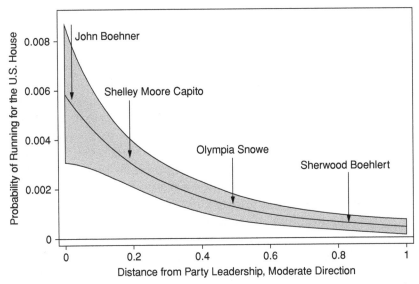

FIGURE 4.4. Predicted probability of running for the U.S. House among Republican state legislators, 2000–2010
*Note:* Values are estimated from the model in Column (3) in Table 4.1. The arrows refer to hypothetical state legislators who have the same ideological scores as various former and current members of Congress. For example, the arrow corresponding to John Boehner represents the probability of running for the U.S. House for a state legislator who has the same ideology score as Boehner.

groups are relevant for polarization, and those on the ideologue side of the leadership will be discussed later in the chapter as well.

The figures that follow present the predicted probability of running for Congress across a range of values of party fit, estimated from the full model in Column (3). All other variables are set at their mean or mode. Patterns of candidate entry differ for Republicans and Democrats, and the results will be discussed separately by party.

Figure 4.4 presents the predicted probability of running for Congress across Republican state legislators. The graph also shows the probabilities for state legislators who have the same ideology scores as various current and former members of Congress, including conservatives like former House Speaker John Boehner and former moderates like Olympia Snowe and Sherwood Boehlert. Boehlert represented upstate New York, and he served in the U.S. House from 1982 until his retirement in 2006. Like other moderate Republicans in office at the time, he was often at odds with the leadership and broke from the party on a variety of social and economic issues. He is perhaps best known for the attention he devoted to environmental policy. Boehlert supported endangered species protection, mandatory greenhouse gas restrictions, and stronger fuel-economy standards, and he was instrumental in adding acid rain provisions to the Clean Air Act of 1990 (*Grist* (staff) 2006).

We can see that the probability of running for Congress differs dramatically across Republican state legislators. The probability that an ideological conformist like Boehner runs for Congress is 0.6 percent, compared with 0.1 percent and 0.05 percent for former moderates like Snowe and Boehlert, respectively.[9] In other words, even across high-quality potential candidates, the likelihood that a state legislator who resembles Boehner runs is six times that for a moderate like Snowe and twelve times that for a moderate like Boehlert. Furthermore, the magnitude of this effect compares with that of an open seat, which has long been regarded as one of the most important determinants of the decision to run among quality candidates. Among Republicans, the predicted probabilities of running when the seat is open and when the incumbent is running are 2.8 percent and 0.2 percent, respectively, which is a 14-fold increase in the likelihood of running.

In short, virtually no moderate Republicans ran for the U.S. House during this time. As shown previously in Figure 4.3, of the 2,617 Republican state legislators in this sample who were at least as liberal as former Senator Olympia Snowe, only 17, or 0.6 percent, sought congressional office between 2000 and 2010. A mere 3 of the 929 (0.3 percent) Republican state legislators resembling Boehlert launched congressional candidacies.

Figure 4.5 shows the results for Democratic state legislators. The values are lower because Democrats are, on average, less likely to run for higher office than their Republican counterparts, but the general patterns are the same.[10] The probability that a Democratic state legislator with the same ideological profile as former DNC chair Debbie Wasserman Schultz (FL) runs for Congress is 0.2 percent, compared with 0.03 percent and 0.02 percent for legislators who resemble John Tanner and

---

[9] Because all variables are set at their mean or mode, these values are state legislators' probabilities of running when there is an incumbent seeking reelection. The low probabilities among state legislators reflect the fact that most instead wait for an open seat. I turn to open seats in the next chapter.

[10] It is unclear why the probability of running is lower for Democrats than it is for Republicans. Part of the disparity is likely due to the slightly better proportion of open seat opportunities for Republicans, but that is beyond the scope of the analysis here.

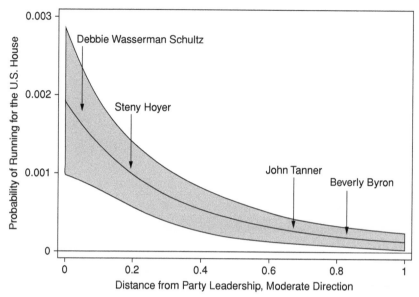

FIGURE 4.5. Predicted probability of running for the U.S. House among Democratic state legislators, 2000–2010

*Note:* Values are estimated from the model in Column (3) in Table 4.1. The arrows refer to hypothetical state legislators who have the same ideological scores as various former and current members of Congress. For example, the arrow corresponding to Debbie Wasserman Schultz represents the probability of running for the U.S. House for a state legislator who has the same ideology score as Schultz.

Beverly Byron, the moderate Democrats discussed above. The likelihood that a state legislator like Wasserman Schultz runs is nearly seven times that for a legislator like Tanner and ten times that for a legislator like Byron. For Democrats, the size of this effect is smaller than that of an open seat, with an open seat expected to result in an 18-fold increase in the probability of running (from 0.05 to 0.9 percent). But it is clear that candidate emergence is much more likely among high-quality potential candidates who conform to the ideology of the party than for those who do not. Ideological moderates are not running for Congress at the same rates as their counterparts with more liberal or conservative preferences.

As noted above, the party fit argument does not work in the same way for those on the ideologue side of the leadership, although the likelihood of running decreases among extreme ideological outliers. Figure 4.6

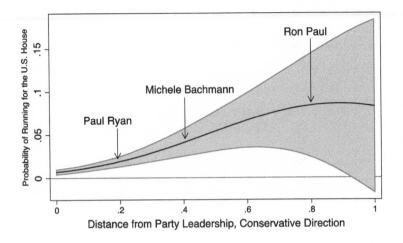

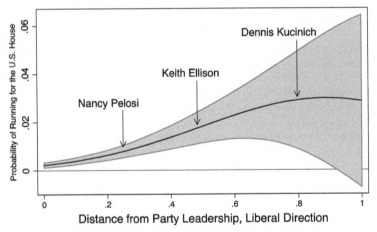

FIGURE 4.6. Predicted probability of running for the U.S. House among conservative Republican and liberal Democratic state legislators, 2000–2010
*Note:* Values are estimated from the model in Column (3) in Table 4.1.

shows the probability of running for the U.S. House among state legislators who are more extreme than the party leadership. The graph shows the probabilities for conservative Republicans who resemble Paul Ryan and Michele Bachmann (MN) and liberal Democrats who resemble Nancy Pelosi and Keith Ellison (MN). All of these individuals are strong partisans who vote with the majority of their party more than 90 percent of the time, although Bachmann and Ellison are at the conservative and liberal ends of their parties (Poole and Rosenthal 2007). Bachmann has been an outspoken leader of the Tea Party movement, and she launched a brief presidential bid in 2012. Like many Republicans, she is pro-life and anti-tax, supportive of increased domestic drilling for oil and natural gas, and opposed to the Affordable Care Act and same-sex marriage. Yet her language is more inflammatory and her tactics are more confrontational than those used by other Republicans. Bachmann has said that President Obama has "anti-American views" and that his administration is running a "gangster government" (Hooper 2010). On the Democratic side, Ellison has not been in the national spotlight like Bachmann, but he is one of the most liberal members in Congress and co-chair of the Congressional Progressive Caucus (CPC). He was a vocal critic of the Iraq War, and he favors minimum wage increases, single-payer government health care, and equal pay for women. Ellison recently joined with his co-chair of the CPC, Representative Raul Grijalva (D-AZ), to introduce the Justice Is Not for Sale Act, which would ban federal contracts with private prisons entirely (Seitz-Wald 2015). Ellison also differs from some of his Democratic colleagues in his embrace of economic populism and resistance to cuts in entitlements.

The patterns in Figure 4.6 suggest that the ranks of conservative Republicans and liberal Democrats in Congress will continue to grow in the future. For a Republican state legislator who resembles Ryan or Bachmann, the probability of running for Congress increases to 1.8 percent and 4.1 percent, respectively. Among Democrats, the likelihood of a state legislator like Pelosi or Ellison seeking congressional office increases to 0.8 percent and 1.7 percent, respectively. Put differently, the probability that a Republican state legislator like Ryan runs for Congress is 18 times that for a legislator like Snowe, and the probability that a Democratic state legislator like Pelosi runs is 26 times that for a legislator like Tanner. The magnitude of these effects is larger than that of an open seat for both Republicans and Democrats.

Yet it is also important not to overstate the substantive impact of very conservative Republicans and very liberal Democrats on polarization, given the ideological distribution of state legislators. As illustrated in Figure 4.1, 65 percent of the Republican sample and 70 percent of the Democratic sample are on the moderate side of the leadership. Of the 239 Republican and 164 Democratic state legislators who ran for Congress from 2000 to 2010, only 14 Republicans were as or more conservative than Bachmann and only 18 Democrats were as or more liberal than Ellison. Put differently, the vast majority of state legislators who ran for Congress were less conservative than Bachmann and less liberal than

Ellison. Aggregate changes in polarization seem to be due in large part to the disproportionate entry and abstention of conformists and moderates, respectively, and in much smaller part to the entry of ideological outliers like Bachmann and Ellison.

More generally, the fact that those on the extreme side of the party are more likely to run suggests that the effect of party fit differs depending on the direction of distance, but it is also possible that potential candidates evaluate their congruence with the party's most outspoken leaders or the expected future location of the party. Party fit is measured here as distance from the congressional leadership, but a case could be made that the loudest Republican voices are at least as conservative as Boehner and the loudest Democratic voices are at least as liberal as Wasserman Schultz. In fact, Nancy Pelosi is 0.25 units away from the party in the liberal direction, and Paul Ryan is 0.20 units away in the conservative direction. In addition, the most recent promotions within both parties have been ideologues. Moderates may therefore project a decrease in the benefits of party membership over time, and ideologues may project an increase in these benefits. The selection of Paul Ryan to replace John Boehner as House Speaker, coupled with the addition of Kevin McCarthy (CA) as Majority Leader and Steve Scalise (LA) as Majority Whip, has moved the leadership further to the right than it was during the time frame here. This is a measurement question, rather than a theoretical one, as there are a variety of ways to conceptualize party fit. But across the board, the predictions do not bode well for moderates or bipartisanship.

The results on the control variables are largely as expected. As discussed above, state legislators are much more likely to run when the seat is open, which conforms to a long line of research on strategic candidate entry (e.g., Jacobson and Kernell 1983). In addition, those who raised more money as state legislative candidates and those with more state legislative experience are more likely to launch a congressional candidacy. The ideology of same-party subconstituencies in the congressional district is negatively related to the decision to run, with Republican state legislators less likely to run in districts with increasingly conservative partisans and Democrats less likely to do so in districts with increasingly liberal partisans. Donor conservatism is also negatively related to candidate emergence. In this sample of high-quality potential candidates, women are no less likely to run for higher office than men, but it is important to remember that there are still very few women in the congressional pipeline (Thomsen 2015).

## Summary

This chapter demonstrated that quality potential candidates from across the ideological spectrum are not emerging at similar rates, and the findings provide empirical support for the party fit argument outlined in Chapter 2. Although a sizeable number of liberal Republicans and conservative Democrats currently serve in state legislative office, they are much less likely to seek congressional office than those at the extremes. These results hold even after controlling for a variety of factors that also shape the decision to run for office, such as seat type, district partisanship, legislator experience, and fundraising ability. The findings are crucial for understanding how the supply of congressional candidates contributes to partisan polarization and why legislative tactics and strategies in Congress have become less accommodating and increasingly confrontational in recent years. The vanishing of conservative Democrats and liberal Republicans not only from Congress but also from the congressional candidate pool means that there are no moderates to shape the policy platforms of the two parties or bend legislation away from the growing liberal and conservative party factions.

The results in this chapter are important for examining how party fit matters for the calculus of candidacy, on average, all else equal. But the modal case here is also when an incumbent is running for reelection. Most state legislators choose not to run against an incumbent and instead wait for the seat to become open (Jacobson 2013). High-quality challengers who beat incumbents are a minority of incoming candidates, and most newly elected replacements enter through open seats, which is why state legislators choose to wait rather than take on an incumbent. In addition, scholars have increasingly pointed to asymmetries in the ideological trajectories of the two parties, and we might be interested in how Republicans and Democrats compare with each other. Because we are concerned with the implications of party fit for both partisan polarization and asymmetric polarization, it is important to take a closer look at open seats and examine candidate emergence by party as well. I turn to these two topics next.

# 5

## Where the Action Is

### Asymmetric Polarization and Open Seats

In 2012, Thomas Mann and Norman Ornstein wrote an editorial in the *Washington Post* titled, "Let's Just Say It: The Republicans Are the Problem." Mann and Ornstein, along with a growing number of political scientists, have argued that the GOP bears a larger part of the burden for the current dysfunction in Congress. They suggest that although both parties have moved away from the center, the Republicans have charged sharply to the right and the Democrats have shifted more modestly to the left (e.g., Hacker and Pierson 2005; McCarty et al. 2006; Carmines 2011). The recent research on asymmetric polarization has, for obvious reasons, generated quite a stir. It is, as Mann and Ornstein (2012, 186) themselves acknowledge, "awkward and uncomfortable, even seemingly unprofessional, to attribute a disproportionate share of the blame for dysfunctional politics to one party or the other."

We might even wonder about the significance of all the finger pointing. Ron Fournier of the *National Journal* claimed that it does not really matter which party is to blame: "This is my fundamental disagreement with partisan journalists and political scientists who dedicate their careers to measuring increments of fault – the GOP's share of blame is 20 percent or 60 percent or 80 percent. Who cares? Not the average voter who merely wants her leaders to work together and get results." Ornstein wrote a deft response to the "Who Cares?" question in the *Atlantic* and countered that it does matter whether polarization is equal on both sides or whether the Republicans are the driving force. He said, "If bad behavior – using the nation's full faith and credit as a hostage to political demands, shutting down the government, attempting to undermine policies that have been lawfully enacted, blocking nominees not on the basis of their qualifications but to nullify the policies they would pursue, using filibusters as weapons of mass obstruction – is to be discouraged or abandoned, those who engage in it have to be held accountable." Attributing the same level of responsibility to two unequal partners in crime leaves voters unable to reward and punish their elected officials accordingly.

We can also look at the data to evaluate differences between the parties. Party averages constructed with Poole and Rosenthal's (2007) DW-NOMINATE scores reveal that the two parties have not followed the same trajectory. The scores range from −1 to 1, with higher values indicating conservative positions. In the 112th Congress (2011–12), the median Republican had a score of 0.61, while the median Democrat had a score of −0.36. In addition, Carmines (2011) finds that from 2000 to 2008, newly elected Democrats were more moderate than Democrats who were continuing their House careers. He notes that this pattern makes "perfect electoral sense," because many of these new Democrats came from swing districts where moderates have a greater chance of success. Patterns on the Republican side, however, have not followed a similar logic. During this same period, newly elected Republicans were more conservative than continuing House Republicans, even in swing seats that were previously held by Democrats (Carmines 2011). In 2010 alone, 77 percent of the newly arriving Republicans were to the right of the median Republican in the previous Congress (Bonica 2010).[1]

While asymmetric polarization is not the primary emphasis of the book, Republicans and Democrats may nevertheless differ in important ways. The previous chapter showed that moderates are less likely to run for Congress than conservative Republicans and liberal Democrats. This chapter instead focuses on the action of polarization, paying particular

---

[1] To be sure, the rate of party change does depend on the data that are used to measure legislator ideology. On the one hand, DW-NOMINATE scores show that since 1980, the mean Democrat moved 0.20 standard deviations to the left while the mean Republican moved 0.44 standard deviations to the right. Yet Bonica's (2014) CFscores reveal sizeable ideological shifts by both parties toward the extremes since 1980. In fact, the CFscores indicate that the mean Democrat moved 0.50 standard deviations to the left while the mean Republican moved 0.31 standard deviations to the right during this time (Bonica 2014, 379). Nevertheless, the CFscores similarly suggest that incoming Republicans have been more conservative than continuing House Republicans from 2000 to 2010 and that the current Republican Party is more conservative than the Democratic Party is liberal. The CFscores range from −1.5 to 1.5, with higher values corresponding to conservative positions. In the 112th Congress, the median Republican had a CFscore of 0.94, while the median Democrat had a score of −0.79. In short, although the particular data do shape the discussion around asymmetric polarization, there is reason to believe that the contemporary GOP is distinct from the Democratic Party.

attention to partisan asymmetries and open seats. First, the bulk of party shifts occur through those who win in open seats, as most newly elected candidates do not enter Congress by defeating incumbents. As a share of incoming replacements, open seat victors are thus a key factor in whether and how much the gulf between the parties widens or diminishes. Second, in light of the partisan differences in the benefits of the office and the distinct characters of the two parties described in Chapter 2, I examine how the impact of ideology varies between Republicans and Democrats. I find that conservative Republicans are more likely to run for Congress than liberal Democrats. The disproportionate emergence of conservative Republicans, particularly in open seats where they are most likely to win, is an additional force behind asymmetric polarization in Congress.

### The Impact of Open Seat Entrants on Polarization

Nonincumbents differ markedly with respect to their chance of success. Gaddie and Bullock (2000, 1) write, "Open seats, not the defeat of incumbents, are the portal through which most legislators enter Congress." Open seat candidates have a far greater probability of winning than challengers, and compared with the relatively few candidates who defeat incumbents, those who are selected in open seats are more likely to spur changes in the makeup of Congress. Indeed, of the approximately 1,000 new members elected between 1980 and 2010, nearly three-fourths entered through open seats, compared with one-fourth who defeated incumbents (Center for Responsive Politics 2014). To understand how party shifts occur, it is crucial to examine the types of candidates who are elected in open seats.

Figure 5.1 presents the percentages of incoming members who were elected to Congress as challengers, open seat candidates, and incumbents from 1980 to 2010. Of course, incumbents dominate the pool of incoming members, but those elected in open seats constitute the vast majority of replacements. These figures vary across election cycles, and the number of freshmen elected in open seats increases noticeably in the elections following reapportionment.[2] However, in every election except 2010, the freshmen elected in open seats outnumbered those elected as challengers, and in most years dramatically so. Sizeable proportions of challengers defeated incumbents in 1980, 1994, 2006, and 2010, but the general pattern is one of open seat winners making up the bulk of the

---

[2] The large number of open seat freshmen in 1992 was also due to retirements prompted by the House banking scandal.

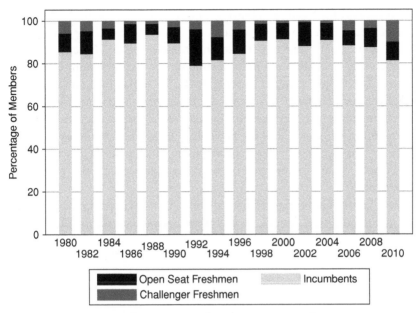

FIGURE 5.1. Incoming members by seat type, 1980–2010
*Source:* Center for Responsive Politics (2014).

replacements. Although challenger victories also contribute to the growing distance between the parties, open seat winners have more weight in shaping these trends due to their greater numbers. Given that members of Congress tend to "die in their ideological boots" (Poole 1998), it is the open seat victors who are steering the party's ideological course.

On the one hand, if the only candidates who run for office come from the ideological extremes, the only candidates who will be elected to office will come from the extremes. Yet at the same time, these decisions to seek congressional office are not equal in their ability to impact aggregate trends in the ideological makeup of Congress. All candidates, incumbents and nonincumbents alike, have moved away from the political center, but the replacements who enter through open seats have the largest effect on recent changes in the ideology of the Republican and Democratic parties in Congress.

## How Ideology Matters for Candidate Entry in Open Seats

As discussed in Chapter 2, a variety of factors influence the calculus of candidacy. Whether or not an incumbent is running for reelection is perhaps the single most relevant factor for high-quality potential candidates considering an electoral bid. This is because open seat candidates have a much better chance of winning than those who challenge incumbents (but see Banks and Kiewiet 1989). Given the huge opportunity costs involved in both running for and serving in Congress, many of the highest caliber candidates choose to run only when there is no incumbent. Indeed, Jacobson (2013) shows that experienced candidates, or those who have previously held elected office, constitute more than half of the candidates for open U.S. House seats but less than one-quarter of those who challenge incumbents. And again, the newly elected replacements entering through open seats are driving much of the rise in polarization.

Ideology has never figured prominently in traditional notions of strategic candidate entry. Among quality potential candidates, the probability of running is expected to be equally low when an incumbent is running and equally high when the seat is open regardless of their ideology (e.g., Jacobson and Kernell 1983; Kazee 1994; Cox and Katz 1996; Levitt and Wolfram 1997; Jacobson 2013; Baumgartner and Francia 2010). To be sure, all quality candidates have a much greater chance of achieving their electoral goals if the congressional seat is open. Incumbent reelection rates are consistently higher than 90 percent, and strategic candidates tend to wait for the incumbent to retire (Jacobson 2013). But if the value of the office differs for ideological conformists and deviants, it is likely that the same electoral opportunity will result in different patterns of candidate emergence across quality potential candidates. What is more, increased attention to ideology within the context of strategic candidate entry is important precisely because challengers and open seat candidates have dramatically different rates of election and dramatically different effects on their party's ideological course.

I use the same dataset of state legislators from the previous chapter to examine whether the probability of running when the seat is open differs across high-quality potential candidates. The figures below show the predicted probability of running for Congress when the seat is open across a range of values of party fit, again broken down by party. The patterns are identical to those in Chapter 4, but the probability of running increases dramatically across candidates when the seat is open.[3]

---

[3] I also interacted party fit with seat type, but the interaction is not significant. Open seats do not have a differential impact on the probability of running for conformists and nonconformists.

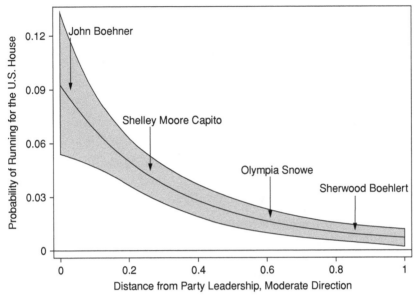

FIGURE 5.2. Predicted probability of running in an open seat among Republican state legislators, 2000–2010
*Note:* Values are estimated from the model in Column (3) in Table 4.1.

Figure 5.2 presents the results for Republicans. The probability that an ideological conformist like former Speaker John Boehner runs for Congress when the seat is open is 9.0 percent, compared with 0.9 percent for a moderate like former Representative Sherwood Boehlert. Even across quality potential candidates, the likelihood that a state legislator like Boehner runs when the seat is open is 10 times that of a moderate like Boehlert. Hardly any moderate Republicans ran for Congress even if the seat was open. Of the 270 Republicans who were at least as liberal as Snowe and faced open seats during this time, only 9 ran for Congress (3.3 percent). The ideological disparity in open seats is particularly important given that most members of Congress enter through this pathway (Gaddie and Bullock 2000).

Figure 5.3 shows the results for Democratic state legislators. The values are lower because Democrats are, on average, less likely to run for higher office than their Republican counterparts, but the general patterns are the same. The probability that a Democratic state legislator with the same ideological profile as Representative Debbie Wasserman Schultz runs for Congress when the seat is open is 2.6 percent, compared with 0.3 percent for a state legislator who resembles a conservative Democrat

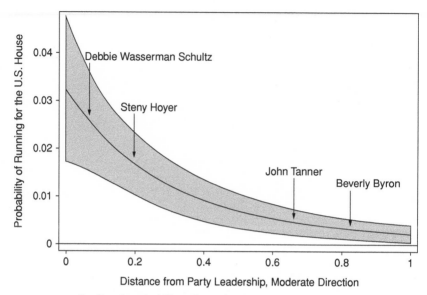

FIGURE 5.3. Predicted probability of running in an open seat among Democratic state legislators, 2000–2010
*Note:* Values are estimated from the model in Column (3) in Table 4.1.

like Beverly Byron. In other words, the likelihood that a state legislator like Wasserman Schultz runs when the seat is open is five times that for a legislator like Tanner and eight times that for a legislator like Byron.

We can see in Figure 5.4 that patterns of candidate entry again reach their height among those on the ideologue side. For Republican state legislators like Paul Ryan or Michele Bachmann, the likelihood of running for congressional office when the seat is open soars to 24 percent and 42 percent, respectively. Among Democrats, the chance that a state legislator like Nancy Pelosi or Keith Ellison seeks congressional office when the seat is open increases to 12 percent and 23 percent, respectively. In other words, the probability that a Republican state legislator like Ryan runs for Congress when the seat is open is nearly 30 times that for a legislator like Boehlert, and the probability that a Democratic state legislator like Pelosi runs is 40 times that for a legislator like Byron.

As discussed in Chapters 2 and 4, it is possible that potential candidates evaluate their congruence with the party's most prominent members or the future composition of the party. For reasons described throughout, party fit is measured as distance from the leadership, but the precise location of the party is difficult to pin down. This is a

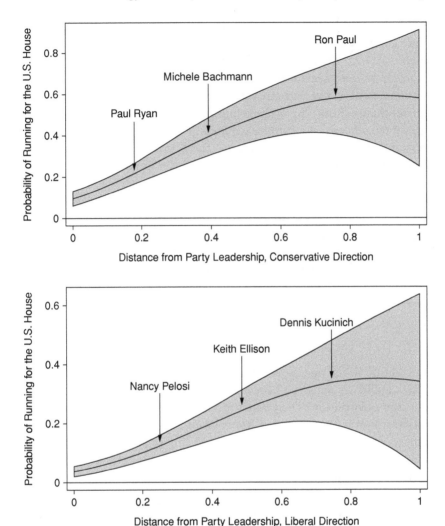

FIGURE 5.4. Predicted probability of running in an open seat among conservative Republican and liberal Democratic state legislators, 2000–2010
*Note:* Values are estimated from the model in Column (3) in Table 4.1.

measurement question, and a case could be made that the most visible and most successful Republican and Democratic members are more conservative and liberal, respectively, than these leadership averages. Moderates may also anticipate a decrease in the future benefits of party membership, and ideologues may anticipate an increase in these benefits. Yet more generally, despite these high probabilities, there are relatively few state legislators at the ideologue end of the distribution, and the bulk of the state legislators who run for Congress resemble the party leadership (see Figure 4.2). Of the 158 Republican and 107 Democratic state legislators who ran in open seats from 2000 to 2010, only 5 Republicans were as or more conservative than Bachmann and 11 Democrats were as or more liberal than Ellison. The overwhelming majority of those who seek congressional office are not extreme ideological outliers, but rather those who resemble the increasingly conservative and liberal party mainstreams.

In sum, candidates from across the ideological spectrum are not emerging at similar rates regardless of seat type. The findings with respect to open seats add nuance to our conception of the strategic politician, and they provide additional support for the argument that the value of the office varies across individuals. The party fit framework also helps to explain why newly elected members are exacerbating the gulf between the parties. The potential candidates who are the most likely to run and the most likely to win are pulling the parties away from the center and toward their respective poles.

## The Asymmetric Decision to Run for Congress

In addition to the open seat entrants described above, incoming Republican candidates may also have a disproportionate impact on the rise in partisan polarization. The general focus of the book is on the decline of moderates in both parties, but Republicans are likely to differ in important ways from Democrats. Grossman and Hopkins (2015, 2016) suggest that ideological orthodoxy is valued more in the Republican Party than in the Democratic Party (see also Freeman 1986). Indeed, the reason that those who study asymmetric polarization are concerned about the intransigence on the Republican side is not that there are too many John Boehners in the party but rather that there are too many Steve Kings (IA) and Justin Amashes (MI). Members of the GOP's Freedom Caucus advocate a confrontational approach on issues such as government spending, abortion, immigration, and the ACA. Boehner's resignation from the Speakership was even spurred by heavy pressure from conservative members to take a harder line on their causes (DeBonis and Kane 2015). In comparison, we hear less discussion about far-left liberals causing trouble for the Democratic leadership or trying to chart a new ideological course for the Democratic Party.

Different patterns of candidate emergence across conservative Republicans and liberal Democrats have important implications for the action of polarization. While the primary concept of interest is a candidate's ideological distance from the party, this chapter examines the relationship between a state legislator's left–right ideology and the decision to run for Congress. We are concerned here with the marginal effect of being a Republican across different values of ideology, as conservative Republicans may be more likely to run for Congress than their liberal Democratic counterparts. It is also important to note that the measurement of party fit can obscure key left–right differences. GOP leaders are more conservative than Democratic leaders are liberal, so equally moderate and extreme legislators will have different values of party fit by party. For example, a moderate Republican like Olympia Snowe is 0.6 units from the GOP, but a similarly moderate Democrat would be 0.4 units from the Democratic Party.

Table 5.1 shows the results with the state legislator's ideology rather than her ideological distance from the party. Ideology is coded so that higher values correspond to increasing Republican liberalism and Democratic conservatism. I also include Shor and McCarty's (2011) measures of state legislator ideology as an additional test. The concept of party fit cannot be directly measured with the Shor and McCarty data because the ideology estimates of the congressional party are not available, but we can still examine how the decision to run for Congress varies across state legislators who are moderates and ideologues. The same controls are used as in the models in Table 4.1. Here I include a dummy variable to account for extreme ideological outliers, measured as those who are more conservative (liberal) than the most conservative Republican (liberal Democratic) member of Congress. Columns (1) and (2) show the results with the Bonica data, and Columns (3) and (4) show the results with the Shor and McCarty data. Columns (2) and (4) include the moderate Republican interaction term, so we can analyze whether the relationship between ideology and candidate emergence differs for Republicans and Democrats.

The results in Columns (1) and (3) echo those in the previous chapter: liberal Republican and conservative Democratic state legislators are less likely to run for Congress than those at the extremes. This relationship emerges with both the Bonica and the Shor and McCarty estimates of state legislator ideology. The coefficient for very extreme ideologues is negative, which lends support to the party fit argument, but it does not reach conventional levels of significance.

Our main interest here is the interaction between party and ideology, and we can see in Columns (2) and (4) that the interaction is negative and

TABLE 5.1. *Asymmetric determinants of running for the U.S. House,*
2000–2010

| | (1) | (2) | (3) | (4) |
|---|---|---|---|---|
| Moderate (Bonica; Republican liberalism, Democratic conservatism) | −3.75** (0.31) | −3.12** (0.34) | – | – |
| Republican | 0.65** (0.20) | −0.40 (0.38) | 0.56** (0.14) | 0.19 (0.22) |
| Republican × Moderate | – | −1.44** (0.47) | – | −0.53* (0.25) |
| Moderate (Shor–McCarty; Republican liberalism, Democratic conservatism) | – | – | −0.69** (0.15) | −0.40† (0.21) |
| Extreme ideologue | −0.99 (0.62) | −0.69 (0.66) | −0.41 (0.45) | −0.42 (0.45) |
| Open congressional seat | 2.85** (0.13) | 2.86** (0.13) | 2.83** (0.11) | 2.83** (0.11) |
| Ideology of same party voters in district (higher = extreme) | −4.31** (0.60) | −4.11** (0.60) | −0.45 (0.44) | −0.38 (0.44) |
| Ideology of average donor in district (higher = conservative) | −0.73** (0.24) | −0.78** (0.25) | −0.39** (0.15) | −0.56** (0.17) |
| Log of mean receipts raised as state legislator | 0.30** (0.08) | 0.32** (0.08) | 0.41** (0.04) | 0.42** (0.08) |
| Number of times run for state legislature | 0.45** (0.04) | 0.45** (0.04) | 0.20** (0.03) | 0.46** (0.04) |
| Female | −0.25 (0.14) | −0.21 (0.14) | 0.11 (0.13) | 0.13 (0.13) |
| Democratic control of state legislature | 0.13 (0.25) | 0.09 (0.26) | −0.20 (0.15) | −0.23 (0.15) |
| Constant | −10.82** (1.22) | −10.99** (1.21) | −10.90** (0.68) | −10.87** (0.68) |
| Number of observations | 30,925 | 30,925 | 29,880 | 29,880 |
| Log likelihood | −1486.24 | −1479.84 | −1693.19 | −1691.12 |

*Note:* Entries are logistic regression coefficients with robust standard errors clustered by individual in parentheses. The dependent variable is coded 1 if the state legislator ran for Congress and 0 if the state legislator instead ran for the state legislature. The models include state and year fixed effects.
** $p < 0.01$, * $p < 0.05$, † $p < 0.10$.

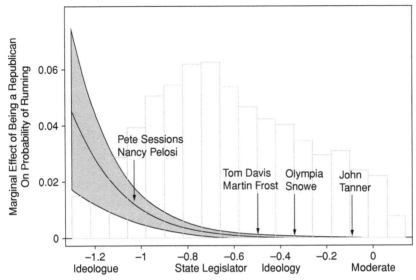

FIGURE 5.5. Marginal effect of being a Republican on the probability of running for the U.S. House, 2000–2010
*Note:* Values are estimated from the model in Column (2) in Table 5.1.

statistically significant.[4] This finding is driven by the fact that conservative Republicans are much more likely to run for Congress than liberal Democrats. Figure 5.5 presents the marginal effect of being a Republican on the probability of seeking congressional office at different values of ideology. The graph shows the difference in the probability of running for Congress among ideologically similar Republicans and Democrats. For example, longtime Republican Representative Pete Sessions (TX) has an ideological score that is similar to that of Democrat Nancy Pelosi. For a Republican state legislator who resembles Sessions or a Democratic state legislator who resembles Pelosi, the probability of running for Congress increases by 1.3 percentage points for the Republican legislator, from 0.6 percent to 1.9 percent. In other words, the probability of running is more than three times higher for conservative potential candidates like Sessions than for liberal potential candidates like Pelosi.

The heightened sense of political ambition among more conservative Republicans sheds additional light on the mechanisms of asymmetric polarization. It is possible that very conservative potential candidates

---

[4] The models are not sensitive to the inclusion of the control variables, and all of the relationships hold with and without the controls.

view the most recent Republican gains as an indication of where the party is heading. Within Congress, the Democratic Party respects the seniority norm to a greater degree, so liberal Democrats may not view their ideology to be as much of a boon to their career prospects. But again, this is a measurement question, and it is difficult to draw a definitive line on how potential candidates view the ideology of the party. Regardless of the specific reason that more conservative Republicans are disproportionately opting into congressional elections, the disparity appears to be part of the explanation for why the Republicans and Democrats have followed different ideological trajectories in recent years.

The marginal effect of being a Republican diminishes when state legislator ideology is greater than −0.6. A more concrete way to interpret this result is to compare former members of Congress who have such an ideological profile. Former Representatives Tom Davis (R-VA) and Martin Frost (D-TX) have ideology scores of −0.5 on the scale here. Both were influential members of their party in the 1990s, with Frost chairing the DCCC from 1995 to 1998 and Davis chairing the NRCC from 1998 to 2002. Both also built reputations as relatively centrist legislators, not quite as moderate as Olympia Snowe or John Tanner, but they leaned toward the ideological middle. In fact, Davis and Frost recently co-authored a book that explores the origins of the current gridlock in Congress and offers suggestions on how to bridge the parties in the future. Yet somewhat ironically, high-quality potential candidates like Davis and Frost are simply not running for Congress. The probability that a state legislator like Davis seeks congressional office is 0.2 percent, and the probability that a state legislator like Frost does so is 0.1 percent. We can see in Figure 5.5 that, unlike state legislators at the extreme end of the spectrum, Republican state legislators who resemble Davis are no more or less likely to run for Congress than Democratic state legislators who resemble Frost. Put differently, they are equally likely not to run.

The shift of both parties away from the center is due to the abstention of moderates from and the selection of ideologues into congressional elections. The disproportionate entrance of very conservative Republicans into the candidate pool is also to blame for the "hard-edged conservatism" that characterizes the GOP today (Hacker and Pierson 2005, 34). The fact that conservatives are especially likely to run means that the disparity between ideologues and moderates is more pronounced on the Republican side.

In light of the particular impact of open seats entrants on polarization discussed at the outset of the chapter, we can also look at the

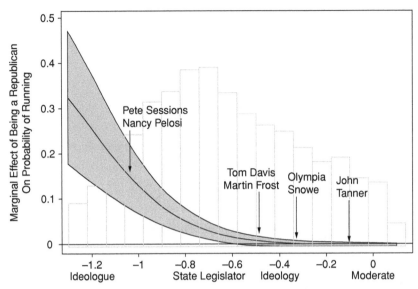

FIGURE 5.6. Marginal effect of being a Republican on the probability of running in an open seat, 2000–2010
*Note:* Values are estimated from the model in Column 2 in Table 5.1.

marginal effect of being a Republican when the seat is open. The results in Figure 5.6 tell the same story. Conservative Republicans are more likely to seek congressional office than their liberal Democratic counterparts when faced with an open seat. For a state legislator like Sessions or Pelosi, the probability of running for Congress increases by 15 percentage points, from 10 to 25 percent, for Republican state legislators. The values among ideologues are very high considering that so few people – even high-quality potential candidates and even when the seat is open – will ever launch a congressional candidacy.

The marginal effect of being a Republican again diminishes among moderate state legislators when the seat is open. Republican state legislators who resemble Tom Davis are no more or less likely to seek congressional office when they face an open congressional seat than Democratic state legislators who resemble Martin Frost. The probability that a Republican state legislator like Davis and a Democratic state legislator like Frost run when the seat is open is 2.7 percent and 2.0 percent, respectively, but the difference is not significant. As discussed previously, the predicted probability of running for Congress increases across quality potential candidates when the incumbent does not seek reelection. Even so, ideologues on both sides, and especially conservative Republicans, exhibit

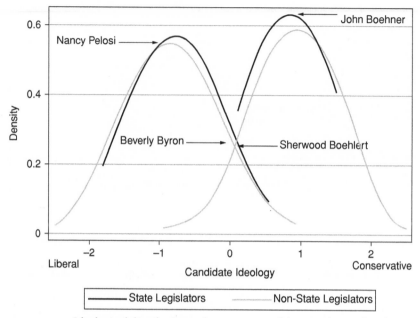

FIGURE 5.7. Ideological distributions of open seat candidates with state legislative and non-state legislative backgrounds, 2000–2010
*Source:* Bonica (2014).

remarkably high levels of political ambition when the congressional seat is open. Given that these individuals are steering the party's ideological course, it is little wonder that the Republican Party has charged rightward in recent years.

## Additional Considerations

The main advantage of the state legislator data is that they include those who ran for Congress and those who could have run but did not, but we might wonder how state legislators compare with the full pool of open seat candidates. It is possible that open seat candidates with state legislative backgrounds differ from those with non-state-legislative backgrounds. Figure 5.7 shows the ideological distributions of state legislators and non-state legislators who ran in open seats from 2000 to 2010. The figure also provides the locations of the legislators discussed above. The ideological profiles of the two groups are only slightly different. The average ideology score of Republican state legislators who ran in open congressional seats is 0.84, compared with 0.95 for those without state legislative experience ($p < 0.05$). Democratic candidates with and without state legislative backgrounds have average scores of −0.75 and −0.86, respectively ($p < 0.10$). We can also see that, regardless of previous political experience, most congressional candidates are ideologically proximate to the party leadership, which is consistent with the argument here. What is notable is the virtual absence of ideological moderates from the candidate pool. Among all open seat candidates, Republicans who are at least as liberal as Sherwood Boehlert composed 4 percent of the Republican runners, and Democrats who are at least as conservative as Beverly Byron composed 5 percent of the Democratic runners.

We might also wonder about electoral factors and whether the makeup of the candidate pool varies across congressional districts. The analysis of state legislators controlled for the ideology of donors and partisans in the state legislator's congressional district, but we can further examine how ideological congruence with the district, and especially district partisans, matters for the decision to seek higher office. Although it is difficult to untangle the effects of district fit and party fit given the increased polarization among party activists and among members of Congress, the idea that "all politics is local" has a prominent place in American politics. Legislators are expected to represent the particular interests of their constituents, and the ideology of congressional candidates is presumed to reflect these district-level differences. Thus, although congressional districts have become increasingly homogeneous and voters are now better sorted, the candidate pool may nevertheless differ across districts. As discussed in Chapter 2, Republicans (Democrats) who run in districts with more conservative Republican (liberal Democratic) partisans may be more conservative (liberal) than those who run elsewhere.

Figure 5.8 presents the ideological distributions of open seat candidates who ran in various districts from 2000 to 2010. I draw on Tausanovitch and Warshaw's (2013) measures of the ideology of Republican and Democratic partisans in each congressional district. The darker lines show the distributions of Republican and Democratic candidates who ran in the 50 districts with the most conservative Republican and liberal Democratic partisans, respectively; the lighter lines show the distributions of candidates who ran in the remaining districts. The ideological profiles of the candidates are again only slightly different. On the Republican side, the average open seat candidate in a more conservative district has an ideology score of 1.00, compared with 0.91 for a Republican in a less conservative district ($p < 0.10$). Among Democrats, the average open seat candidate in a more and less liberal district has a score of −1.01 and

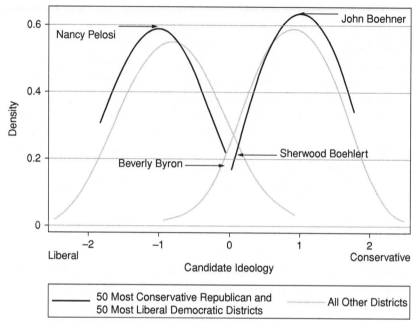

FIGURE 5.8. Ideological distributions of open seat candidates across congressional districts, 2000–2010
*Sources:* Bonica (2014); Tausanovitch and Warshaw (2013).

−0.83, respectively ($p < 0.05$). Thus, while Republican and Democratic open seat candidates are more extreme in districts with the most conservative and liberal partisans, respectively, the disparity is rather small.

These results provide additional evidence that the ideological makeup of the candidate pool is contributing to the polarization of the two parties in Congress. The composition of open seat congressional candidates is similar across those with and without state legislative backgrounds. The fact that state legislators in both parties are more moderate, albeit slightly, than non-state legislators suggests that the analysis of state legislators above may even understate how patterns of candidate entry matter for polarization. In addition, the virtual disappearance of ideological moderates from the candidate pool across congressional districts suggests that the calculus of a congressional candidacy has become increasingly nationalized. This may also be a product of the nationalization of congressional elections more generally (e.g., Herrnson 2004; Jacobson 2013). More research is needed to examine how local interests and variation across congressional districts matter, or fail to matter, for patterns of candidate entry in the contemporary partisan era.

## Open Seat Runners vs. Open Seat Winners

The emphasis of this chapter is on the ideological makeup of open seat candidates and partisan variation between Republicans and Democrats. However, running for office, or having the potential to shape the party's course, is still different from winning a race, or actually shaping the party's course. Of course, it is possible that those who are more likely to run in open seats are not more likely to win. If moderates are less likely to run but more likely to win, then these skewed patterns of candidate emergence may not have as great an impact on actual changes in polarization. It is also possible that state legislators who win in open seats are different from non-state legislators who win in open seats, in which case state legislators might be a less relevant pool for the action of polarization. To address these concerns, this final section examines the ideological profile of state legislators who entered Congress through open seats and the ideological profile of incoming state legislators and non-state legislators who were elected in open seats.

Figure 5.9 shows the average ideology of state legislators elected in open seats and continuing House incumbents, broken down by party. It is not the case that state legislators elected in open seats are more polarized than continuing members in every election year. But for the most part, and particularly on the Republican side, newly elected state legislators are pulling their parties away from the political center. Republican state legislators who entered through open seats were more conservative than continuing House members in four of the six elections and ideologically indistinguishable in two elections (2000 and 2008). In comparison, Democratic open seat victors were more ideologically diverse. They were more liberal than continuing Democrats in three of the elections but also more conservative than continuing members in 2002 and 2004, which helps account for why the Democratic Party did not move during that time. Aggregate partisan changes occur only gradually due to the large carryover of incumbents, and replacements slowly contribute to shifts in the party's center of gravity.

The second consideration is whether the ideological profile of incoming state legislators who were elected in open seats differs from that of non-state legislators who were elected in open seats. It is possible that open seat winners with state legislative backgrounds differ from winners

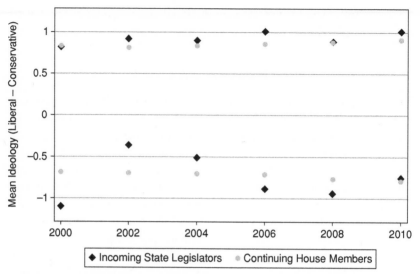

FIGURE 5.9. State legislators elected in open seats and continuing U.S. House members, 2000–2010
*Sources:* Bonica (2014); Jacobson (2013).

with non-state legislative backgrounds. Figure 5.10 shows the average ideology of former state legislators who entered from open seats compared with those who did not have state legislative backgrounds. In some years, incoming candidates without state legislative experience are more extreme than those with such experience, but these differences are only statistically significant among Democrats in 2000, when state legislators were actually more liberal than nonlegislators. Among Republicans, there is virtually no difference among open seat victors with and without state legislative backgrounds. The state legislative pool appears to be an appropriate sample from which to examine how candidate entry matters for polarization. Again, the main advantage of the state legislator data is that it includes those who ran for Congress and those who could have run for Congress but did not, but it is helpful to examine patterns of candidate entry among non-state legislators as well.

Taken together, the findings suggest that open seat winners are, albeit slowly, contributing to the rise in partisan polarization in Congress. In most of these cycles, newly elected replacements on both sides are pulling the parties away from the center (see also Fleisher and Bond 2004; Theriault 2006; Carmines 2011). This pattern is especially clear among incoming Republicans, where open seat victors with state legislative as well as

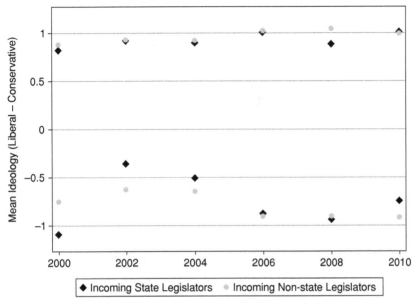

FIGURE 5.10. State legislators and non-state legislators elected in open seats, 2000–2010
*Sources:* Bonica (2014); Jacobson (2013).

non-state-legislative backgrounds have steadily moved the party to the right. Incoming Democrats elected in open seats are more ideologically diverse, but they are also pulling the party left in some election years. These gradual replacement processes are spurring ideological changes in Congress and contributing to the asymmetry of partisan polarization in recent years.

## Summary

This chapter focused on the action of polarization. Newly elected replacements are the driving force behind the rise in polarization, yet not all incoming candidates have the same impact on the future direction of the party. Those who enter through open seats constitute a larger share of newly elected members, and they have a greater impact on the party's ideological course. The opting out of moderates in open seats is therefore crucial for understanding how the parties are moving further and further apart. The findings also contribute to the growing literature on asymmetric polarization. Although moderates on both sides are unlikely to run for Congress, conservative Republican state legislators are more likely to seek higher office than their liberal Democratic counterparts. The disproportionate entry of conservative Republicans into the candidate pool, especially in open seats where they are more likely to win, sheds additional light on why the parties have followed different trajectories in recent years.

Yet we might also wonder whether open seat candidates differ across districts and whether congressional candidates with state legislative backgrounds differ in important ways from those without state legislative backgrounds. A closer consideration of these questions reveals little ideological variation in open seat candidates across congressional districts. In addition, the state legislators who run and win are ideologically similar to the non-state legislators who do so. The implications are twofold: first, state legislators are an appropriate pool from which to examine the action of polarization; and second, candidate emergence is increasingly uniform across districts, which is consistent with the growing nationalization of congressional elections that has occurred over the past few decades.

# 6

## Ideological Moderates Won't Stay in Congress

The Tuesday Group of moderate Republicans was formed in 1994, shortly after the GOP takeover of the House. Its membership included about 40 Republicans, and they met for lunch weekly in the basement of the Capitol. The group sought to provide a counterbalance to the growing right wing of the party, and its members have historically been more liberal on a range of issues such as environmental protection, reproductive rights, and social welfare policy. Similar groups of moderates have existed on the Democratic side, and the Blue Dog Coalition is perhaps the best known of these today. Members of the Blue Dog Coalition have tended to be more conservative on gun restrictions, abortion, and immigration, and they often join with Republicans in their support for tax cuts and defense spending. The influence of these groups has waxed and waned over the years, but neither the Blue Dog Coalition nor the Tuesday Group has much political clout these days. Following the 2010 elections, the *New Republic* ran an article on the Tuesday Group titled "Tuesday Mourning." In 2012, *Politico* similarly observed in the months leading up to the election that the "Blue Dog Dems face extinction."

The rise in partisan polarization and the declining influence of these coalitions have had important effects on moderates' ability to achieve their goals in office. Indeed, when Olympia Snowe announced her retirement from Congress, she emphasized how limited she thought she would be, as a moderate, in her effectiveness as a legislator. And Snowe is far from the only moderate to call it quits in recent years. She is part of a broader phenomenon of ideological centrists choosing to leave congressional office. One moderate Republican whom I interviewed recounted the day he informed his colleagues of his decision to retire from the House of Representatives: "I'll never forget the day that I announced [my retirement]. I came back [to Washington], and I would always sit in this certain section of the House. It's like a school cafeteria; you sit in the same place, with people that are ideologically aligned with you. The [conversation] wasn't so much, 'We're sorry to see you go,' but it was like, 'Maybe I should go, or maybe I should go, or maybe I should go'" (28 February 2013).

The calculus of candidacy framework used to understand the decision to run for office is also applicable to the decision to seek reelection. During their time as legislators, it is safe to assume that the benefits of serving outweighed the costs. But there are serious costs, both personal and professional, to being a member of Congress. Incumbents have reached a high level of professional success, and most of them have ample career opportunities available to them when they leave office. One former moderate described how his decision to retire affected his quality of life: "I'm making over a million bucks a year. It's a nice life now. I'm going to the ball game today ... I got to take my dogs on a walk. It's a whole different way of looking at things" (1 April 2013). Another member agreed, "For me, I'm happier than I've been in years. My schedule's better, I'm making more money, I don't have anybody yelling and screaming at me all the time" (28 February 2013). One member even referenced Snowe's retirement from the Senate: "I'm sorry for the party, but I thought she was smart [to retire]. She felt, 'Where am I going, what more can I do?' I think her timing was pretty good" (22 January 2013).

The emphasis on candidate emergence in the previous chapters is due to the fact that replacement processes are responsible for much of the rise in polarization (e.g., Fleisher and Bond 2004; Roberts and Smith 2003; Theriault 2006; Carmines 2011). Yet the types of members who are being replaced are also relevant for the pace of polarization. This chapter further tests the party fit argument and examines how ideological conformity with the party matters for the decision to seek reelection. If members no longer receive the party, policy, and personal benefits of the office, they have fewer reasons to stay. A variety of factors influence the decision to leave office, such as age, health, and the desire to spend more time with their family. Here I show that, from 1982 to 2010, liberal Republican and conservative Democratic members of Congress are also more likely to retire than ideological conformists. This relationship is especially apparent in the polarized era when it became increasingly difficult for moderates to achieve their goals. While the exit of moderates

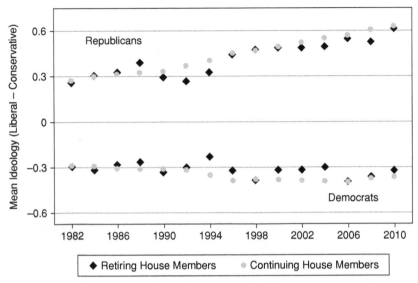

FIGURE 6.1. Ideology of retiring and continuing U.S. House members, 1982–2010
*Sources:* Poole and Rosenthal (2007); Evans and Swain (2012).

has only exacerbated the gulf between the parties, it is easy to see why moderates are opting out of congressional politics.

## Patterns of Member Retirement over Time

The previous chapters relied on Bonica's (2014) CFscores because they are the only available ideology estimates for winners as well as losers from 1980 to 2010. The CFscores also allowed an examination of the ideology of state legislators who did and did not run for Congress from 2000 to 2010. This chapter instead draws on Poole and Rosenthal's (2007) DW-NOMINATE scores for member ideology. DW-NOMINATE scores are available for all members of Congress, and they are the most widely used measures of legislator ideology in congressional scholarship. As discussed earlier, CFscores and DW-NOMINATE scores are highly correlated but they show somewhat different patterns with respect to asymmetric polarization, with CFscores revealing similar shifts by both parties away from the center and DW-NOMINATE scores suggesting a sharper rightward shift by the GOP and a more modest leftward shift by the Democrats.

Figure 6.1 displays the average DW-NOMINATE scores of members who retired and continuing House members from 1982 to 2010. The

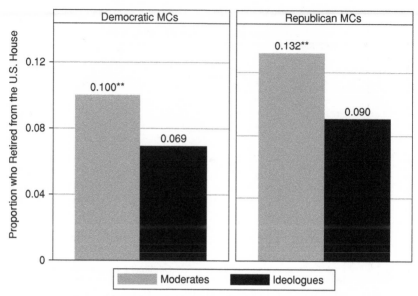

FIGURE 6.2. Proportion of moderates and ideologues who retired from the U.S. House, 1982–2010
*Sources:* Poole and Rosenthal (2007); Evans and Swain (2012).
** $p$ < 0.01. Statistical significance denotes differences between moderates and ideologues by party.

dramatic ideological shift on the Republican side is immediately apparent. It is also clear that, in most election cycles, retiring Republicans are to the left of continuing House Republicans and retiring Democrats are to the right of continuing House Democrats. For both Republicans and Democrats, the average score of retiring members was more moderate than that of continuing members in 11 of the 15 Congresses. These differences are statistically significant on the Republican side in 1992, 1994, 2004, and 2008, and they are significant on the Democratic side in 1994, 1996, 2002, and 2004 ($p$ < 0.10). In not a single election during this time were retiring members significantly more extreme than members who remained in office. Although aggregate shifts in party ideology over the past three decades have been gradual, these skewed retirement patterns have contributed to the rate of partisan polarization in Congress.

In addition, we can look at the proportion of ideologues and moderates who retired from the U.S. House between 1982 and 2010. Figure 6.2 shows the proportion of MCs in the moderate quartile of their party who voluntarily left office, as well as the proportion of conservative Republican and liberal Democratic MCs who did so. Snowe, Boehlert, Tanner, and Byron were all in the moderate quartile when they held office. Among Republicans and Democrats, moderates are significantly more likely to retire from the House than ideologues. Roughly 7 percent of liberal Democrats left office, versus 10 percent of moderate Democrats. Similarly, 9 percent of conservative Republicans, compared to 13 percent of moderate Republicans, retired from congressional office during this time ($p < 0.01$ for both parties).

What is also remarkable is how the ideology of retirees in the 1980s differs from that of retirees in the 2000s. Republican MCs who left office in the 1980s had an average score of 0.31, whereas their counterparts who did so in the 2000s had an average ideology score of 0.52 ($p < 0.01$). Democratic MCs who retired were less variable, with an average score of −0.29 in the 1980s and −0.34 in the 2000s ($p < 0.11$). The overall numbers of GOP retirees differed substantially during these periods as well. In the five Congresses from 1982 to 1990, 76 Republican members retired from office, compared with 121 Republican members who retired in the five Congresses from 2002 to 2010. In contrast, relatively equal numbers of Democrats left office in these two periods, with 68 Democratic MCs leaving between 2002 and 2010 and 71 leaving between 1982 and 1990. This means, too, that there were more opportunities for Republican prospective candidates to run in open seats than there were for Democratic prospective candidates. And as Chapters 4 and 5 demonstrated, conservative Republican state legislators are much more likely to run for Congress than moderate Republicans.

The short story is that those in the ideological middle are disproportionately likely to leave congressional office. What is more, even the moderate members of Congress who are retiring today are more extreme than the moderate members who retired 30 years ago. With each election cycle, there are fewer and fewer moderates, and the moderates who remain are less likely to seek reelection than those at the extremes. The recent retirements of moderate Democratic Representatives Jim Matheson (UT), Mike McIntyre (NC), and Heath Shuler (NC), along with moderate Republican Representatives JoAnn Emerson (MO), Frank Wolf (VA), and Steve LaTourette (OH), have only pulled the parties further apart. In the 2016 cycle, Republicans Richard Hanna and Chris Gibson and Democrat Steve Israel, all relatively moderate legislators from New York, left congressional office as well.

## The Decision to Retire from the U.S. House

This section uses the DW-NOMINATE data to further examine how party fit matters for member retirement and partisan polarization. The dataset extends from the 97th Congress to the 111th Congress (election years 1982–2010), and it includes every member who resigned or was up for reelection in each two-year cycle (Evans and Swain 2012).[1] I use logistic regression to analyze the decision to leave the U.S. House, and the dependent variable is coded 1 if the member did not seek reelection to the House and 0 if she did seek reelection. "Left the House" includes those who retired, resigned, or sought or accepted another office; "Sought reelection" includes those who were reelected and those who were on the primary ballot but were defeated in the primary or general election.[2] There are a total of 6,535 individual decisions to retire from the House (3,001 Republicans and 3,534 Democrats), and 573 legislators chose to do so during this time period (302 Republicans and 271 Democrats).[3] For Republicans, the number of retirements per Congress ranged from a low of 10 in the 100th Congress (1987–88) to a high of 30 in the 110th Congress (2007–08); the Democrats had a low of 7 retirements in the 106th Congress (1999–2000) and a high of 42 in the 102nd Congress (1991–92).

The independent variable of interest is the legislator's ideological fit with her party, again measured as ideological distance from the party leadership. The main expectation is that increasing distance from the party is positively associated with member retirement. I include a squared term to allow for a nonlinear relationship, and party fit is interacted with direction of distance. In additional specifications, I use the member's

---

[1] Sean Evans and John Swain compiled the dataset; they collected the data from ICPSR's *Roster of U.S. Congressional Officeholders and Biographical Characteristics of Members of the U.S. Congress, 1789–1996, Merged Data, Study #7803* and the *Biographical Directory of the U.S. Congress*. I follow the coding procedures in Evans and Swain (2012) unless noted otherwise.

[2] Given the definition of a candidacy outlined in Chapter 2, the main consideration was whether the individual was on the primary ballot as a House candidate. However, I also ran the models with "Left All Political Office" as the dependent variable, which excludes those who sought or accepted another office. This coding decision is partially a question of what "the party" is. The party is understood here to be chamber-specific, but the legislative institution also has implications for legislators' ability to achieve their goals (members can be more independent as governors or senators, for example). I focus on the likelihood of leaving the House here, as the research question concerns empirical trends in the House.

[3] This figure is slightly higher than the retirement rate cited in other studies (e.g., Lawless and Theriault 2005), because I include those who seek higher office in the analysis here.

left–right ideology rather than her ideological distance from the party, coded so that higher values correspond to increasing Republican liberalism and Democratic conservatism. In those models, I include a dummy variable for the five percent most extreme MCs in both parties. Because the data span a longer time period than the state legislator dataset, we can also analyze changes in the relationship between moderate ideology and retirement over time. The left–right ideology models also include a dummy for the period from 1990 to 2010, and I interact member ideology with this variable to examine differences under higher and lower levels of polarization.

The retirement literature has highlighted a variety of electoral, institutional, and personal factors that shape the decision to leave office. First, the benefits of holding office are lower for older MCs, those serving in the minority, and those who took a term limits pledge (e.g., Hibbing 1982; Brace 1985; Ansolabehere and Gerber 1997; Lawless and Theriault 2005; Evans and Swain 2012). Members who were involved in a scandal are also more likely to retire from office (Alford et al. 1994; Jacobson and Dimock 1994). Second, incumbents who won their last election by a small margin and MCs whose districts are seriously altered by redistricting have fewer incentives to seek reelection (e.g., Bullock 1972; Kiewiet and Zeng 1993; Groseclose and Krehbiel 1994; Hall and Van Houweling 1995; Moore and Hibbing 1998). I also control for the partisan tilt of the district, measured as the same party presidential vote share, as MCs from more favorable partisan districts are less likely to retire than MCs from less favorable ones. Third, MCs in party and committee leadership positions are less likely to retire (Groseclose and Krehbiel 1994; Hall and Van Houweling 1995), while senior members who were denied committee chair positions or lost their chair positions due to institutional reforms are more likely to do so (Lawless and Theriault 2005; Evans and Swain 2012).[4]

The results are shown in Table 6.1. Most of the control variables conform to the expectations described above, but not all are statistically significant. Older legislators, those who took a term limits pledge, and those who were involved in a scandal are more likely to leave the House. In addition, female MCs are less likely to retire than their male counterparts, though this effect is driven by Democratic women. The probability of leaving office is higher for legislators serving in the minority, for members

---

[4] See Evans and Swain (2012) for a full description of these variables. None of the control variables are correlated at levels above 0.35.

TABLE 6.1. *Determinants of retiring from the U.S. House, 1982–2010*

|  | (1) | (2) | (3) | (4) |
|---|---|---|---|---|
| Distance from party in Congress | 0.23 | 3.39* | – | – |
|  | (0.41) | (1.55) |  |  |
| Distance from party × ideologue side | – | −5.70* | – | – |
|  |  | (2.58) |  |  |
| Distance from party squared | – | −7.01 | – | – |
|  |  | (3.63) |  |  |
| Distance from party squared × ideologue side | – | 11.05 | – | – |
|  |  | (5.99) |  |  |
| Ideologue side | – | 0.03 | – | – |
|  |  | (0.21) |  |  |
| Moderate (Republican liberalism; Democratic conservatism) | – | – | 0.74* | −0.41 |
|  |  |  | (0.32) | (0.61) |
| Polarized Congress (1990–2010) | – | – | – | 1.07** |
|  |  |  |  | (0.36) |
| Moderate × polarized Congress | – | – | – | 1.51* |
|  |  |  |  | (0.65) |
| Extreme ideologue | | | −0.07 | −0.08 |
|  |  |  | (0.26) | (0.26) |
| Woman | −0.30 | −0.31* | −0.33* | −0.32* |
|  | (0.16) | (0.15) | (0.16) | (0.16) |
| Age | 0.03** | 0.03** | 0.03** | 0.03** |
|  | (0.00) | (0.00) | (0.00) | (0.00) |
| Republican | 0.31** | 0.25** | 0.35** | 0.39** |
|  | (0.09) | (0.09) | (0.09) | (0.10) |
| Involvement in a scandal | 1.07** | 1.07** | 1.07** | 1.08** |
|  | (0.23) | (0.23) | (0.23) | (0.23) |
| Previous vote share | 0.11 | 0.03 | 0.01 | 0.07 |
|  | (0.35) | (0.36) | (0.36) | (0.36) |
| Same party presidential vote share | −0.02** | −0.01 | −0.01 | −0.01 |
|  | (0.00) | (0.01) | (0.01) | (0.01) |
| Hostile redistricting | 0.66** | 0.64** | 0.64** | 0.63** |
|  | (0.25) | (0.25) | (0.25) | (0.25) |
| Party leader or committee chair | −0.34 | −0.30 | −0.32 | −0.32 |
|  | (0.20) | (0.20) | (0.20) | (0.20) |
| Serving in minority | 0.35** | 0.34** | 0.30** | 0.30** |
|  | (0.10) | (0.10) | (0.10) | (0.10) |
| Took a term limits pledge | 0.58** | 0.65** | 0.63** | 0.65** |
|  | (0.17) | (0.18) | (0.17) | (0.18) |
| Removed from chair position | 1.93** | 1.86** | 1.92** | 1.92** |
|  | (0.43) | (0.43) | (0.43) | (0.43) |
| Denied chair despite seniority | 1.04* | 1.05* | 1.08** | 1.09** |
|  | (0.42) | (0.41) | (0.41) | (0.41) |
| Constant | −3.68** | −4.34** | −3.54** | −4.49** |
|  | (0.40) | (0.45) | (0.40) | (0.45) |
| Number of observations | 6,535 | 6,535 | 6,535 | 6,535 |
| Log likelihood | −1837.68 | −1828.48 | −1834.68 | −1831.89 |

*Note:* Entries are logistic regression coefficients with robust standard errors clustered by individual in parentheses. The dependent variable is coded 1 if the member of Congress left the House and 0 otherwise. Congress fixed effects are included in all of the models.
**$p < 0.01$, *$p < 0.05$.

who lost their chair positions due to reforms, and for senior members who were denied chair positions. Electoral factors also affect the decision to retire, as MCs whose districts were altered by redistricting are more likely to leave office. As well, same-party presidential vote share is negative and significant in the model in Column (1), meaning that members in more favorable partisan districts are less likely to retire, but this is not significant in the other models.

With respect to the party fit variables, it is remarkable how congruent the results are with those in the previous analyses of state legislators. As shown in Column (1), increasing distance from the party is positively signed but does not reach conventional levels of significance. However, as in the previous chapters, direction of distance clearly matters during the time frame here. The results in Column (2) indicate that increasing distance from the party in the moderate direction is positively related to member retirement, whereas increasing distance from the party in the ideologue direction is negatively related to member retirement.[5]

Figure 6.3 shows the probability of retiring from the House across members with different values of party fit; Republicans and Democrats are displayed in the top and bottom panels, respectively. The values of party fit in the model are fluid and varying within members over time, but the member placements here are simply their average distance from the leadership during their tenure in office. We see substantial ideological variation across members in their probability of retirement, with non-conformists more likely to leave office than those who conform to the party. For a Republican MC who resembles former Minority Leader Bob Michel (IL) or former Appropriations Chair Bob Livingston (LA), the probability of retiring is 6.9 percent and 7.4 percent, respectively, compared with 9.2 percent for a moderate like Olympia Snowe. Democratic MCs are less likely to retire than Republicans, on average, but the likelihood for a member who resembles former Speaker Tom Foley (WA) or current Minority Whip Steny Hoyer (MD) is 5.3 percent and 5.4 percent, respectively, compared with 7.3 percent for a moderate like John Tanner. These skewed retirement patterns result in fewer and fewer moderates who anchor the parties at the middle.

In comparison, Figure 6.4 displays the probability of retirement across conservative Republican and liberal Democratic members. Again, these values of party fit are members' average distance from the leadership while

---

[5] Again, the models are not sensitive to the inclusion of the control variables, and the relationships hold with and without the controls.

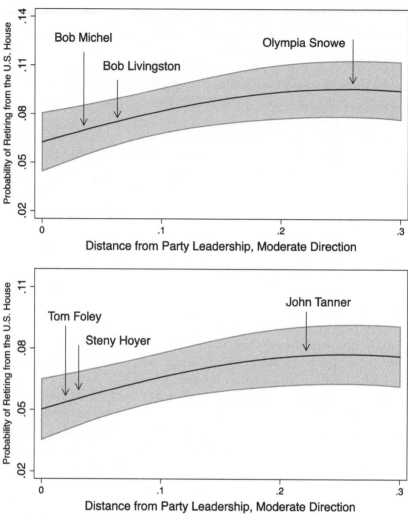

FIGURE 6.3. Predicted probability of retiring from the U.S. House among Republican and Democratic members, 1982–2010
*Note:* Values are estimated from the model in Column (2) in Table 6.1.

in office, so although John Boehner was 0.02 units from the leadership on the ideologue side when he left office, his average score is 0.06 units because the party moved in his direction over time. Among Republican MCs, the probability that an MC such as Boehner retires from office is 5.8 percent, and this value decreases to 5.3 percent and 5.1 percent for members such as Paul Ryan and former Majority Leader Tom DeLay

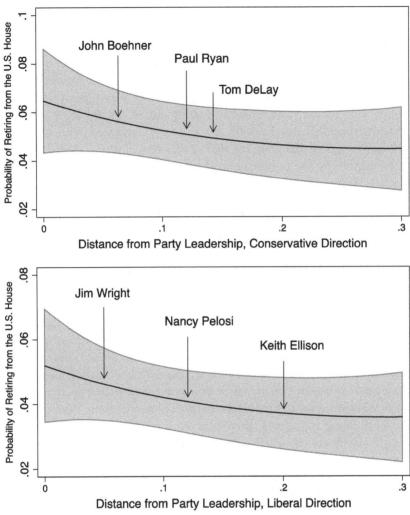

FIGURE 6.4. Predicted probability of retiring from the U.S. House among conservative Republican and liberal Democratic members, 1982–2010
*Note:* Values are estimated from the model in Column (2) in Table 6.1.

(TX), respectively. On the Democratic side, the probability of leaving the House chamber is 4.6 percent for an MC who resembles former House Speaker Jim Wright (TX), 4.1 percent for an MC who resembles Nancy Pelosi, and 3.8 percent for an MC who resembles Keith Ellison.

The degree of party fit for members of Congress changed over time as the parties evolved. In fact, Bob Michel was at the center of the GOP for much of the 1980s, but he became increasingly distant from the caucus in the early 1990s. Michel recognized this shift, and when he retired in 1994, he remarked, "My style of leadership, my sense of values, my whole thinking process ... is giving way to a new generation" (quoted in Povich 1993). The transition from relative conformist to ideological outsider resonates with the insights from the interviews, as those in the center were hit the hardest as the parties shifted toward the extremes. As former member Ray LaHood (2015, 285–6) lamented in his memoir, "Newer members today are cut from a different cloth ... My brand of Republicanism – the pragmatic kind practiced by Everett Dirksen, Bob Michel, Howard Baker, and Bob Dole – has become marginalized." For the members who had served in Congress for decades, the value of the office even changed during their tenure.

Moreover, those in the extreme wings of both parties became "better fits" in their party delegation as polarization increased. As discussed previously, the Republican Study Committee and the Congressional Progressive Caucus experienced huge changes in political fortune during this time. Conservatives like Paul Ryan and Tom Delay became increasingly close to the Republican mainstream as the caucus moved to the right, and liberals like Nancy Pelosi and Keith Ellison became increasingly close to the Democratic mainstream as the caucus moved to the left. Indeed, one limitation of the models above is that, although the analysis offers the most appropriate test of the party fit argument, the data in some ways mask what it means to fit with the party. Those who were a good fit for the GOP in the 1980s and those who are a good fit for the GOP today are quite distinct in their left–right political ideology. And this distinction is an important part of the rise in polarization.

The above analyses shed less light on historical variation in patterns of member retirement, but we can also use these data to examine changes in the relationship between moderate ideology and retirement over time. The relationship might even be insignificant in the 1980s when there were still a sizeable number of moderates in Congress. To explore this question, the model in Column (3) of Table 6.1 includes the member's ideology rather than her ideological distance from the party. As expected, moderate ideology is positively associated with the decision to leave office, but our main concern here is variation in this relationship over time. Figure 6.5 shows the coefficients and confidence intervals from the models for each year (see Lawless and Pearson 2008 for a similar approach). Two notable patterns emerge. First, the relationship between moderate ideology and retirement is insignificant throughout the 1980s. Second, moderates were

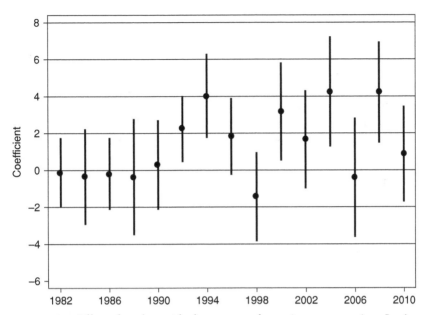

FIGURE 6.5. Effect of moderate ideology on member retirement over time: Logistic regression coefficients and confidence intervals
*Note:* The coefficients are calculated from the model in Column (3) in Table 6.1 by cycle.

more likely to retire as the divisions between the parties intensified. In 5 of the 10 sessions between 1992 and 2010, liberal Republicans and conservative Democrats were significantly more likely to leave office than those at the extremes. The results in Column (4) similarly show that when ideology is interacted with the period from 1990 to 2010, the interaction is significant but moderate ideology itself is not. It appears that the retirement of moderates is a more recent propelling force behind polarization.

These patterns conform to the insights from the interviews. As noted previously, one member said that being a moderate was "pretty cool" early on, but it became increasingly difficult and frustrating as the parties drifted apart. In the 1980s, moderates were able to build bipartisan coalitions and shape the legislative agenda. The moderate factions gradually lost their clout over the next two decades, and life in Congress became more and more challenging as the parties polarized. Their waning numbers made it harder to influence policy outcomes, reap party rewards, and bond with like-minded colleagues. Even accounting for a host of electoral factors, ideological moderates are more likely to leave congressional office, particularly in recent years. The disproportionate retirement of moderates from office has further widened the gulf between the two parties.

## Electoral Considerations

Electoral vulnerability also plays a prominent role in the decision to leave office. Most of the moderates I interviewed believed they would have won reelection, but it is difficult to ascertain how large electoral considerations loomed in their decision to retire. Furthermore, the distinction between running and retiring can also be murkier than one might expect. One member described the trajectory of a fellow colleague: "[The member's] district rolled over from being a moderate Republican district to a strong Democrat district. She held it as long as she could, and she was not going to run. The White House cut a deal with her to run, and if she lost they would give her a post somewhere, which they did" (7 February 2013). It is impossible to know whether those who retired would have lost if they had run, and it is also difficult to say whether those who ran and lost actually wanted to retire but were compelled to seek reelection for some reason.

We can nevertheless briefly examine the electoral situations of retiring and nonretiring members. In particular, we might expect to see differences in the incumbent's previous vote share between members who do and do not seek reelection. The electoral disparities between retiring and nonretiring members are not especially pronounced. Among Republican MCs, those who chose to retire received 64.1 percent of the vote share in the previous election, on average, and those who sought reelection received 64.2 percent of the vote.[6] Of all the Republicans who retired, those in the liberal quartile of the party garnered 64.2 percent of the vote in the previous election, compared with 64.0 percent for their conservative co-partisans who also retired. Slight differences emerge on the Democratic side, but they are not especially glaring. Among Democratic MCs, retiring members received 65.7 percent of the vote in the previous election, on average, and nonretiring members received 67.1 percent ($p < 0.10$). And of the Democrats who retired, those in the conservative quartile of the party received 63.7 percent of the vote in the previous

---

[6] These averages exclude races in which the incumbent was uncontested. These races were omitted because they inflate the averages, but the patterns are the same when uncontested elections are included (the percentages are just higher).

election, compared with 66.7 percent for their liberal counterparts ($p < 0.05$).

In addition, the moderates who retired did not receive fewer votes in the previous election than the moderates who ran for reelection. The Republican MCs in the most liberal quartile of the party who chose to retire received 64.2 percent of the vote in the previous election, on average, compared with 64.0 percent for the liberal Republicans who sought reelection. Similarly, the Democratic MCs in the most conservative quartile of the party who retired from Congress garnered 63.7 percent of the vote in the previous election, and the conservative Democrats who ran for reelection received 62.9 percent of the vote in the previous election. These differences are not statistically significant.

Nevertheless, the growing nationalization of congressional elections and the increase in straight-ticket voting is likely to hurt those in the ideological middle the most. Jacobson (2015) provides a rich analysis of the decline in Democrats representing Republican-leaning districts and Republicans representing Democratic-leaning districts. He finds that, from 2012 to 2014, only 44 percent of incumbents who represented districts that leaned to the challenger's party were reelected, compared with 79 percent of MCs from balanced districts. Even so, most of the moderates in Congress had already vanished by this point. In fact, through the 1990s and 2000s, 86 percent and 76 percent of members in districts that leaned to the challenger's party were reelected, respectively, compared with 92 percent and 88 percent of members from balanced districts (Jacobson 2015, 867). The differences are apparent but again not overwhelmingly large. As discussed previously, the evidence that moderates have historically been penalized at the ballot box is mixed, and the size of the effect of ideology is small across studies (e.g., Ansolabehere et al. 2001; Canes-Wrone et al. 2002; Brady et al. 2007; Hirano et al. 2010; Hall and Snyder 2015).

Boatright's (2013) detailed study of congressional primaries similarly demonstrates that incumbents who do face primary challenges – even ideological primary challenges – are not affected all that much. They may lose a few votes in the general election, but generally in cases where the challenge was actually a nonideological one. Incumbents also suffer no further damage in the next election, and their vote share changes little overall. In addition, members of Congress are no more likely to retire after a primary challenge than are unthreatened members, and they do not appear to change their voting record in response to a primary challenge (Boatright 2013).

Although all incumbents "run scared" (Fenno 1978), the probability of reelection is high across members in the contemporary context. Moderates are likely to face a tougher reelection campaign in the current polarized era, and the quantitative analyses above also account for a variety of electoral factors, including the incumbent's previous vote share, the partisan tilt of the district, and hostile redistricting patterns. These variables collectively seek to capture the electoral vulnerability of the member. Again, the argument is not that electoral considerations do not matter, but rather that the benefits of the office also matter, and increasingly so, for the decision to run for and remain in congressional office.

### The Pull of the Party Club

The disproportionate retirement of ideological moderates makes sense within the context of party fit, but it is nevertheless puzzling in some ways. As discussed in Chapter 2, Krehbiel's (1991, 1993) theory of legislative organization suggests that policy outcomes should reflect the preferences of the median member of the chamber. We might therefore posit that liberal Republicans and conservative Democrats are more likely to influence policy and more likely to remain in office than those at the extremes. At the very least, and even for those who think parties are the key agenda setters, we might expect moderates to flex their muscles to a greater degree than they have in recent years.

So why haven't they? One moderate Republican said, "Moderates tend to be pleasant, genteel people. There was a reluctance to stand up and get in their face when we were being marginalized. And like any relationship where you continually are on the short end of the stick, unless the person getting the bad end of the deal speaks up for himself, you're going to embolden the person to continue to give you the short end of the stick" (28 February 2013). This was perhaps in part due to their declining numbers as well. Of the two moderate Republicans who were able to move up in leadership, both were cautious in terms of how much they dissented from the party. One, for example, chose not to criticize the party in public: "I knew that was a compromise I had to make in order to advance" (23 January 2013). The other said, "I learned to just keep quiet unless I was asked where the moderates are going. There were several of us moderates who were whips. But we all learned to keep quiet unless we were asked" (7 February 2013). These decisions were strategic, because they knew the party could ultimately revoke their positions at any time.

Moderates did push back from time to time. One Republican told a story about a current representative who was initially denied a subcommittee chair position, and "the only way [he eventually got it] was by threatening to be a pain in the ass for two years" (28 February 2013). As the accounts in Chapter 2 illustrated, they were also willing to withhold their votes and demand policy concessions on some issues. But in general, moderates seemed to use a different set of tactics than their ideologically extreme counterparts. This was likely due to a multitude of factors, including their diminishing numbers, the potential denial of party rewards, and an alternative approach to policymaking that emphasized negotiation and compromise. It is nevertheless tempting to wonder how the congressional environment might be different today had moderates stepped out from behind the scenes and caused a public stir as well.

To be sure, although most of the moderates described the congressional environment as "steadily deteriorating" (14 January 2013), not all of them minded going against the grain. As one high-level staffer commented, "Some people get a charge out of being a martyr, always swimming upstream, being a maverick. For some people, that's all they need" (22 January 2013). For example, one former moderate said he enjoyed going against the pack, but then he laughed and said that in the end he got his membership revoked. One House staffer noted that the moderate member he worked for relished his role to some degree but that he ultimately "got tired of it" (8 March 2013). Features of the institution are likely to matter as well, and the House in particular "is not an institution that rewards or is designed to reward maverick behavior" (22 January 2013). Indeed, I did not speak with a single moderate on either side who seemed eager to go into the fray each time, and the fact that moderate Republicans and Democrats became increasingly loyal to the party during this period suggests that bucking the party was not the most preferred strategy (Roberts and Smith 2003).

## Summary

This chapter demonstrated that in the contemporary context, ideologically moderate members of Congress are more likely to retire from office than those at the extremes. The results look very similar to those in the previous chapters, and they are robust to the inclusion of a variety of electoral variables, such as the incumbent's previous vote margin and district partisanship. In addition, the relationship is particularly apparent in the polarized era. The power and influence of liberal Republicans and conservative Democrats waned as their numbers diminished, and it became increasingly difficult for them to achieve their goals in office. While not too long ago, ideological moderates were "eating high on the hog," the nature of congressional service has worsened for those in the political center, and the value of the office has steadily declined. With each election cycle, there are fewer and fewer moderates in office who not only are faced with the decision to run for reelection but also choose to do so.

To be sure, both electoral and nonelectoral factors influence the decision to retire from office. The contribution of party fit is to recognize the nonelectoral benefits of the office, and more specifically, the changing nature of the value of congressional service during this time period. In addition to the quantitative findings in this chapter, the qualitative data used throughout the book also illustrate how, for ideological moderates, the nonelectoral benefits of the office have diminished as the ideological gulf between the parties has widened. The experiential aspect of serving in Congress has yet to be discussed in the context of member goals, but the interviews indicate that in the current polarized environment, being the odd member out is, in a word, miserable.

# 7

## The Growing Partisan Gap in Women's Representation

Amid the concern over the rise in partisan polarization, a second development in Congress has, by comparison, gone largely unnoticed: The number of Democratic women has increased dramatically since the 1980s while the number of Republican women has barely grown. Contemporary patterns of female representation have a distinctly partisan flavor. Of the 247 House Republicans in the 114th Congress, a mere 22, or 9 percent of the party delegation, are women. The 2010 elections, popularly dubbed the "Year of the Republican Woman," did result in an absolute gain of seven Republican women in Congress, but as a proportion of their party, the female delegation increased by only 0.3 percent from the previous Congress. The percentage of women in the Republican Party has hovered between 6 and 10 percent since the mid-1980s, and the victories of GOP women pale in comparison to those of women in the Democratic Party. There is a record high of 62 Democratic women in the 114th Congress, and women comprise one-third of the House Democratic caucus.

Women in Congress are now nearly three times as likely to be Democrats, but this is a recent trend in American politics. Figure 7.1 displays the historical trajectory of women's representation by party. Throughout the 1980s, women were evenly distributed between the parties. In 1980, 11 Democratic women and 10 Republican women were elected to Congress; in 1984, there were 12 Democratic women and 11 Republican women; and by 1988, these numbers had increased only slightly to 16 women on the Democratic side and 13 on the Republican side (CAWP 2015). In 1990, the figures began to split, with the Democrats electing 19 women to Congress and the Republicans electing 9

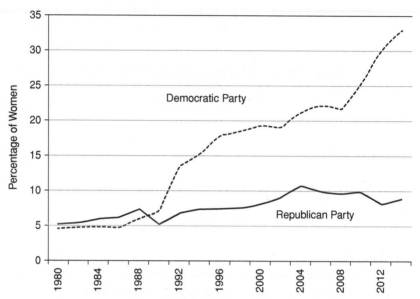

FIGURE 7.1. Women in the U.S. House by party, 1980–2014
*Source:* Center for American Women and Politics (CAWP) (2015).

women. The "Year of the Woman" elections in 1992 led to the first significant jump in women legislators, but it is important to note that these gains were primarily within the Democratic Party. The number of Democratic women in Congress increased from 19 to 35, and the percentage of women in the Democratic Party doubled from 7 to 14 percent. In contrast, the number of Republican women rose from 9 to 12. What is perhaps most striking is that the Democratic Party has seen an increase in the number of women elected to Congress in 8 of the 11 elections since 1992 (Cooperman and Oppenheimer 2001). The percentage of women in the Democratic Party is an amazing six times larger than it was just 25 years ago. In short, to the extent that we are concerned about the dearth of women in office, the problem is by and large a Republican one. If women were represented in the GOP at levels similar to those in the Democratic Party, there would be 82 women in the Republican caucus, a full 60 more than there are today. The United States would move up 45 spots in the global rankings and be placed 26th worldwide (Inter-parliamentary Union 2016).

The question "Why are there so few women in politics?" has motivated more than three decades of political science scholarship. The underrepresentation of women in elected office remains as relevant now as it was

30 years ago, particularly in the American context. At the national legislative level, the United States is ranked 99th worldwide, with women comprising only 19 percent of the House of Representatives (Inter-parliamentary Union 2016). The laggard status of women in American politics stands in stark contrast to levels of female representation cross-nationally. The United States ranks well below the Nordic countries, where women hold approximately 40 percent of national legislative seats, but it also trails behind much of the rest of the world. Just to reach the global average of 22.9 percent (Inter-parliamentary Union 2016), the United States would have to retain all of its current female members and elect an additional 15 women to Congress. Most recently, it took five election cycles for the number of women in Congress to increase by such a margin. And this is simply to achieve the global average; gender parity remains much further down the road.

The plateau in women's representation has generated widespread concern, but less attention has been paid to the growing partisan disparity discussed above. This chapter shows that the opting out of moderates from the congressional politics has important implications for contemporary patterns of women's representation as well. The analyses are simply extensions of the party fit argument and the candidate entry patterns described in the previous chapters. Two general insights emerge. First, conservative men outnumber conservative women in state legislative office more than five to one, and there are few Republican women in the eligibility pool who are a good fit for the contemporary GOP. Second, the Republican women in Congress in the 1980s and 1990s were in the moderate wing of the party, and they were disproportionately affected by the rightward shift of the GOP. The findings shed light on why the number of women in Congress has diverged so sharply along partisan lines and why the ideological gulf between Republican and Democratic women has widened during this time.

## Historical Background of Women in Congress

The first woman to serve in Congress, Jeanette Rankin (R-MT), was elected to office in 1916, before women even had the right to vote. For the next several decades, though, Congress remained almost exclusively male. The social and political conditions were less than favorable to women's entry into office because politics was deemed a male arena. A Gallup poll conducted in 1945 showed that only 32 percent of Americans – 26 percent of men and 38 percent of women – agreed that not enough capable women were holding important government jobs (Erskine 1971, 280). With respect to Congress, results from a 1946 Roper poll demonstrated that 75 percent of men and 67 percent of women thought that members of Congress should nearly always be men (Erskine 1971, 280). In fact, many of the women who did serve in Congress prior to the 1970s were widows of congressmen who died in office.

The first wave of congresswomen was overwhelmingly characterized by the "bereaved widow as placeholder" stereotype. Parties and civic organizations promoted this storyline in order to hold onto the seat and avoid disputes about the proper successor (Kincaid 1978; Palmer and Simon 2008). For instance, Mae Ella Nolan (R-CA), the first congressional widow, was convinced to run for her deceased husband's seat by local civic leaders. She ran and won, served in Congress from 1923 to 1925, and chose not to seek reelection, citing her distaste for political life (Palmer and Simon 2008). Similarly, in 1938, Elizabeth Gasque (D-SC) was persuaded by local and state party officials to finish her husband's term, and they even covered the filing fee. She captured 96 percent of the vote but was never sworn into office and did not receive any committee assignments. Gasque returned to South Carolina at the end of her term (Wasniewski 2006). However, there were other women who succeeded their husbands and went on to have long careers. Edith Nourse Rogers (R-MA) served 18 terms, from 1925 to 1960, after first winning her husband's seat. Frances Bolton (R-OH) held office for 15 terms, from 1940 to 1969. Margaret Chase Smith (R-ME), who was persuaded by her fatally ill husband to run for his seat, served five terms in the House and went on to serve four terms in the Senate (Wasniewski 2006).

Perceptions of the frequency of widows' succession to office are somewhat inflated, but the congressional widow pathway was a widely recognized route to office for female MCs who served prior to the 1970s (Gertzog 1995). This may in part be due to the differential victory rates of widows and nonwidows at that time. Between 1916 and 1964, 28 of the 32 widows (88 percent) who were appointed to their husbands' seats won their races, compared with 16 percent of nonwidows who were victorious (Gertzog 1995). Widows and nonwidows were likely viewed differently in the eyes of party officials and the American public, with widows deemed to be acceptable women candidates (Fox 2014).

Since then, the widow route has been much less common. The 1960s and 1970s resulted in the emergence of a second type of female candidate who "turned her attention from civic volunteerism to politics" (Fox

2014, 193). While roughly half of the female legislators who served in the U.S. House between 1916 and 1964 were widows (Fox 2014), only 8 percent of those elected between 1972 and 2006 were widows (Palmer and Simon 2008). The rise of the women's movement and the emergence of women in the pipeline professions of law, business, and education occurred alongside increases in the number of women seeking congressional office. For instance, the number of women running in congressional primaries between 1970 and 1974 went from 42 to 105, and the number of women winning general elections grew from 12 to 18 (Palmer and Simon 2008, 23). These figures continued to grow slowly but steadily for the next two decades.

Whereas congressional widows were assumed to continue their husbands' policy agendas, few of the female members elected in this second phase of candidacies owed their positions to their husbands (Burrell 1994; Gertzog 1995). Moreover, women's issues became part of the political discourse in the 1960s and 1970s. Many of these female legislators saw their gender as politically relevant, and they established the Congressional Women's Caucus in 1977 (Costain 1992). The initial policy impact of the Caucus was minimal, perhaps in part because of the shared belief that they were not intended to be a "disciplined unit trying to forge unanimity on women's issues" (Gertzog 1995, 186).

The ideological differences between female MCs at that time were often bridged in pursuit of common policy goals. In a comprehensive analysis of bill sponsorship patterns between the 1960s and the 1980s, Wolbrecht (2000) finds that women in both parties were more likely to co-sponsor women's rights legislation than their male counterparts, and little difference existed between Republican and Democratic women in their advocacy of women's rights. This policy activism extended to a range of issues, such as the prohibition of wage discrimination against women, the establishment of rape prevention centers, increased support of programs for female business owners, and greater availability of abortion-related services (Wolbrecht 2000, 81). Swers (2002) shows that even into the 103rd and 104th Congresses (1993–96), Democratic and moderate Republican congresswomen were more supportive of women's issues than their male co-partisans. Women devoted more attention to and focused more of their resources on issues such as breast cancer research, violence against women, and childcare tax credits. Similarly, Swers (2002) finds that moderate Republican women in the 104th Congress sought to temper their party's proposals on welfare reform by offering amendments to expand childcare enforcement.

The trajectories of women in Congress began to diverge in the early 1990s. As detailed above, the 1992 "Year of the Woman" elections resulted in a large increase in the number of female members of Congress, but most of these gains were on the Democratic side. The percentage of Democratic women has increased steadily since then as well, while the percentage of Republican women has remained at a standstill. A few high-profile Republican women have received extensive media attention, but in general, the Democrats have made sizeable gains in female representation at the state and federal levels and the Republicans have lagged behind.

What the numerical disparity does not reveal is the dramatic change in the ideological profile of women in Congress, and particularly among Republican women. In the 1980s and 1990s, GOP women were a moderate faction in their party, and many were stalwart leaders in a variety of policy areas, including, but not limited to, women's issues. Nancy Johnson (R-CT) was the first Republican woman named to the powerful Ways and Means Committee. Sue Kelly (R-NY) served on the Financial Services Committee for more than a decade and eventually became a subcommittee chair. These Republican women hailed mainly from the Northeast and the Midwest, and they were part of the moderation coalition during that time. This group of Republican women (and men) banded together in their support of environmental regulation, labor protection, and reproductive health care. They put pressure on the party leadership and worked to shape and adjust policies before they came to the floor. These women mattered not only for the aggregate level of female representation, but also for the day-to-day operations of Congress, the process of legislating and governing, and the nature of policy outcomes.

Figure 7.2 shows the average DW-NOMINATE scores of male and female members of Congress from 1982 to 2010. Democratic women have consistently been to the left of their male co-partisans, but the ideological changes among Democratic women have been relatively minor. From 1982 to 2010, the average ideology of female Democrats shifted from −0.33 to −0.42. The fate of women in the GOP has been much different. The average ideology score of Republican women soared from 0.19 in the 97th Congress (1981–82) to 0.61 in the 111th Congress (2009–10). Although Republican women were to the left of their male counterparts throughout the 1980s and 1990s, this difference has now disappeared (Frederick 2009). An article in *Slate* described the 2010 cohort of GOP women as follows: "Most of [them] have children – or, rather, 'the Lord blessed them' with children and their 'most important

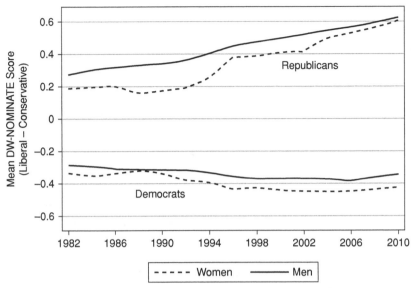

FIGURE 7.2. Ideology of male and female U.S. House members by party, 1982–
2010
*Source:* Poole and Rosenthal (2007).

job is being a mom.' They hate Obamacare, wasteful government spend-
ing, and open borders. More than anything, though, they hate Nancy
Pelosi" (Rosin and Malone 2010). The Connie Morellas (MD) and Nancy
Johnsons (CT) of yesterday have been replaced by the Martha Robys
(AL) and Marsha Blackburns (TN) of today. The Republican women in
Congress today are mirror ideological images of their male co-partisans.

Over the last 20 years, there has been a complete ideological makeover
of women in the GOP. Virtually all of the Republican women who held
office in the 1980s and 1990s have, either by choice or by defeat, left
congressional politics. Of the 22 Republican women in the 114th House,
only 2 of them – Ileana Ros-Lehtinen (FL) and Kay Granger (TX) – have
been in office since before 2000. The average election year of these 22
women is 2006 (CAWP 2013). In comparison, of the 62 Democratic
women in the House, 21 have been in Congress since before 2000.
The stability and change in the ideology of Democratic and Republican
women, respectively, is in large part a reflection of the carryover of
Democratic women and the turnover of Republican women in recent
years. Importantly, the longevity in tenure has also allowed Democratic
women to rise to increasingly powerful positions. Nancy Pelosi reached

new heights as the former Speaker of the House and current minority leader. And when the Democrats held the majority in the 110th and 111th Congresses (2007–11), there were four and three House committees, respectively, that were chaired by women. In comparison, in the 114th Congress (2015–16), only 1 of the 21 committee chair positions is held by a woman. Candice Miller (R-MI) heads the lower-tier House Administration Committee, but even her initial appointment in 2012 came days after the first 19 positions had all been doled out to men (Sherman 2012).

These distinct periods of female candidacies highlight the ways in which the larger social and political context matter for the representation of women in office. The third phase of female candidates has resulted in the election of women who are first and foremost partisans. Against a backdrop of rising partisan polarization and heightened levels of party loyalty, women in the contemporary Congress look very much like their male co-partisans. Throughout the 1980s, the ideological distance between female MCs was smaller than it was for men, but the distance between women now exceeds that between men (Frederick 2009). In fact, over the last two decades, the ideological gulf between Democratic and Republican women in Congress has increased with nearly every election cycle. This is due to both the increasing conservatism of female Republicans and, to a lesser extent, the increasing liberalism of female Democratic MCs. These aggregate changes have been spurred by the election of new female candidates who come from the ideological extremes and the retirement and defeat of moderate women, especially moderate Republican women.

### An Extension of the Party Fit Argument to Women's Representation

The research design here is especially advantageous for examining the partisan gap in women's representation. Due to the emphasis on the underrepresentation of women in politics, gender scholars have largely focused on comparisons between male and female candidates (e.g., Burrell 1994; Darcy et al. 1994; Seltzer et al. 1997; Lawless and Fox 2005, 2010; Crespin and Deitz 2010). But as Schreiber (2012, 550) notes, "We know little about the differences among women who seek elective positions of power." This chapter offers the first empirical analysis of the decision to run for Congress across women in the pipeline, and it provides the first empirical examination of how ideology influences the entry of female candidates and the retention of female incumbents. Importantly, the design allows an examination of within-party variation across women and sheds light on why some women run for and remain in office and others do not.

### Gender Dynamics in the Pipeline to Congress

This section builds on the analyses of state legislators in Chapters 4 and 5. The results will not be presented again, but two points are of particular relevance. First, gender is insignificant across models. Male and female state legislators are equally likely to run for Congress, with 1.3 percent of men and 1.3 percent of women doing so. This result conforms to recent findings on gender and candidate emergence at the federal level. For example, Maisel and Stone (2014) show that gender does not have an effect on the probability of running for Congress in their pool of potential congressional candidates (see also Maestas et al. 2006). Lawless and Fox (2010) similarly find that equal percentages of men and women in their sample ran for federal office. It may be that existing accounts of women's underrepresentation – which seek to explain why women are less likely to run for office than men (e.g., Niven 1998; Lawless and Fox 2005, 2010; Sanbonmatsu 2006; Kanthak and Woon 2015) – are more applicable at lower levels of office than at the congressional level.[1] Female state legislators are a highly select group of women: they are already politically ambitious, they have already overcome any aversion to elections they may have had, and they have likely been recruited by party elites at earlier points in their careers. Indeed, among these eligible congressional candidates, women are just as likely to seek higher office as their male counterparts.

The second and more crucial point is that some women are dramatically more likely to run for Congress than others. Figure 7.3 presents the predicted probability of running for Congress among male and female Republican state legislators across a range of ideology scores. The values are calculated from the model in Chapter 5. The patterns are the same for men and women, and the confidence intervals overlap across all values of state legislator ideology. The main divide is clearly along ideological, rather than gender, lines. Among Republicans, the probability that a moderate female state legislator resembling Olympia Snowe runs for Congress is 0.1 percent, compared to 1.7 percent for a conservative woman resembling Marsha Blackburn. In other words, the probability

---

[1] Gender scholars have highlighted three main explanations for why women are underrepresented in office: women have lower levels of political ambition than men, they are more averse to elections, and they are less likely to be recruited by party leaders. These explanations may be less relevant at the federal level, however, for reasons noted here.

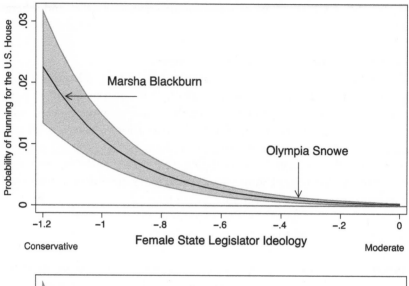

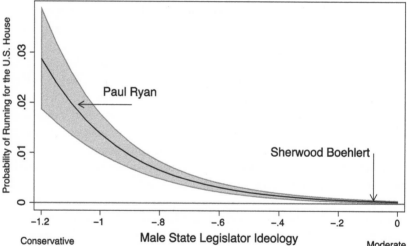

FIGURE 7.3. Predicted probability of running for the U.S. House among male and female Republican state legislators, 2000–2010

*Note:* Predicted values are from the model in Column 1 in Table 5.1. The arrows refer to hypothetical state legislators who have the same ideological scores as various former and current members of Congress.

that a state legislator like Blackburn runs for Congress is 17 times greater than that for a state legislator like Olympia Snowe.

The male and female members of Congress referenced in Figure 7.3 differ on a range of policy issues, but reproductive health care is a particularly stark example. During her time in office, Snowe had a consistently pro-choice record and had long supported the federal funding of family planning programs. At an awards ceremony in 2014, Cecile Richards, the president of Planned Parenthood, called Snowe one of the "bravest and fiercest defenders of women in American history" (Goodman 2014). Sherwood Boehlert is also pro-choice, and when he was in Congress, he received consistently high ratings from Planned Parenthood and NARAL Pro-Choice America for his positions. In comparison, Marsha Blackburn, Paul Ryan, and virtually all of the Republicans in office today are pro-life, and Blackburn has been at the forefront of recent Republican efforts to defund Planned Parenthood (O'Brien 2015). Blackburn and Ryan both have 100 percent lifetime ratings from the National Right to Life Committee and 0 percent lifetime ratings from Planned Parenthood and NARAL (Project Vote Smart 2016).

Figure 7.4 presents the results for male and female Democratic state legislators across a range of ideology scores. Democrats are less likely to run for Congress than Republicans, but the general pattern is again the same for men and women. Democratic women are actually less likely to run for Congress than Democratic men (see Appendix C), but the slight gender difference in the likelihood of running for Congress is dwarfed by the ideological differences across men and women. Among Democrats, the probability that a moderate female state legislator resembling Beverly Byron runs for Congress is 0.01 percent, compared to 0.6 percent for a liberal woman resembling Nancy Pelosi. Similar intraparty differences on abortion policy emerge among the Democratic members of Congress referenced in Figure 7.4. Byron and Tanner are pro-life Democrats and they often broke with their party on reproductive issues when they were in office (Wasniewski 2006; Project Vote Smart 2016). In comparison, Nancy Pelosi and rising progressive star and Maryland Senator Chris Van Hollen are strong supporters of abortion rights. Van Hollen is a longtime protégé of Pelosi, and he has been a high-profile defender of liberal policies since his election to the House in 2002 (Weiner 2016). In virtually all of the Congresses in which they have served, both Pelosi and Van Hollen have received 100 percent ratings from Planned Parenthood and NARAL and 0 percent ratings from the National Right to Life Committee (Project Vote Smart 2016). In short, the main takeaway from this section is that similar types of men and women are equally likely, or equally unlikely, to run for congressional office.

We might wonder, then, why women are still underrepresented in congressional office if similar types of men and women are equally likely (or

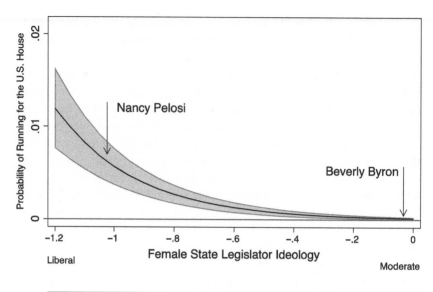

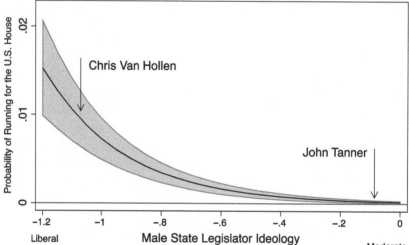

FIGURE 7.4. Predicted probability of running for the U.S. House among male and female Democratic state legislators, 2000–2010
*Note:* Predicted values are from the model in Column 1 in Table 5.1. The arrows refer to hypothetical state legislators who have the same ideological scores as various former and current members of Congress.

almost equally likely) to run for Congress. This observation is particularly puzzling given the recent turn in the literature toward women not running for office as the leading explanation for the plateau in female representation. Part of the answer, at least with respect to Congress, harkens back to the first wave of gender research and involves looking at the makeup of the pipeline to congressional office. Lawless and Fox (2005, 2010) disproportionately stratified by sex, so they started with equal numbers of men and women in their pool of potential candidates. But gender differences in the eligibility pool can be key, especially at increasingly high levels of office. The most common pipeline to Congress for both male and female MCs is state legislative office, and men continue to dominate state legislatures. In addition, given the dramatic variation across men and women, the ideological leanings of male and female state legislators are most relevant to the number of male and female runners. Just as Lawless and Fox (2005, 2010) described the gendered winnowing of the candidate pool at various stages of a political candidacy, we can think about a similar ideological winnowing of the congressional candidate pool. If there is a dearth of conservative Republican and liberal Democratic women in the congressional pipeline, the number of women who seek elected office will remain lower than the number of men who do so. These patterns would occur even if men and women were equally likely to run for office.

Figure 7.5 presents the gender breakdown of Republicans and Democrats in the conservative and liberal halves of the state legislative pool, respectively.[2] As shown in Chapters 4 and 5, these state legislators are the most likely to run for higher office. The vast majority of female ideologues are Democrats, with Democratic women outnumbering Republican women nearly two and a half to one (2,832 vs. 1,181). Republican women make a small appearance in the state legislative pool, and there are more than five times as many men as women in the conservative half of the GOP pool (5,987 vs. 1,181). The rates of running are similar across these Republican men and women, at 2.4 and 2.1 percent, respectively, but because there are so many more men, this translates into a huge gender difference in candidacies: 143 conservative Republican men actually ran for Congress, compared with 25 conservative women. Republican women are more likely to be in the moderate half of the party than either Republican men or Democratic women ($p < 0.10$ and $p < 0.01$, respectively), but the differences are not as large as the numerical disparity between male and female conservatives in Figure 7.5.[3]

---

[2] Extreme ideological outliers, measured as state legislators who are more extreme than the most conservative or liberal member of their party in Congress, are excluded from this group.

[3] Among Republicans, 52 percent of women and 50 percent of men are in the moderate half of the state legislator pool ($p < 0.10$). Republican women comprise 18 percent of the moderate half of the state legislative pool compared with 16 percent of the conservative

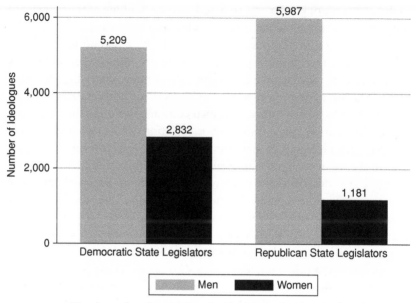

FIGURE 7.5. Number of male and female ideologues in the pipeline by party, 2000–2010
*Source:* Bonica (2014).

Among Democrats, the gender gap is significantly smaller in the pool of liberal state legislators, which is 35 percent women and 65 percent men (2,832 vs. 5,209). Virtually the same percentage of liberal Democratic men and women also ran for Congress (1.4 percent and 1.6 percent, respectively). Democratic women are actually more likely to be in the liberal half of the state legislator pool than their male co-partisans: 61 percent of Democratic women versus 44 percent of Democratic men are in the liberal half of the pool (*p* < 0.01). As illustrated in Figure 7.5, the number of Democratic men in the liberal half of the pool is still much greater than the number of women, but the disproportionately liberal ideological leanings of Democratic women result in a much larger supply of female potential congressional candidates on the Democratic side. And as we would expect, the gender disparity in the number of men and women candidates who emerged from this sample is indeed smaller

half of the state legislator pool shown in Figure 7.5. Among women, 39 percent of the Democratic women are in the moderate half of the state legislator pool compared with 52 percent of the Republican women (*p* < 0.01).

among Democrats: 44 female state legislators and 74 male state legislators ran for Congress.

In sum, the makeup of the pipeline continues to matter for contemporary patterns of women's representation. Although male and female ideologues are virtually equally likely to seek higher office, the gender disparity in the number of conservative Republican and liberal Democratic men and women in state legislatures results in the election of more men, particularly Republican men, to congressional office. The pool of eligible congressional candidates is far from reaching gender parity, and even if women were more likely to run than men, a greater number of men would still be on the ballot. Male state legislators outnumber their female counterparts in both parties, but Democratic women comprise a significantly larger share of ideologically suitable candidates than Republican women. The greater number of liberal Democratic women means that there are simply more women who are likely to run.

### Gender Dynamics in Retirement Patterns

This section builds on the findings in Chapter 6 and addresses differential retention rates of Republican and Democratic women in Congress. Republican women have served fewer terms in office than Democratic women in recent years, but what is especially noteworthy is how these patterns have changed over time. Between the 97th and 102nd Congresses (1981–92), just prior to the 1992 "Year of the Woman" elections, Republican and Democratic women both spent an average of 4.5 terms in Congress. Since then, the average length of service for Democratic women has grown markedly, from 4.5 terms to 5.2 terms, while the growth rate has been much slower for Republican women, increasing from 4.5 to 4.8 terms. The disparity in the sheer number of Republican and Democratic women with extensive congressional experience is even more striking. Figure 7.6 shows the total number of women in each Congress who have served at least four terms in office.[4] Throughout the 1980s and 1990s, the number of Republican and Democratic women with at least eight years of experience in Congress was virtually the same. These trends have diverged sharply over the past decade, in part because of the 1992 cohort, but this figure has increased on the Democratic side in nearly every Congress since then as well.

---

[4] The same pattern emerges when the number of women who have served for longer periods (i.e., 5–10 terms) is examined. For example, of the 19 women in the 111th Congress who have been in office for at least 8 terms, 16 are Democrats and 3 are Republicans.

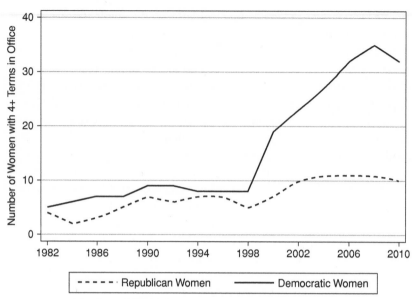

FIGURE 7.6. Number of Republican and Democratic women with four or more terms in office, 1982–2010
*Source:* Data from Evans and Swain (2012).

Chapter 6 showed that moderates are more likely to retire from the House than their counterparts at the extremes. Female MCs are actually less likely to retire than male MCs, but Democratic women were largely driving this effect. Republican men and women are not statistically different during this period. Like the previous section, we see substantial variation across women as well as men in their likelihood of retirement. Table 7.1 displays the predicted probability of leaving the House for various male and female members of Congress.[5] For Republican women, the likelihood of retirement increases more than twofold with a shift from Marsha Blackburn to Olympia Snowe. A similar pattern emerges among male MCs as well: the probability that a moderate like Steve LaTourette decides to leave the House chamber is much larger than that for a conservative like Paul Ryan. The probability of retiring is significantly lower for Democratic women than it is for Democratic men, but the more notable pattern is the substantial variation across male and female MCs.

[5] The values were calculated from the ideology model in Column (4) in Table 6.1. Because of this, some of the predicted values are different from those in the previous chapter, which were calculated from the model in Column (2). However, the general patterns are clearly the same.

TABLE 7.1. *Predicted probability of retiring from the U.S. House by gender and party, 1982–2010*

| Republican women | | Republican men | |
|---|---|---|---|
| Marsha Blackburn (TN) | 4.1% | Paul Ryan (WI) | 6.3% |
| Shelley Moore Capito (WV) | 6.7% | John Boehner (OH) | 7.4% |
| Olympia Snowe (ME) | 9.8% | Steven LaTourette (OH) | 10.5% |
| Connie Morella (MD) | 11.1% | Sherwood Boehlert (NY) | 13.7% |
| Democratic women | | Democratic men | |
| Maxine Waters (CA) | 3.2% | Keith Ellison (MN) | 5.3% |
| Nancy Pelosi (CA) | 3.9% | Chris Van Hollen (MD) | 6.9% |
| Marcy Kaptur (OH) | 4.9% | Steny Hoyer (MD) | 7.2% |
| Beverly Byron (MD) | 7.6% | John Tanner (TN) | 9.2% |

*Note:* Republicans are ordered from ideologically conservative to ideologically liberal. Democrats are ordered from ideologically liberal to ideologically conservative.

Moderate Democrats are also more likely to leave the House chamber than their liberal co-partisans. For male and female moderate Democrats like John Tanner and Beverly Byron, the probability of voluntarily leaving the House is about double what it is for liberal Democrats like Maxine Waters and Keith Ellison.

Yet it is again important to consider how the ideological distribution of women in both parties overlaps with member retirement patterns. The 19 Republican congresswomen who served in the 1980s and 1990s were nearly 4 times more likely to be in the liberal half of the party delegation than in the conservative half. Of the 15 GOP women in the liberal half, 14 decided not to seek reelection to the House, compared with 1 of 4 women in the conservative half of the Republican delegation. Across the entire sample (1982–2010), 16 of the 24 Republican women in the liberal half of the GOP delegation retired from the House (67 percent), as opposed to 161 of the 294 Republican men in the liberal half of the GOP who also retired (55 percent). The gender differences in retirement rates are not significant, but due to the comparative size of their ranks, the result was to disproportionately cut the ground out from under Republican women.

On the Democratic side, there were 32 women in the conservative half of the party during this time period, compared with 69 women in the liberal half of their party. The increased probability of retirement among ideological moderates therefore had less of an effect on Democratic women given their more liberal leanings. The comparatively low turnover of Democratic women is why the number of Democratic women has continued to grow steadily over the last three decades. Unlike their female counterparts in the GOP, the carryover of Democratic women has enabled them to rise to increasingly powerful positions in the chamber. Having a greater number of women not only in elected office but also in positions of influence is significant for the substantive representation of women as well.

The dramatic changes in the centers of gravity of the parties have had differential effects for Republican and Democratic women. As the Republican Party became more conservative, the Republican women in office grew increasingly isolated. Conversely, as the Democratic Party moved to the left, the Democratic women in office became closer to the party mainstream. The value of congressional service changed in divergent ways for Republican and Democratic women due to the shifting ideological makeup of the parties. Although the party fit argument is a gender-neutral story – in terms of both candidate entry and member retirement – it is one that has very important gendered implications.

## Summary

This chapter united the partisan polarization and gender and politics literatures by demonstrating that the opting out of moderates from congressional politics has additional effects for contemporary patterns of women's representation. Furthermore, the rise in partisan polarization has had clear gendered consequences despite the fact that ideologically similar men and women follow the same patterns of candidate entry. In fact, the disparity across women in the decision to run for and remain in Congress is much greater than the disparity between men and women. Conservative Republican women run at rates similar to those for conservative Republican men, and liberal Democratic women do so at rates similar to those for liberal Democratic men.

The analyses explore two mechanisms for how polarization has contributed to the partisan gap among women in Congress, both of which call attention to the ideological distribution of women. First, Republican women are underrepresented among conservative state legislators, and these individuals are the most likely to run for Congress. Second, the Republican women in Congress in the 1980s and 1990s were disproportionately in the moderate wing of the party, and these individuals became increasingly worse off as the party shifted to the right. On the Democratic side, women comprise a larger proportion of the pool of liberal state legislators. In addition, most of the Democratic women in Congress have been in the liberal wing of the party, and they have retained a sizeable number of seats over time. The ideological distributions of men and women have important consequences for women's representation and for the types of women who are elected to Congress in the contemporary partisan era.

The entry of male and female ideologues into congressional office and the exit of male and female moderates from office have also contributed to the dramatic ideological changes among women, particularly Republican women. The GOP women who served in Congress in the 1980s and 1990s were disproportionately from the ideological middle, and as the party moved to the right, the women and men who replaced them instead came from the extremes. These replacement and retirement processes resulted in a standstill in women's numerical representation in the GOP as well as a complete ideological makeover of Republican women. On the Democratic side, women have continued to grow their ranks because the party has both retained those who were elected in the 1990s and elected new women to office in recent years. In order for the partisan gap to diminish, the Republican Party will need to retain existing female members and elect new women to the party as well. The entry of conservative women into Congress in recent years, coupled with the growing number of conservative women in state legislatures (Carroll 2003; Carroll and Sanbonmatsu 2013), bodes well for the future of female representation in the Republican Party.

# 8

## Toward a Less Polarized Congress?

The emergence of high-quality political candidates is critical to the health of American democracy. As much as politicians are disparaged and even loathed, we rely on them to deliberate, legislate, and lead the nation. Although 98 percent of the population will never seek, let alone hold, elected office, the 2 percent that do can alter the content of political debate and shape public policies that affect us all. Political candidates are a small minority of the population, but they are a minority that has a profound impact on the direction of the country. As Maestas and Stewart (2012, 25) note, "Understanding why specific candidates run for Congress is an important step toward understanding who makes legislative decisions and why." The decision to run for office is, in short, a consequential one.

While democracy is "unthinkable" or "unworkable" without political parties (Schattschneider 1942; Aldrich 1995), it is all but impossible without candidates. Representative government relies upon a supply of individuals who wish to hold elected office. Electoral competition instills the democratic process with legitimacy, and elections are the principal mechanism that voters use to hold political leaders accountable and evaluate government performance. One way that public policy is responsive to changes in public preferences is through the replacement of elected officials (Stimson, MacKuen, and Erikson 1995), but the replacement mechanism only works if new candidates decide to run for office (Maestas and Stewart 2012). The democratic ideal deeply depends on, and indeed takes for granted, the existence of a vibrant and healthy pool of candidates from which voters can choose. If the only candidates who are willing to run for office are as extreme as those in office, this has serious consequences for the nature of legislative deliberation and the scope of policy outcomes.

The "my way or the highway" ideologies that pervade Congress today have generated widespread academic and public concern, and those who seek to restore bipartisanship in Congress have not sat idly by. Reformers have advocated a variety of policy changes in the legislative and electoral process. Most of their attention has been directed at redistricting procedures, campaign finance regulations, and primary election rules. First, several states have sought to eliminate or reduce the role of partisan politics in the redistricting process. Four states – Arizona, California, Idaho, and Washington – now use independent commissions to draw congressional districts. Members of these commissions are not legislators or public officials, and in some states, additional restrictions are made on commissioners to further limit their link to the legislature (Levitt 2015). It is widely assumed that when politicians are involved in redistricting, they will adjust district lines to their advantage. The expectation is that independent commissions will create districts that are more competitive and do not heavily favor one party or candidate. Removing partisan politics from the redistricting process is believed to foster greater competition and pull candidates closer to the ideological center.

States have also experimented with the way that political campaigns are financed. Arizona, Connecticut, and Maine have passed new "clean election laws," which provide full public funding to state legislative candidates, and 14 states offer some kind of public funding to candidates (NCSL 2015). Support for public funding programs is rooted in the idea that elections will be more competitive if candidates have equal access to campaign funds. Moreover, candidates are expected to be representative of and responsive to the public rather than a small subset of ideologically extreme donors who fund their campaigns. Public funding programs and campaign finance reforms are also projected to have a moderating effect on candidates and pull them toward the ideological center.

The policy reforms that have generated the most excitement involve changes to primary election systems. Three states – California, Louisiana, and Washington – use the "top-two primary" to elect congressional candidates. Candidates of all parties run in the same primary, and the top two vote getters advance to the general election regardless of their party. The expectation is that the top-two primary reduces the impact of extreme primary voters on candidate selection, and reformers believe that moderate candidates are more likely to make it out of a top-two primary and advance to the general election. The top-two primary has received widespread support from current policymakers, and New York Senator Charles Schumer recently wrote an editorial in the *New York Times* advocating the end of partisan primaries and the nationwide adoption of the top-two primary. Schumer and others who suggest that the primary system is at the root of partisan polarization have embraced the top-two primary as a relatively workable panacea for congressional polarization.

Other prominent political leaders have weighed in as well. In 2007, former Senate Majority Leaders Howard Baker, Tom Daschle, Bob Dole, and George Mitchell founded the Bipartisan Policy Center, an organization that unites former policymakers from across the ideological spectrum. In 2014, the Center released a series of recommendations for how to restore bipartisanship in Congress, including a return to a five-day workweek in Washington, the regular scheduling of joint caucuses, and the creation of opportunities for bipartisan dialogue and socialization among members (BPC 2014).

All of these reforms focus either on the inner workings of Congress or on the rules of electoral participation, but the policies that have been enacted and implemented have not been particularly effective in combating polarization. As discussed at the outset, none of the recent reforms have resulted in the election of more moderate candidates. Neither independent redistricting commissions nor clean election laws have yielded an increase in moderate candidates or officeholders, and the most surprising null findings have emerged from recent analyses of the top-two primary in California (Kousser et al. 2017; Masket and Miller 2014; Hall 2015; Ahler et al. 2016).

In some ways, the types of solutions being posited reflect the current state of academic research on polarization. On the one hand, we have a much improved understanding of what is, and especially what is not, likely to be responsible for the rise in polarization. One of the great contributions of the recent wave of polarization research is to evaluate the merit of the conventional wisdom and journalistic claims, and the findings cast serious doubt on the most commonly cited culprits for polarization, such as gerrymandering, big money in politics, and primary election systems. Yet at the same time, scholars have also focused almost exclusively on either institutional-level or mass-level explanations for why the distance between the parties has continued to grow.

Very few people are talking about the ideological makeup of the candidates who run for Congress. None of the proposed solutions have called for more ideological moderates to launch congressional candidacies, nor do they even reference the current supply of congressional candidates. Academics and practitioners alike tend to assume that the problem lies either with members of Congress or with the electorate. This book seeks to challenge that assumption.

Ideological moderates have overwhelmingly opted out of congressional elections. They currently make up an incredibly small proportion of the candidates who are on the ballot, and their numbers have only continued to diminish over time. It is not the case that individuals like Olympia Snowe and John Tanner do not exist. But it is the case that they do not run for Congress. Furthermore, despite the perks of incumbency, moderates serving in Congress in recent years have been disproportionately likely to call it quits. These patterns of candidate entry are an important yet largely untold part of the polarization story. This book offers a new perspective on the polarization puzzle by examining the types of candidates who run for Congress and the choices that voters are given when they go to the polls. Regardless of whether, how much, or why the public is divided, it is difficult to see how partisan polarization in Congress will fade any time soon if moderates do not run for office.

The main theoretical contribution of the book is to introduce the concept of party fit into the calculus of candidacy. The party fit argument suggests that ideological conformity with the party influences the decision to seek elected office. Party fit matters for legislators' ability to shape the policy agenda, advance within the chamber, and forge bonds with fellow members of their party. It matters for whether they want to be on the party team. The value of the office differs across individuals depending on whether they can achieve their goals, and the benefits of holding office change as the parties shift positions. Those in the ideological center are abstaining from congressional politics because it is no longer worth it for them to run for or hold congressional office. In fact, most of the former moderates I interviewed were glad they had served in the 1980s and 1990s but were relieved not to be there today. In the contemporary Congress, it is difficult, if not impossible, for moderates to influence policy outcomes and advance in the chamber, and there are fewer and fewer like-minded colleagues to work and interact with in office.

These many, many individual decisions to run for and remain in office have a profound impact on the ideological makeup of the institution as a whole. The patterns of candidate entry described here are the microprocesses that have sustained and contributed to the hyperpartisanship that now pervades Congress. One implication of these trends is that the two parties increasingly lack the moderate policy perspectives they once had. The policy agendas of the parties are no longer influenced by conservative Democrats like Tanner or liberal Republicans like Snowe. Even relatively moderate legislators have a difficult time shaping the party's course in the contemporary partisan era. It is hard to believe that policy outcomes will not be affected by the continual decline of moderates in office. Party leaders do not have to bend policies like they used to in order to get moderates on board, nor do they have to craft policies with an eye toward the preferences of the moderate factions. The absence of moderates is even more troublesome as leaders pursue increasingly internal legislative strategies.

The rise in partisan polarization has consequences not only for the types of policies that emerge on legislative agenda, but also for the design and implementation of these policies. Mettler (2011) notes that, in the current legislative environment, policies that disguise or subvert the government's role have proven easier to enact than other policies because they face fewer institutional obstacles. The hurdles involved in enacting new tax breaks, for example, are lower than those associated with new direct spending programs (Howard 1997). The ways in which public policies are delivered have important effects for perceptions of government, levels of political engagement, and the quality of democratic citizenship (Campbell 2002; Mettler 2005, 2011; Soss 1999). Policies such as the G.I. Bill, which are highly visible and universalistic, can stimulate political participation and promote a sense of political efficacy among recipients, while those that are hidden from the public's view perpetuate the notion that government is divorced from the lives of the citizenry (Mettler 2005, 2011). These sharp partisan divisions have created a gulf between the government and the public, in part because of the features of contemporary public policies.

A particularly grave implication of the opting out of moderates from Congress is its effect on political debate and discussion. Even into the 1990s, moderates actively tried to keep the House on the course of civility. Republican Ray LaHood organized several bipartisan congressional retreats in the late 1990s and early 2000s with the expressed goal of restoring civility and comity in the institution. The first retreat was held in March 1997 in Hershey, Pennsylvania, and 197 House members participated. Spouses and children also attended so that legislators could build personal bonds. Members identified various ways to improve the functioning of the House, such as moving the toxic one-minute speeches from the beginning of the day to the end, convening regular meetings of the two parties' leaders, and holding joint sessions of the party conferences. By some measures, the retreat had improved the climate in the House (Jamieson and Falk 1998). But party leaders largely ignored their requests and failed to make institutional changes. LaHood organized a total of four civility retreats in eight years, but enthusiasm and participation waned as rancor and bitterness in the institution increased (LaHood 2015). LaHood retired from Congress in 2008. Columnist David Broder wrote about LaHood's retirement and singled out his ability to "cultivate the kind of personal relationships that build trust across partisan and ideological lines." The exodus of the LaHoods, Snowes, and Tanners from congressional politics will leave a mark on policy outcomes and legislative debate in the years ahead.

## Force for Partisan Polarization

The party fit argument is complementary to elite-level and mass-level explanations for polarization, yet we know less about the varying impact of these explanations over time. As Rohde (2016) notes, scholars have assumed that these causal forces have had significant effects throughout the development of polarization, but it is likely that some have been more and less consequential at different stages of the process. With respect to the party fit argument, it is difficult to pin down the specific tipping point and identify when the benefits of congressional service became too low for moderates to run for or remain in office. Furthermore, the interviews illustrated that individual members also have different levels of tolerance for outsider status. However, we can briefly consider when patterns of candidate entry have had a greater effect on the evolution of polarization over time.

Figure 8.1 presents the numbers of newly elected Republican and Democratic moderates, conformists, and ideologues in three periods: 1980–1992, 1994–2004, and 2006–2010. On the Republican side, moderates include MCs who are more liberal than Shelley Moore Capito (WV); conformists include those who are more conservative than Capito and less conservative than Marsha Blackburn (TN); ideologues include those who are more conservative than Blackburn. Among Democrats, moderates include MCs who are more conservative than Steny Hoyer (MD); conformists include those who are more liberal than Hoyer and

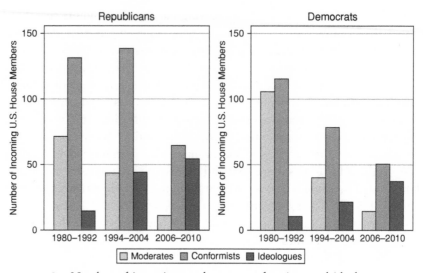

FIGURE 8.1 Number of incoming moderates, conformists, and ideologues over time
*Sources:* Bonica (2014) and Center for Responsive Politics (2014).

less liberal than Chris Van Hollen (MD); and ideologues include those who are more liberal than Van Hollen.[1] Between 1980 and 1992, 105 of the 230 newly elected Democrats (46 percent) were more conservative than Hoyer. Between 1994 and 2004, the proportion of moderates dropped significantly to 29 percent of incoming members (40 of 139); and between 2006 and 2010, the number diminished further to 14 (of 101 incoming Democrats). Among Republicans, 71 of the 216 Republicans elected between 1980 and 1992 (33 percent) were more liberal than Capito. Between 1994 and 2004, the proportion of moderates decreased to 19 percent of new members (43 of 225); and between 2006 and 2010, the number declined to 11 (of 129 incoming Republicans).

A generous definition of moderate is used here to illustrate just how entrenched partisan polarization is. Hoyer and Capito are very different from the liberal Republicans and conservative Democrats of yesteryear who are the main focus of this book. Yet even relatively moderate

---

[1] The trends do not depend on the specific individuals who are used as ideologues, conformists, and moderates. The same pattern occurs if moderates and ideologues are measured as those who are one standard deviation to the right or left of the party leadership, for example.

candidates who resemble Hoyer and Capito comprise a much smaller fraction of House newcomers today than they did thirty years ago.

Although the bulk of newly elected members resemble the party mainstream across this time period, we can also see that ideologues have followed a much different trajectory than moderates. As moderates lost the leverage and bargaining power they once had, liberal Democrats and conservative Republicans gained. Only 4 percent of incoming Democrats were more liberal than Van Hollen prior to the 1994 elections (10 of 230), but this figure soared to 37 percent between 2006 and 2010 (37 of 101). Among Republicans, 14 of 216 incoming members were more conservative than Blackburn between 1980 and 1992 (6 percent), but the number of incoming Blackburns constituted 42 percent of newly elected Republicans between 2006 and 2010 (54 of 129). In fact, we can see that ideologues advanced more quickly on the Republican side, particularly in the period between 1994 and 2004. The disparity between ideologues and even relatively moderate members has only continued to widen in recent years, especially in the GOP. Between 2006 and 2010, incoming Republican ideologues outnumbered moderates nearly five to one (54 to 11), and incoming Democratic ideologues outnumbered moderates more than two and a half to one (37 to 14). These distinct partisan patterns are consistent with the finding in Chapter 5 that conservative Republicans in the pipeline are more likely to seek higher office than liberal Democrats.

To further examine the rate of polarization, Figure 8.2 shows the average ideology of newly elected replacements and continuing House members from 1980 to 2010. Incoming Republican members were more conservative than continuing Republicans in 15 of the 16 elections during this time, and incoming Democrats were more liberal than continuing Democrats in 13 of these elections. Newly elected members have consistently pulled the parties away from the center, but aggregate shifts in party ideology have varied as well. Neither party moved all that much in the 1980s, which conforms to the retirement patterns highlighted in Chapter 6. Ideological moderates were not more likely to retire than their co-partisans in the 1980s, and the bulk of their departures came in the 1990s and 2000s. Of the 187 retiring Democratic members who were at least as conservative as Hoyer, 93 left office between 1992 and 2000 and 43 left between 2002 and 2010. On the Republican side, 168 members who were at least as liberal as Capito retired between 1982 and 2010, with 69 leaving office between 1992 and 2000 and 35 leaving between 2002 and 2010. Much of the changes in party ideology were spurred by

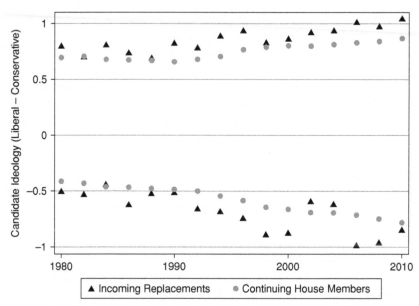

FIGURE 8.2 Ideology of incoming House members and continuing members, 1980–2010
*Sources:* Bonica (2014) and Center for Responsive Politics (2014).

incoming and exiting members in the 1990s, although the ideological gulf has continued to widen in the 2000s. It is difficult to see how moderate coalitions of legislators could resurge in light of this wave of retirements and the dearth of moderate newcomers.

The quantitative and qualitative data tell a similar story: being in the ideological middle was somewhere between tolerable and "pretty cool" in the 1980s and early 1990s because moderates were able to influence the policy agenda, reap party rewards, and bond with like-minded colleagues. As the party delegations evolved, however, liberal Republicans and conservative Democrats increasingly found themselves on the losing side of policy and partisan battles. The argument advanced here sheds additional light on how polarization has increased and intensified in recent years. Partisan polarization has been a slow and gradual process, and the same factors that set polarization into motion are not necessarily also responsible for its persistence and growth (Rohde 2016). For moderates, the nature of congressional service changed significantly in the 1990s, and the value of the office has continued to diminish into the 2000s. The John Tanners and Olympia Snowes of yesteryear have gradually left congressional office, and not even relatively moderate legislators have entered in their place. By comparison, ideologues have steadily gained ground within both party delegations, and especially within the GOP. These replacement and retirement processes have important implications for the widening of the partisan divide in Congress. The ideological skew among incoming candidates and retiring incumbents does not bode well for the future of bipartisanship.

## The Intersection of Ideology and Gender

A separate contribution of this book is to show how differential patterns of candidate emergence matter for the representation of particular groups. If potential candidates and MCs who belong to a specific group are clustered in one end of the ideological distribution, they may, individually, be more or less inclined to run for and remain in office than those who do not belong to that group. And collectively, their level of representation may be lower or higher than it would be if the group members were more evenly ideologically dispersed. In this case, Republican women are the group that is disproportionately affected by the changing political environment. For one, very few conservative women hold state legislative office, so the probability that a "Republican type" will both be in the congressional pipeline and be a woman is low. In addition, Republican women in Congress in the 1980s and 1990s were more likely to be in the moderate wing of the party, and the rightward shift of the GOP resulted in a large turnover of women in the party caucus. These patterns help to account for the growing partisan disparity in female representation, the stagnation in the overall number of women in Congress, and the recent ideological makeover of women in the Republican Party.

The partisan imbalance of women in Congress has serious consequences for the types of policies that are pursued in the legislative arena as well as for the representation of historically marginalized groups in the policymaking process. In terms of policy outcomes, Swers (2002) finds that gender plays a significant role not only in determining how legislators vote on women's issues, but also in shaping the extent to which legislators participate in various stages of the legislative process, such as sponsoring bills, drafting amendments, and speaking on the floor (see also Dodson 2006). In addition, women define the legislative agenda and discuss policy issues in different ways than their male colleagues (Wolbrecht 2002). For example, Nancy Johnson worked to frame childcare policy and child support enforcement as an effort to promote the independence of poor women (Hawkesworth et al. 2001). These findings suggest that as more women hold office, policy will better represent women's interests and new issues will emerge on the legislative agenda.

The fact that conservative Republican and liberal Democratic women are more likely to select into congressional office and also choose to stay there has additional effects on the nature of policy outcomes, and particularly on debates over women's issues. Democratic women in Congress approach women's issues from a completely different vantage point than Republican women. Although women's issues have historically been associated with feminist values, conservative women in office are instead likely to pursue policies that are linked with traditional family values (Osborn 2012; Swers 2013). And even in cases where women would be inclined to find common ground, the gulf in the political middle further limits the legislative opportunities for them to do so. In terms of gender scholarship, we may need to revisit how we conceptualize the substantive representation of women.

The implications of this growing partisan disparity in female representation also extend beyond policymaking. Women of all ideological stripes are members of a historically disadvantaged group in American politics, but there are crucial differences between women that must be taken into account (Schreiber 2014). In fact, Elder (2008, 4) claims that "The more important measure of women's power is arguably their representation within their respective party delegations." Republican women in Congress have policy priorities and concerns that differ from those of both Democratic women and Republican men (Burrell 1994; Swers and Larson 2005), but they lack the numerical strength to influence their party's policy direction (Elder 2008, 2012). If women are excluded from one of the two major parties in American politics, this seriously constrains the influence that women can have in Congress. At a theoretical, empirical, and normative level, there is reason to be concerned about the laggard status of Republican women, particularly in light of the advances made by women in the Democratic Party.

## Looking toward the Future

The paralysis in Washington is due in large part to the rule of ideological hardliners and the ruin of ideological centrists. The past few Congresses have been among the least productive in the modern era, and the 112th Congress (2011–12) passed fewer bills than any Congress in more than six decades (Ornstein et al. 2014). Members of Congress have delayed action on a range of pressing issues such as minimum wage legislation, immigration, and paid employment leave. And the public wants Congress to address these issues. For instance, 76 percent of Americans – 58 percent of Republicans, 76 percent of Independents, and 91 percent of Democrats – support an increase in the minimum wage (Dugan 2013). Three in four Americans favor workplace proposals that require employers to provide paid sick leave and vacation (Newport 2016). A majority of Americans, Republicans and Democrats alike, support a variety of immigration reform proposals, including a multifaceted pathway to citizenship as well as increased border security (Newport and Wilke 2013). Polls conducted after the Orlando shooting showed that 75 percent of Republicans, 80 percent of Independents, and 84 percent of Democrats believe that banning gun sales to suspected terrorists would be an effective way to prevent future incidents (Jones 2016). Yet a series of gun control proposals offered by both Republican and Democratic senators in the wake of the attack failed because they could not muster enough bipartisan support (Demirjian 2016).

What remains unclear is how we will get out of this situation. Members today fail to see "the value of listening, bargaining, negotiating, or compromising. Theirs is the language of battle, of take-no-prisoners... Every skirmish must be won, no matter how small the stakes" (LaHood 2015). What is more, conservative Republicans and liberal Democrats in Congress are looking to further expand their ranks. The Freedom Caucus, a group of around 40 of the most conservative Republicans, has been targeting open seats and meeting with prospective candidates, and leaders believe it is "realistic" for the caucus to grow by 20 to 30 members (Meyer 2016). Leaders of the Congressional Progressive Caucus also have high hopes. In an interview with Minnesota Public Radio, Keith Ellison said that he and fellow co-chair Raul Grijalva (AZ) are trying to turn the caucus into a liberal version of the Republican Study Committee. Among their goals is to raise money to help elect progressive candidates (Neely 2011). The shift away from the center does not seem to be slowing down any time soon.

To be sure, a return to an era in which large numbers of liberal Republicans and conservative Democrats are elected to Congress is unlikely, at least in the short run. Significant ideological changes have unfolded in the electorate, and the American public is, at best, sorted into distinct partisan camps, and at worst, housed at opposite ends of the spectrum. But it was also not long ago that moderates were running and winning.

Olympia Snowe was among the last to go in 2012, and with an approval rating of 57 percent, she left office as one of the most popular senators in the country. Furthermore, the on-the-ground efforts by those who seek reform stem from a broader public desire to elect less divisive candidates. There is a demand for politicians who adopt a give-and-take approach to policymaking. The real irony is that Congress's record low approval ratings stem from the inability and unwillingness of members to work across party lines (Hibbing and Theiss-Morse 1995; Ramirez 2009).

The election of ideological moderates is not a sure-fire way to end government gridlock and partisan warfare. An increase in the number of moderates, or a decrease in the number of ideologues, will not necessarily enhance the quality of representation. Nor will moderates, or any member for that matter, pass policies that always reflect the will of "the people." However, the presence of ideological moderates would almost certainly expand the scope of the policy agenda and change the tenor of legislative debate. It is difficult to imagine how some issues could even emerge on the agenda today given the continual push toward the ideological extremes. For instance, following the 2010 elections, 86 percent of the newly elected Republicans were opposed to any climate change legislation that increased government revenue, and 91 percent of them swore to never allow an income tax increase on any individual or business, regardless of deficits or war (Keyes 2010).

The forecast of this book is not overly bright for those who yearn for compromise, bipartisanship, and comity in Washington. It will likely take an unexpected shock to the political environment and many elections for the parties to shift from their current course. What is cause for optimism, though, is that the findings contribute to our understanding of how, specifically, polarization is intensifying with nearly each election cycle. And it is crucial that we identify the mechanisms that are responsible for changes in congressional polarization. Only then, when we have pinpointed the various reasons that the number of liberal Republicans and conservative Democrats has declined, can we begin to address and counteract the movement of both parties toward the ideological extremes.

Scholars have been an active part in uncovering these forces, and they have weighed in with ideas on how to minimize polarization in the future. A host of leading political scientists recently came together to focus specifically on the solutions to partisan polarization (Persily 2015a). Several of their proposals aim to facilitate the election of moderate candidates. For example, Prior and Stroud (2015) propose reforms that target and mobilize moderate voters, and Bonica (2015) recommends giving voters a "data-driven voter guide" so they can identify the ideological distance between candidates and themselves. Others would instead seek to strengthen political parties, embolden party leaders, enhance the role of party organizations in the nomination process, and provide public funding to parties (McCarty 2015; Pildes 2015; Persily 2015b). But there is no "magic bullet" (Persily 2015a). Our current situation is the product of a multitude of long-run historical forces, and many reforms will be needed to counteract the decades-long shift away from the ideological center.

One additional lesson suggested here is that those who bemoan partisan polarization in Congress should focus on recruiting and supporting ideologically moderate candidates. Some, but not enough, political elites are already doing this. For example, the Republican Main Street Partnership is an organization that, according to its website, "supports Republican candidates who are committed to governing and making Washington work again." The organization launched a fundraising arm last year to fight Tea Party influence, and they have helped Republican incumbents fend off Tea Party challengers. Unlike conservative groups like the Club for Growth, the organization has not spent money to challenge a sitting member of Congress (Cornwell 2014). However, the defeat of ideologues in Congress, combined with the recruitment of moderates in the congressional pipeline and the support of moderate incumbents, seems like a potentially promising recipe.

But the main lesson is that partisan polarization in Congress is not going anywhere, at least in the short run, unless political elites and the American public do something to end it. The "take no prisoners" mode of political competition that prevails in Congress today has a negative effect on the nature of policy outcomes, the tenor of legislative debate, and the quality of representative democracy. In his final State of the Union address, President Obama said, "[Democracy] doesn't work if we think the people who disagree with us are all motivated by malice. It doesn't work if we think that our political opponents are unpatriotic or trying to weaken America. Democracy grinds to a halt without a willingness to compromise ... Our public life withers when only the most extreme voices get all the attention." This book does not seek to glorify ideological moderates or the time period in which they served. But it does advocate a renewal of the middle ground in American politics. This aspiration is neither novel nor controversial. One of the moderate Republicans I interviewed said she hopes that "like the Phoenix, the moderates will rise from the ashes" (22 January 2013). Many Americans, probably most, would agree with this statement, but we must also acknowledge that moderates are not likely to rise on their own.

# Appendix A

## Interviews with Political Elites

I interviewed 22 political elites; 18 of them were former members of Congress and 4 were party elites or former staffers of members of Congress. Two of these MCs had been recruiters for their respective parties as well. Of these 18 members, 12 were Republicans and 6 were Democrats. It was important for me to interview a significant number of male and female Republicans, so I could more fully grapple with whether the value of the office differed for moderate Republican men and moderate Republican women as the parties drifted apart. My general goal was to interview approximately 20 ideological moderates who were in Congress under varying degrees of partisan polarization, so I could understand how the nature of congressional service changed for those in the political center as the parties drifted apart.

The members were selected based on their DW-Nominate scores. I reviewed the entire membership of the U.S. Association of Former Members of Congress (FMC), and I chose all of the individuals who were in the moderate quartile of their party when they were in office. I then divided this group of approximately 60 individuals into a few smaller groups based on their ideology, seniority, geography, and tenure in office. I prioritized members who had served in the U.S. House for longer periods of time. All had served at least two terms (most had served at least five terms), were in office in the 1990s and/or 2000s, and were less than 85 years of age. As noted in Chapter 1, most belonged to at least one of the moderate groups in Congress, such as the Tuesday Group and the Republican Main Street Partnership on the Republican side or the Blue Dog Coalition and the New Democrat Coalition on the Democratic side. They represented a range of geographical areas, though many of the

Republicans came from the Northeast and many of the Democrats came from the South due to historical patterns of partisan alignment.

The U.S. Association of Former Members of Congress (FMC) contacted these individuals on my behalf, and I followed up with those who agreed to speak with me. Virtually everyone who received emails from the FMC agreed to be interviewed; only a couple of them declined. I also contacted additional members who were frequently mentioned in other interviews, again with the assistance of the FMC. A few of the members also recommended that I speak with former members of their staff, and they put me in touch with these individuals. Prior to the interviews, I informed the participants that we would discuss the role of moderates in the House of Representatives. I said I was particularly interested in how moderates have influenced the policymaking process in recent decades and how growing partisan polarization has affected their ability to do so. The project received an exception from IRB review by the Institutional Review Board at Cornell University (Protocol ID# 1110002564).

The majority of the interviews were conducted in person; a few were conducted over the phone. Most of the conversations took place in Washington, DC, as many former members still live in the DC area. I made several trips to Washington, DC, in the winter and spring of 2013. I also made a few trips around the Northeast during this time, where some of the members currently reside. The interviews with former staff members were also conducted in Washington in the spring of 2013. All participants were informed that the interviews would be anonymous, and all signed consent agreements or gave written consent via email. The interviews were recorded and transcribed (except one), and I took notes during the interviews as well.

The claims were not verified by more than one source because the questions focused largely on personal experience. As noted in Chapter 2, some of the moderates even discussed how other moderates were treated, and inconsistencies emerged on occasion. For example, one moderate described her own experiences as follows: "Some of [my co-partisans] genuinely liked me and respected what I was doing, but they were all nice to me. Nobody was ever nasty." However, this member came up in another interview and was described as being shunned and ridiculed. Conversely, one member suggested that two of the other moderates I spoke with were not ridiculed, but those members themselves gave several examples of the negative interactions they had with partisan colleagues. In general, I opted to discuss the member's own portrayal of events given the emphasis on individual perceptions and personal experience.

# Appendix B

## Attraction to a Career in the U.S. House, across State Legislators (with Interaction between Ideology and Chance of Winning)

|  | All | Republicans | Democrats |
|---|---|---|---|
| Ideological moderate | −0.15 | −0.40* | −0.06 |
| (Republican liberalism; Democratic conservatism) | (0.11) | (0.18) | (0.18) |
| Chance of winning nomination | 0.33** | 0.48** | 0.24 |
|  | (0.11) | (0.17) | (0.15) |
| Ideological moderate × chance of winning nomination | 0.03 | −0.05 | 0.16 |
|  | (0.10) | (0.18) | (0.13) |
| Distance from voters in House district | 0.03 | −0.35* | 0.27 |
|  | (0.11) | (0.17) | (0.17) |
| Contacted by political party | 0.37** | 0.48* | 0.32† |
|  | (0.12) | (0.21) | (0.16) |
| Relative value of House seat | 0.24* | 0.26 | 0.27† |
|  | (0.11) | (0.17) | (0.14) |
| In professionalized state legislature | −0.09 | 0.03 | −0.14 |
|  | (0.10) | (0.16) | (0.14) |
| Faces term limits | 0.00 | −0.24 | 0.20 |
|  | (0.21) | (0.34) | (0.29) |
| Campaign cost index | −0.27* | −0.11 | −0.39* |
|  | (0.12) | (0.18) | (0.16) |
| Family cost index | −0.48** | −0.57** | −0.42** |
|  | (0.11) | (0.18) | (0.16) |
| Female | −0.42† | −0.62 | −0.46 |
|  | (0.25) | (0.48) | (0.33) |
| Age | −0.91** | −0.94** | −0.82** |
|  | (0.12) | (0.18) | (0.16) |
| Constant | 0.06 | 0.10 | 0.02 |
|  | (0.13) | (0.20) | (0.18) |
| Number of observations | 577 | 275 | 302 |
| Log likelihood | −309.30 | −132.47 | −167.91 |

*Source:* 1998 Wave of the Candidate Emergence Study (Maestas et al. 2006).
*Note:* Entries are logistic regression coefficients with standard errors in parentheses. The dependent variable is 1 if the state legislator is attracted to a career in the U.S. House and 0 if not.
** $p < 0.01$, * $p < 0.05$, † $p < 0.10$.

# Appendix C

## Determinants of Running for the U.S. House across State Legislators, by Party (2000–2010)

| | Republican state legislators | | | Democratic state legislators | | |
|---|---|---|---|---|---|---|
| | (1) | (2) | (3) | (4) | (5) | (6) |
| Distance from party in Congress | −2.67** (0.58) | −5.57** (0.85) | −7.31** (1.67) | −1.93** (0.56) | −4.89** (0.63) | −4.44** (1.88) |
| Distance from party × ideologue side | — | 10.72** (1.31) | 15.18** (2.64) | — | 9.05** (0.94) | 11.26** (2.67) |
| Distance from party squared | — | — | 2.17 (1.87) | — | — | −0.40 (1.78) |
| Distance from party squared × ideologue side | — | — | −6.83† (3.55) | — | — | −2.79 (2.75) |
| Ideologue side | — | 0.36 (0.25) | −0.07 (0.33) | — | 0.28 (0.31) | −0.01 (0.45) |
| Open congressional seat | 2.87** (0.16) | 2.91** (0.17) | 2.92** (0.17) | 2.89** (0.20) | 3.00** (0.22) | 2.99** (0.22) |
| Ideology of same party voters in district (higher = extreme) | 0.14 (1.95) | −0.31 (2.12) | −0.06 (2.19) | −0.10 (0.95) | −2.41* (0.99) | −2.55* (0.99) |
| Ideology of average donor in district (higher = conservative) | −0.41 (0.39) | −0.67 (0.40) | −0.65 (0.41) | −0.44 (0.44) | −0.91* (0.44) | −0.94* (0.44) |

| | (1) | (2) | (3) | (4) | (5) | (6) |
|---|---|---|---|---|---|---|
| Log of mean receipts | 0.29** | 0.45** | 0.45** | 0.44** | 0.52** | 0.52** |
| | (0.11) | (0.11) | (0.11) | (0.12) | (0.13) | (0.13) |
| Raised as state legislator | 0.33** | 0.51** | 0.51** | 0.37** | 0.62** | 0.62** |
| | (0.05) | (0.05) | (0.05) | (0.06) | (0.08) | (0.08) |
| Number of times run for state legislature | -0.04 | -0.15 | -0.12 | -0.08 | -0.57** | -0.60** |
| | (0.19) | (0.20) | (0.20) | (0.19) | (0.20) | (0.20) |
| Female | 0.26 | 0.17 | 0.16 | -0.16 | -0.08 | -0.07 |
| | (0.31) | (0.31) | (0.31) | (0.45) | (0.49) | (0.49) |
| Democratic control of state legislature | -10.92** | -13.85** | -14.03** | -26.35** | -27.27** | -27.19** |
| | (2.62) | (2.84) | (2.90) | (1.74) | (2.12) | (2.15) |
| Number of observations | 14,404 | 14,404 | 14,404 | 16,521 | 16,521 | 16,521 |
| Log likelihood | -917.75 | -801.52 | -799.35 | -661.33 | -564.11 | -562.71 |
| State and year fixed effects | Yes | Yes | Yes | Yes | Yes | Yes |

*Note:* Entries are logistic regression coefficients with robust standard errors clustered by individual in parentheses. The dependent variable is coded 1 if the state legislator ran for the U.S. House and 0 if the state legislator ran for the state legislature again.

$^{**} p < 0.01, ^* p < 0.05, ^\dagger p < 0.10.$

# References

Abramowitz, Alan I. 2010. *The Disappearing Center: Engaged Citizens, Polarization, and American Democracy*. New Haven, CT: Yale University Press.

Abramowitz, Alan I. and Kyle L. Saunders. 2008. "Is Polarization a Myth?" *Journal of Politics* 70(2): 542–55.

Abramowitz, Alan I. and Steven Webster. 2015. "All Politics Is National: The Rise of Negative Partisanship and the Nationalization of U.S. House and Senate Elections in the 21st Century." Presented at the annual meeting of the Midwest Political Science Association.

Abramson, Paul R., John H. Aldrich, and David W. Rohde. 1987. "Progressive Ambition among United States Senators: 1972–1988." *Journal of Politics* 49(1): 3–35.

Ahler, Douglas J., Jack Citrin, and Gabriel S. Lenz. 2016. "Do Open Primaries Improve Representation? An Experimental Test of California's 2012 Top-Two Primary." *Legislative Studies Quarterly* 41(2): 237–68.

Aldrich, John H. 1980. *Before the Convention: Strategies and Choices in Presidential Nomination Strategies*. Chicago: University of Chicago Press.

Aldrich, John H. 1995. *Why Parties? The Origin and Transformation of Party Politics in America*. Chicago: University of Chicago Press.

Aldrich, John H. 2011. *Why Parties? A Second Look*. Chicago: University of Chicago Press.

Aldrich, John H. Andrew Ballard, Joshua Lerner, and David Rohde. 2015. "Does the Gift Keep On Giving? House Leadership PAC Donations before and after Majority Status." Presented at the annual meeting of the Midwest Political Science Association.

Aldrich, John H. and Melanie Freeze. 2011. "Political Participation, Polarization, and Public Opinion: Activism and the Merging of Partisan and Ideological Polarization." In *Facing the Challenge of Democracy: Explorations in the Analysis of Public Opinion and Political Participation*, eds. Paul M. Sniderman and Benjamin Highton. Princeton, NJ: Princeton University Press.

Aldrich, John H. and David W. Rohde. 2001. "The Logic of Conditional Party Government: Revisiting the Electoral Connection." In *Congress Reconsidered*, eds. Lawrence Dodd and Bruce Oppenheimer. Washington, DC: CQ Press.

Aldrich, John H. and Danielle M. Thomsen. Forthcoming. "Party, Policy, and the Ambition to Run for Higher Office." *Legislative Studies Quarterly*.

Alford, John R., Holly Teeters, Daniel S. Ward, and Rick K. Wilson. 1994. "Overdraft: The Political Cost of Congressional Malfeasance." *Journal of Politics* 56(3): 788–801.

Ansolabehere, Stephen. 2011. "Run for Office." *Boston Review* 1 May 2011. http://bostonreview.net/stephen-ansolabehere-run-for-office. Accessed 1 September 2015.

Ansolabehere, Stephen and Alan Gerber. 1997. "Incumbency Advantage and the Persistence of Legislative Majorities." *Legislative Studies Quarterly* 22(2): 161–78.

Ansolabehere, Stephen, James M. Snyder, Jr., and Charles Stewart III. 2001. "Candidate Positioning in U.S. House Elections." *American Journal of Political Science* 45(1): 136–159.

Bafumi, Joseph and Michael C. Herron. 2010. "Leapfrog Representation and Extremism: A Study of American Voters and Their Members in Congress." *American Political Science Review* 104(3): 519–42.

Banks, Jeffrey S. and D. Roderick Kiewiet. 1989. "Explaining Patterns of Candidate Competition in Congressional Elections." *American Journal of Political Science* 33(4): 997–1015.

Barber, Michael J. and Nolan McCarty. 2015. "Causes and Consequences of Polarization." In *Solutions to Political Polarization in America*, ed. Nathan Persily. New York: Cambridge University Press.

Bartels, Larry M. 2000. "Partisanship and Voting Behavior, 1952–1996." *American Journal of Political Science* 44(1): 35–50.

Baumgartner, Jody C. and Peter L. Francia. 2010. *Conventional Wisdom and American Elections: Exploding Myths, Exploring Misconceptions*. Lanham, MD: Rowman & Littlefield.

Beckel, Michael. 2010. "Who's Backing the New Top Blue Dogs' Bark, Bite?" *OpenSecrets.org* 22 November 2010. https://www.opensecrets.org/news/2010/11/whos-backing-the-new-top-blue-dogs/. Accessed 9 June 2016.

Bipartisan Policy Center. 2014. "Governing in a Polarized Era: A Bipartisan Blueprint to Strengthen Our Democracy." Report. Washington, DC: Bipartisan Policy Center. http://bipartisanpolicy.org/wp-content/uploads/sites/default/files/files/BPC%20CPR%20Governing%20in%20a%20Polarized%20America.pdf.

Black, Gordon S. 1972. "A Theory of Political Ambition: Career Choices and the Role of Structural Incentives." *American Political Science Review* 66(1): 144–59.

Bland, Scott. 2014. "Moderate Democrats Are Becoming Extinct." *National Journal* 8 January 2014. https://www.nationaljournal.com/s/63880. Accessed 23 March 2014.

Boatright, Robert G. 2013. *Getting Primaried: The Changing Politics of Congressional Primary Challenges*. Ann Arbor: University of Michigan Press.

Bond, Jon R., Cary Covington, and Richard Fleisher. 1985. "Explaining Challenger Quality in Congressional Elections." *Journal of Politics* 47(2): 510–29.

Bonica, Adam. 2010. "Introducing the 112th Congress." *Ideological Cartography* 5 November 2012. https://ideologicalcartography.com/2010/11/05/introducing-the-112th-congress/. Accessed 1 December 2012.

Bonica, Adam. 2013. "Ideology and Interests in the Political Marketplace." *American Journal of Political Science* 57(2): 294–311.

Bonica, Adam. 2014. "Mapping the Ideological Marketplace." *American Journal of Political Science* 58(2): 367–86.

Bonica, Adam. 2015. "Data Science for the People." In *Solutions to Political Polarization in America*, ed. Nathan Persily. New York: Cambridge University Press.

Brace, Paul. 1984. "Progressive Ambition in the House: A Probabilistic Approach." *Journal of Politics* 46(2): 556–71.

Brace, Paul. 1985. "A Probabilistic Approach to Member Retirement from the U.S. Congress." *Legislative Studies Quarterly* 10(1): 107–24.

Brady, David W., Hahrie Han, and Jeremy C. Pope. 2007. "Primary Elections and Candidate Ideology: Out of Step with the Primary Electorate?" *Legislative Studies Quarterly* 32(1): 79–105.

Brodey, Sam. 2015. "How Keith Ellison Made the Congressional Progressive Caucus into a Political Force That Matters." *MinnPost* 21 July 2015. https://www.minnpost.com/dc-dispatches/2015/07/how-keith-ellison-made-congressional-progressive-caucus-political-force-matter. Accessed 9 June 2016.

Broockman, David. 2014. "Mobilizing Candidates: Political Actors Strategically Shape the Candidate Pool with Personal Appeals." *Journal of Experimental Political Science* 1(2): 104–19.

Bullock, Charles S. 1972. "House Careerists: Changing Patterns of Longevity and Attrition." *American Political Science Review* 66(4): 1295–300.

Burden, Barry. 2004. "Candidate Positioning in U.S. Congressional Elections." *British Journal of Political Science* 34(2): 211–27.

Burrell, Barbara C. 1994. *A Woman's Place Is in the House: Campaigning for Congress in the Feminist Era*. Ann Arbor: University of Michigan Press.

Campbell, Andrea Louise. 2002. "Self-Interest, Social Security, and the Distinctive Participation Patterns of Senior Citizens." *American Political Science Review* 96(3): 565–74.

Canes-Wrone, Brandice, David W. Brady, and John F. Cogan. 2002. "Out of Step, out of Office: Electoral Accountability and House Members' Voting." *American Political Science Review* 96(1): 127–40.

Carmines, Edward G. 2011. "Review Symposium: Class Politics, American Style." *Perspectives on Politics* 9(3): 645–7.

Carnes, Nicholas. 2012. Congressional Leadership and Social Status (CLASS) Dataset, v. 1.9 [computer file]. Available from the author, http://nicholas.carnes@duke.edu.

Carnes, Nicholas. 2013. *White-Collar Government: The Hidden Role of Class in Economic Policy Making.* Chicago: University of Chicago Press.

Carroll, Susan J. 2003. "Have Women State Legislators in the United States Become More Conservative? A Comparison of State Legislators in 2001 and 1988." *Atlantis: A Women's Studies Journal* 27(2): 128–39.

Carroll, Susan J. and Kira Sanbonmatsu. 2013. *More Women Can Run: Gender and Pathways to the State Legislatures.* New York: Oxford University Press.

Carson, Jamie L., Michael H. Crespin, Charles J. Finocchiaro, and David W. Rohde. 2007. "Redistricting and Party Polarization in the U.S. House of Representatives." *American Politics Research* 35(6): 878–904.

Carson, Jamie L. and Jason M. Roberts. 2013. *Ambition, Competition, and Electoral Reform: The Politics of Congressional Elections Across Time.* Ann Arbor: University of Michigan Press.

Center for American Women and Politics (CAWP). 2013. Excel spreadsheet of all women who ran for the U.S. House in 2010. New Brunswick, NJ: Center for American Women and Politics. Additional data collected by the author.

Center for American Women and Politics (CAWP). 2015. "Women in the U.S. Congress Fact Sheet." New Brunswick, NJ: Center for American Women and Politics.

Center for Responsive Politics. 2014. Database of new House members. Received 10 February 2014.

Cohen, Marty, David Karol, Hans Noel, and John Zaller. 2008. *The Party Decides: Presidential Nominations before and after Reform.* Chicago: University of Chicago Press.

Congressional Quarterly. 2014. "CQ Roll Call's Vote Studies – 2013 In Review." *Congressional Quarterly* 3 February 2014. http://media.cq.com/votestudies. Accessed September 2015.

Cooperman, Rosalyn and Bruce I. Oppenheimer. 2001. "The Gender Gap in the House of Representatives." In *Congress Reconsidered*, 7th ed., eds. Lawrence C. Dodd and Bruce I. Oppenheimer. Washington, DC: CQ Press.

Cornwell, Susan. 2014. "Michigan Race Highlights Tea Party versus Establishment Struggle." Reuters 9 March 2014. http://www.reuters.com/article/us-usa-politics-teaparty-idUSBREA280NO20140309. Accessed 23 March 2014.

Costain, Anne. 1992. *Inviting Women's Rebellion: A Political Process Interpretation of the Women's Movement.* Baltimore: Johns Hopkins University Press.

Cox, Gary W. and Jonathan N. Katz. 1996. "Why Did the Incumbency Advantage in U.S. Elections Grow?" *American Journal of Political Science* 40(2): 478–97.

Cox, Gary W. and Mathew D. McCubbins. 1993. *Legislative Leviathan: Party Government in the House.* Berkeley: University of California Press.

Cox, Gary W. and Mathew D. McCubbins. 2005. *Setting the Agenda: Responsible Party Government in the U.S. House of Representatives.* New York: Cambridge University Press.

Crespin, Michael H. and Janna L. Deitz. 2010. "If You Can't Join 'Em, Beat 'Em: The Gender Gap in Individual Donations to Congressional Candidates." *Political Research Quarterly* 63(3): 581–93.

Darcy, Robert, Susan Welch, and Janet Clark. 1994. *Women, Elections, and Representation*, 2nd ed. Lincoln, NE: University of Nebraska Press.

DeBonis, Mike and Paul Kane. 2015. "House Speaker John Boehner to Resign at End of October." *Washington Post* 25 September 2015. https://www.washingtonpost.com/news/powerpost/wp/2015/09/25/boehner -resigns/?utm_term=.e4cc634d3bd3. Accessed 9 June 2016.

Demirjian, Karoun. 2016. "Senate Votes Down Gun Control Proposals in Wake of Orlando Shootings." *Washington Post* 20 June 2016. https://www .washingtonpost.com/news/powerpost/wp/2016/06/20/senate-heads-for-gun -control-showdown-likely-to-go-nowhere/?utm_term=.29028087bd92. Accessed 25 June 2016.

Desilver, Drew. 2013. "Current Congress Is Not the Least Productive in Recent History, but Close." Pew Research Center 3 September 2013. http://www.pewresearch.org/fact-tank/2013/09/03/current-congress-is-not -the-least-productive-in-recent-history-but-close/. Accessed 23 March 2014.

Diaz, Kevin. 2009. "Collin Peterson's Blue Dogs Bark at 'Public Option.'" *Star Tribune* 13 September 2009. http://www.startribune.com/collin- peterson-s-blue-dogs-bark-at-public-option/59188657/. Accessed 9 June 2016.

Dodson, Debra L. 2006. *The Impact of Women in Congress*. New York: Oxford University Press.

Dominguez, Casey. 2011. "Does the Party Matter? Endorsements in Congres- sional Primaries." *Political Research Quarterly* 64(3): 534–44.

Downs, Anthony. 1957. *An Economic Theory of Democracy*. New York: Harper and Row.

Dugan, Andrew. 2013. "Most Americans for Raising Minimum Wage." Gallup 11 November 2013. http://www.gallup.com/poll/165794/americans-raising -minimum-wage.aspx. Accessed 9 June 2016.

(*The*) *Economist*. 2016. "The Centre Cannot Hold." *The Economist* 16 Jan- uary 2016. http://www.economist.com/news/united-states/21688393-two -moderate-members-congress-explain-why-they-are-leaving-centre-cannot -hold. Accessed 9 June 2016.

Elder, Laurel. 2008. "Whither Republican Women: The Growing Partisan Gap among Women in Congress." *The Forum* 6(1): Article 13.

Elder, Laurel. 2012. "The Partisan Gap among Women State Legislators." *Journal of Women, Politics, and Public Policy* 33(1): 65–85.

Erikson, Robert S. 1971. "The Advantage of Incumbency in Congressional Elec- tions." *Polity* 3(3): 395–403.

Erikson, Robert S. and Gerald C. Wright, Jr. 1989. "Voters, Candidates, and Issues in Congressional Elections." In *Congress Reconsidered*, 4th ed., eds. Lawrence C. Dodd and Bruce I. Oppenheimer. Washington, DC: Congres- sional Quarterly Press.

Erikson, Robert S. and Gerald C. Wright, Jr. 2000. "Representation of Con- stituency Ideology in Congress." In *Continuity and Change in House Elec- tions*, eds. David W. Brady, John F. Cogan, and Morris P. Fiorina. Stanford, CA: Stanford University Press.

Erskine, Hazel. 1971. "The Polls: Women's Role." *Public Opinion Quarterly* 35(2): 275–90.

Evans, C. Lawrence and Walter J. Oleszek. 1999. "The Strategic Context of Congressional Party Leadership." *Congress and the Presidency* 26(1): 1–20.

Evans, Sean F. and John W. Swain. 2012. "The Impact of Reform on Retirement from the U.S. House of Representatives, 1945–2010." Presented at the annual meeting of the Midwest Political Science Association.

Fabian, Jordan. 2010. "House Roll Call on Healthcare Bill: 34 Dems Vote Against." *The Hill* 22 March 2010. http://thehill.com/blogs/blog-briefing-room/news/88211-house-roll-call-on-healthcare-bill-34-dems-vote-against. Accessed May 2016.

Fenno, Richard F. 1973. *Congressmen in Committees*. Boston: Little, Brown.

Fenno, Richard F. 1978. *Home Style: House Members in Their Districts*. New York: Longman.

Fiorina, Morris P. 1974. *Representatives, Roll Calls, and Constituencies*. Lexington, MA: Lexington.

Fiorina, Morris P., with Samuel J. Abrams. 2009. *Disconnect: The Breakdown of Representation in American Politics*. Norman, OK: University of Oklahoma Press.

Fiorina, Morris P., Samuel J. Abrams, and Jeremy C. Pope. 2006. *Culture War? The Myth of a Polarized America*. New York: Pearson/Longman.

Fleisher, Richard and John R. Bond. 2004. "The Shrinking Middle in the US Congress." *British Journal of Political Science* 34(3): 429–51.

Fox, Richard L. 2014. "Congressional Elections: Women's Candidacies and the Road to Gender Parity." In *Gender and Elections*, 3rd ed., eds. Susan J. Carroll and Richard L. Fox. New York: Cambridge University Press.

Frederick, Brian. 2009. "Are Female House Members Still More Liberal in a Polarized Era? The Conditional Nature of the Relationship Between Descriptive and Substantive Representation." *Congress and the Presidency* 36(2): 181–202.

Freeman, Jo. 1986. "The Political Culture of the Democratic and Republican Parties." *Political Science Quarterly* 101(3): 327–56.

Fulton, Sarah A., Cherie D. Maestas, L. Sandy Maisel, and Walter J. Stone. 2006. "The Sense of a Woman: Gender, Ambition, and the Decision to Run for Office." *Political Research Quarterly* 59(2): 235–48.

Gaddie, Ronald Keith and Charles S. Bullock III. 2000. *Elections to Open Seats in the U.S. House: Where the Action Is*. Lanham, MD: Rowman and Littlefield.

Geer, John. 1988. "Assessing the Representativeness of Electorates in Presidential Primaries." *American Journal of Political Science* 32(4): 929–45.

Gerber, Elisabeth R. and Rebecca B. Morton. 1998. "Primary Election Systems and Representation." *Journal of Law, Economics, and Organization* 14(2): 304–24.

Gertzog, Irwin. 1995. *Congressional Women: Their Recruitment, Integration, and Behavior*, 2nd ed. Westport, CT: Praeger Press.

Goodman, Matt. 2014. "At Planned Parenthood Luncheon, Former GOP Senator Says Partisanship Damages Women's Healthcare." *Dallas/Fort Worth Healthcare Daily* 8 April 2014. Accessed 9 June 2016.

*Grist*. 2006. "An Interview with Retiring Rep. Sherwood Boehlert, a GOP Leader on Environmental Protection." Grist 29 April 2006. Web. Accessed 9 June 2016.

Grofman, Bernard, William Koetzle, and Anthony J. McGann. 2002. "Congressional Leadership 1965–96: A New Look at the Extremism versus Centrality Debate." *Legislative Studies Quarterly* 27(1): 87–105.

Groseclose, Tim and Keith Krehbiel. 1994. "Golden Parachutes, Rubber Checks, and Strategic Retirement from the 102nd House of Representatives." *American Journal of Political Science* 38(1): 75–99.

Grossman, Matt and David A. Hopkins. 2015. "Ideological Republicans and Group Interest Democrats: The Asymmetry of American Party Politics." *Perspectives on Politics* 13(1): 119–39.

Grossman, Matt and David A. Hopkins. 2016. *Asymmetric Politics: Ideological Republicans and Group Interest Democrats*. New York: Oxford University Press.

Grynaviski, Jeffrey D. 2010. *Partisan Bonds: Political Reputations and Legislative Accountability*. New York: Cambridge University Press.

Hacker, Jacob S. and Paul Pierson. 2005. *Off Center: The Republican Revolution and the Erosion of American Democracy*. New Haven, CT: Yale University Press.

Hacker, Jacob S. and Paul Pierson. 2014. "After the 'Master Theory': Downs, Schattschneider, and the Rebirth of Policy-Focused Analysis." *Perspectives on Politics* 12(3): 643–62.

Hacker, Jacob S. and Paul Pierson. 2015. "Confronting Asymmetric Polarization." In *Solutions to Political Polarization in America*, ed. Nathan Persily. New York: Cambridge University Press.

Hall, Andrew. 2014. "How the Public Funding of Elections Increases Candidate Polarization." Working Paper, Harvard University.

Hall, Andrew B. and James Snyder. 2015. "Candidate Ideology and Electoral Success." Working Paper, Harvard University.

Hall, Richard L. and Robert P. Van Houweling. 1995. "Avarice and Ambition in Congress: Representatives' Decisions to Run or Retire from the U.S. House." *American Political Science Review* 89(1): 121–37.

Harris, Douglas B. and Garrison Nelson. 2008. "Middlemen No More? Emergent Patterns in Congressional Leadership Selection." *PS: Political Science and Politics* 41(1): 49–55.

Hawkesworth, Mary, Kathleen J. Casey, Krista Jenkins, and Katherine E. Kleeman. 2001. *Legislating by and for Women: A Comparison of the 103rd and 104th Congresses*. New Brunswick, NJ: Center for American Women and Politics.

Heberlig, Eric, Marc Hetherington, and Bruce Larson. 2006. "The Price of Leadership: Campaign Money and the Polarization of Congressional Parties." *Journal of Politics* 68(4): 992–1005.

Herrnson, Paul S. 1986. "Do Parties Make a Difference? The Role of Party Organizations in Congressional Elections." *Journal of Politics* 48(3): 589–615.

Herrnson, Paul S. 2004. *Congressional Elections: Campaigning at Home and in Washington.* Washington, DC: CQ Press.

Herrnson, Paul S. 2010. "The Evolution of National Party Organizations." In *The Oxford Handbook of Political Parties,* eds. L. Sandy Maisel and Jeffrey M. Berry. New York: Oxford University Press.

Hetherington, Marc J. 2001. "Resurgent Mass Partisanship: The Role of Elite Polarization." *American Political Science Review* 95(3): 619–31.

Hetherington, Marc J. 2009. "Review Article: Putting Polarization in Perspective." *British Journal of Political Science* 39(2): 413–48.

Hibbing, John R. 1982. "Voluntary Retirement from the U.S. House of Representatives: Who Quits?" *American Journal of Political Science* 26(3): 467–84.

Hibbing, John R. and Elizabeth Theiss-Morse. 1995. *Congress as Public Enemy: Attitudes toward American Political Institutions.* New York: Cambridge University Press.

Hirano, Shigeo, James M. Snyder, Jr., Stephen Ansolabehere, and John Mark Hansen. 2010. "Primary Elections and Partisan Polarization in the U.S. Congress." *Quarterly Journal of Political Science* 5(2): 169–91.

Hirano, Shigeo, Gabriel S. Lenz, Maksim Pinkovskiy, and James M. Snyder, Jr. 2015. "Voter Learning in State Primary Elections." *American Journal of Political Science* 59(1): 91–108.

Hooper, Molly K. 2010. "Bachmann Standing by 'Gangster Government.'" *The Hill* 22 April 2010. http://thehill.com/homenews/house/ 93697-bachmann-standing-by-gangster-gov. Accessed 9 June 2016.

Howard, Christopher. 1997. *The Hidden Welfare State: Tax Expenditures and Social Policy in the United States.* Princeton, NJ: Princeton University Press.

Huey-Burns, Caitlin and Scott Conroy. 2013. "Why Would Anyone Run for Congress These Days?" *Real Clear Politics* 24 October 2013. http://www.realclearpolitics.com/articles/2013/10/24/why_would_ anyone_run_for_congress_these_days.html. Accessed March 2014.

Inter-Parliamentary Union. 2016. "Women in National Parliaments, 2016." http://www.ipu.org/wmn-e/world.htm. Accessed November 2016.

Jacobson, Gary C. 1989. "Strategic Politicians and the Dynamics of U.S. House Elections, 1946–1986." *American Political Science Review* 83(3): 773–93.

Jacobson, Gary C. 2000. "Party Polarization in National Politics: The Electoral Connection." In *Polarized Politics: Congress and the President in a Partisan Era,* eds. Jon R. Bond and Richard Fleisher. Washington, DC: CQ Press.

Jacobson, Gary C. 2013. *The Politics of Congressional Elections,* 8th ed. New York: Pearson.

Jacobson, Gary C. 2015. "It's Nothing Personal: The Decline of the Incumbency Advantage in U.S. House Elections." *Journal of Politics* 77(3): 861–73.

Jacobson, Gary C. and Michael A. Dimock. 1994. "Checking Out: The Effects of Bank Overdrafts on the 1992 House Elections." *American Journal of Political Science* 38(3): 601–24.

Jacobson, Gary C. and Samuel Kernell. 1983. *Strategy and Choice in Congressional Elections,* 2nd ed. New Haven, CT: Yale University Press.

Jamieson, Kathleen Hall and Erika Falk. 1998. "Civility in the House of Representatives: An Update." Philadelphia: Annenberg Public Policy Center.

Jenkins, Kent. 1990. "Byron's Credentials on the Line." *Washington Post* 5 July 1990. https://www.washingtonpost.com/archive/local/1990/07/05/byrons -credentials-on-the-line/43274086-459b-4d2a-b298-512512c760f4/?utm _term=.77f33b0ba23e. Accessed 1 September 2015.

Jessee, Stephen and Neil Malhotra. 2010. "Are Congressional Leaders Middlepersons or Extremists? Yes." *Legislative Studies Quarterly* 35(3): 361–92.

Jones, Jeffrey M. 2016. "Republicans, Democrats Interpret Orlando Incident Differently." *Gallup* 17 June 2016. http://www.gallup.com/poll/192842/ republicans-democrats-interpret-orlando-incident-differently.aspx. Accessed 20 June 2016.

Kabaservice, Geoffrey. 2012. *Rule and Ruin: The Downfall of Moderation and the Destruction of the Republican Party, from Eisenhower to the Tea Party.* New York: Oxford University Press.

Kane, Paul. 2014. "Blue Dog Democrats, Whittled Down in Number, are Trying to Regroup." *Washington Post* 15 January 2014. https://www.washingtonpost.com/politics/blue-dog-democrats-whittled -down-in-number-are-trying-to-regroup/2014/01/15/37d4e7e2-7dfd-11e3 -95c6-0a7aa80874bc_story.html?utm_term=.79705721c5eb. Accessed May 2016.

Kanthak, Kristin and Jonathan Woon. 2015. "Women Don't Run? Election Aversion and Candidate Entry." *American Journal of Political Science* 59(3): 595–612.

Karol, David. Forthcoming. "Parties and Leaders in American Politics." In *Leadership in American Politics*, eds. Jeffery A. Jenkins and Craig Volden. Lawrence, KS: University of Kansas Press.

Kazee, Thomas. 1994. *Who Runs for Congress? Ambition, Context, and Candidate Emergence.* Washington, DC: CQ Press.

Keyes, Scott. 2010. "Report: Meet the 2010 Freshman GOP Class." *Think Progress* 3 November 2010. https://thinkprogress.org/report-meet-the-2010 -gop-freshman-class-967851ad506d#.4sq9h4h5b. Accessed 23 March 2014.

Kiewiet, D. Roderick and Mathew D. McCubbins. 1991. *The Logic of Delegation: Congressional Parties and the Appropriations Process.* Chicago: University of Chicago Press.

Kiewiet, D. Roderick and Langche Zeng. 1993. "An Analysis of Congressional Career Decisions: 1947–1986." *American Political Science Review* 87(4): 928–41.

Kincaid, Diane. 1978. "Over His Dead Body: A Positive Perspective on Widows in the U.S. Congress." *Western Political Quarterly* 31(1): 96–104.

King, David C. and Richard J. Zeckhauser. 2002. "Punching and Counterpunching in the U.S. Congress: Why Party Leaders Tend to Be Extremists." Presented at the Conference on Leadership 2002: Bridging the Gap Between Theory and Practice, The Center for Public Leadership, Cambridge, MA.

Kingdon, John. 1981. *Congressmen's Voting Decisions.* New York: Harper & Row.

Klarner, Carl. 2013. "State Partisan Balance Data, 1937–2011." http://hdl.handle .net/1902.1/20403 IQSS Dataverse Network [Distributor] V1. Accessed January 2013.

Kousser, Thad, Justin Phillips, and Boris Shor. Forthcoming. "Reform and Representation: A New Method Applied to Recent Electoral Changes." *Political Science Research and Methods*.

Krehbiel, Keith. 1991. *Information and Legislative Organization*. Ann Arbor, MI: University of Michigan Press.

Krehbiel, Keith. 1993. "Where's the Party?" *British Journal of Political Science* 23(2): 235–66.

La Raja, Raymond L. 2010. "Party Nominating Procedures and Recruitment – State and Local Level." In *The Oxford Handbook of Political Parties*, eds. L. Sandy Maisel and Jeffrey M. Berry. New York: Oxford University Press.

LaHood, Ray, with Frank H. Mackaman. 2015. *Seeking Bipartisanship: My Life in Politics*. Amherst, NY: Cambria Press.

Lawless, Jennifer L. 2012. *Becoming a Candidate: Political Ambition and the Decision to Run for Office*. New York: Cambridge University Press.

Lawless, Jennifer L. and Richard L. Fox. 2005. *It Takes a Candidate: Why Women Don't Run for Office*. New York: Cambridge University Press.

Lawless, Jennifer L. and Richard L. Fox. 2010. *It Still Takes a Candidate: Why Women Don't Run for Office*. New York: Cambridge University Press.

Lawless, Jennifer L. and Kathryn Pearson. 2008. "The Primary Reason for Women's Underrepresentation? Reevaluating the Conventional Wisdom." *Journal of Politics* 70(1): 67–82.

Lawless, Jennifer L. and Sean M. Theriault. 2005. "Will She Stay or Will She Go? Career Ceilings and Women's Retirement from the U.S. Congress." *Legislative Studies Quarterly* 30(4): 581–96.

Layman, Geoffrey C. and Thomas M. Carsey. 2002. "Party Polarization and 'Conflict Extension' in the American Electorate." *American Journal of Political Science* 46(4): 786–802.

Layman, Geoffrey C., Thomas M. Carsey, John C. Green, Richard Herrera, and Rosalyn Cooperman. 2010. "Activists and Conflict Extension in American Party Politics." *American Political Science Review* 104(2): 324–46.

Lee, Frances E. 2009. *Beyond Ideology: Politics, Principles, and Partisanship in the U.S. Senate*. Chicago: University of Chicago Press.

Levendusky, Matthew. 2009. *The Partisan Sort: How Liberals Became Democrats and Conservatives Became Republicans*. Chicago: University of Chicago Press.

Levitt, Justin. 2015. "Who Draws the Lines?" All About Redistricting. Web. Accessed 15 September 2015.

Levitt, Steven D. and Catherine D. Wolfram. 1997. "Decomposing the Sources of Incumbency Advantage in the U.S. House." *Legislative Studies Quarterly* 22(1): 45–60.

Lofgren, Mike. 2011. "Goodbye to All That: Reflections of a GOP Operative Who Left the Cult." *Truthout* 3 September 2011. http://www.truth-out.org /opinion/item/3079:goodbye-to-all-that-reflections-of-a-gop-operative-who -left-the-cult. Accessed September 2015.

Maestas, Cherie D., Sarah A. Fulton, L. Sandy Maisel, and Walter J. Stone. 2006. "When to Risk It? Institutions, Ambitions, and the Decision to Run for the U.S. House." *American Political Science Review* 100(2): 195–208.

Maestas, Cherie and Melissa Stewart. 2012. "Recruitment and Candidacy: Ambition, Strategy, and the Choice to Run for Congress." In *New Directions in Congressional Politics*, ed. Jamie L. Carson. New York: Routledge.

Maisel, Sandy and Walter J. Stone. 2014. "Candidate Emergence Revisited: The Lingering Effects of Recruitment, Ambition, and Successful Prospects among House Candidates." *Political Science Quarterly* 129(3): 429–47.

Mann, Thomas E. and Norman J. Ornstein. 2012. *It's Even Worse Than It Looks: How the American Constitutional System Collided with the New Politics of Extremism*. New York: Basic Books.

Manning, Jennifer E. and R. Eric Peterson. 2013. "First Term Members of the House of Representatives and Senate, 64th–113th Congresses." Report from the Congressional Research Service. Washington, DC.

Masket, Seth E. 2009. *No Middle Ground: How Informal Party Organizations Control Nominations and Polarize Legislatures*. Ann Arbor, MI: University of Michigan Press.

Masket, Seth E. and Michael G. Miller. 2014. "Does Public Election Funding Create More Extreme Legislators? Evidence from Arizona and Maine." *State Politics and Policy Quarterly* 15(1): 24–40.

Masket, Seth and Michael G. Miller. 2015. "Is Public Funding Really Electing Extremists?" *Monkey Cage* 22 January 2015. https://www.washingtonpost.com/news/monkey-cage/wp/2015/01/22/is-public-funding-really-electing-extremists/?utm_term=.2bdd6bb2f000. Accessed 9 June 2016.

Mayhew, David R. 1974. *Congress: The Electoral Connection*. New Haven, CT: Yale University Press.

McCarty, Nolan. 2015. "Reducing Polarization by Making Parties Stronger." In *Solutions to Political Polarization in America*, ed. Nathan Persily. New York: Cambridge University Press.

McCarty, Nolan, Keith Poole, and Howard Rosenthal. 2006. *Polarized America: The Dance of Ideology and Unequal Riches*. Cambridge, MA: Massachusetts Institute of Technology Press.

McCarty, Nolan, Keith T. Poole, and Howard Rosenthal. 2009. "Does Gerrymandering Cause Polarization?" *American Journal of Political Science* 53(3): 666–80.

McGhee, Eric, Seth Masket, Boris Shor, Steve Rogers, and Nolan McCarty. 2014. "A Primary Cause of Partisanship? Nomination Systems and Legislator Ideology." *American Journal of Political Science* 58(2): 337–51.

McIntyre, Joyce K. 2000. "New York State of Mind: After Running Family Business, Amory Houghton Serves as Renegade U.S. Representative." *Harvard Crimson* 5 June 2000. http://www.thecrimson.com/article/2000/6/5/new-york-state-of-mind-after/. Accessed 19 June 2013.

Mettler, Suzanne. 2005. *Soldiers to Citizens: The G.I. Bill and the Making of the Greatest Generation*. New York: Oxford University Press.

Mettler, Suzanne. 2011. *The Submerged State: How Invisible Government Policies Undermine American Democracy*. Chicago: University of Chicago Press.

Meyer, Theodoric. 2016. "Inside the Freedom Caucus' Growth Plans." *Politico* 3 April 2016. http://www.politico.com/story/2016/04/freedom-caucus-house -conservatives-221481. Accessed 9 June 2016.

Moore, Michael K. and John R. Hibbing. 1998. "Situational Dissatisfaction in Congress: Explaining Voluntary Departures." *Journal of Politics* 60(4): 1088–1107.

National Conference of State Legislatures. 2013. "Number of State Legislators and Length of Terms (in Years)." http://www.ncsl.org/research/about-statelegislatures/number-of-legislators-and-length-of-terms.aspx. Accessed January 2013.

National Conference of State Legislatures (NCSL). 2015. "Overview of State Laws on Public Financing." http://www.ncsl.org/research/ elections-and-campaigns/public-financing-of-campaigns-overview.aspx# candidates. Accessed January 2015.

Neely, Brett. 2011. "Ellison's Tune-Up of Caucus Could Shift Democratic Party." *MPRnews* 5 October 2011. http://www.mprnews.org/story/2011/ 10/05/ellison-progressive-caucus. Accessed 9 June 2016.

Newport, Frank. 2016. "Americans Favor Idea of Increased Overtime Eligibility." *Gallup* 3 June 2016. http://www.gallup.com/poll/192287/americans -favor-idea-increased-overtime-eligibility.aspx. Accessed 9 June 2016.

Newport, Frank and Joy Wilke. 2013. "Immigration Reform Proposals Garner Broad Support in U.S." *Gallup* 19 June 2013. http://www.gallup.com/ poll/163169/immigration-reform-proposals-garner-broad-support.aspx. Accessed 23 March 2014.

Niven, David. 1998. "Party Elites and Women Candidates: The Shape of Bias." *Women and Politics* 19(2): 57–80.

Norrander, Barbara. 1989. "Ideological Representativeness of Presidential Primary Voters." *American Journal of Political Science* 33(3): 570–87.

O'Brien, Cortney. 2015. "'Disturbed' by Planned Parenthood Video, House GOP Launch Investigation." *Townhall* 15 July 2015. http://townhall.com /tipsheet/cortneyobrien/2015/07/15/house-gop-disturbed-by-planned-parent hood-video-launch-investigation-n2025903. Accessed 9 June 2016.

Ornstein, Norman J., Thomas E. Mann, Michael J. Malbin, Andrew Rugg, and Raffaela Wakeman. 2014. *Vital Statistics on Congress*. Washington, DC: Brookings Institution.

Osborn, Tracy L. 2012. *How Women Represent Women: Political Parties, Representation, and Gender in the State Legislatures*. New York: Oxford University Press.

Palmer, Barbara and Dennis Simon. 2008. *Breaking the Political Glass Ceiling: Women and Congressional Elections*, 2nd ed. New York: Routledge.

Patterson, Samuel C. 1963. "Legislative Leadership and Political Ideology." *Public Opinion Quarterly* 27(3): 399–410.

Pearson, Kathryn. 2015. *Party Discipline in the U.S. House of Representatives*. Ann Arbor, MI: University of Michigan Press.

Persily, Nathan. 2015a. *Solutions to Political Polarization in America*, ed. Nathan Persily. New York: Cambridge University Press.

Persily, Nathan. 2015b. "Stronger Parties as a Solution to Polarization." In *Solutions to Political Polarization in America*, ed. Nathan Persily. New York: Cambridge University Press.

Pew Research Center. 2014. Political Polarization in the American Public. Washington, DC: Pew Research Center.

Pildes, Richard H. 2015. "Focus on Political Fragmentation, Not Polarization: Re-empower Party Leadership." In *Solutions to Political Polarization in America*, ed. Nathan Persily. New York: Cambridge University Press.

Polsby, Nelson W. 2004. *How Congress Evolves: Social Bases of Institutional Change*. New York: Oxford University Press.

Poole, Keith T. 1998. "Changing Minds? Not in Congress!" GSIA Working Paper 1997–22. Carnegie–Mellon University.

Poole, Keith T. and Howard Rosenthal. 2007. *Ideology and Congress*. New Brunswick, NJ: Transaction Publishers.

Povich, Elaine S. 1993. "GOP House Leader Rep. Michel To Retire: Peoria Lawmaker Known for Conciliatory Style." *Chicago Tribune* 5 October 1993. http://articles.chicagotribune.com/1993-10-05/news/9310050149-1-michel-veto-strategy-house-floor. Accessed September 2015.

Prior, Markus and Natalie Jomini Stroud. 2015. "Using Mobilization, Media, and Motivation to Curb Political Polarization." In *Solutions to Political Polarization in America*, ed. Nathan Persily. New York: Cambridge University Press.

Project Vote Smart. 2016. "Candidate Ratings and Endorsements." Project Vote Smart. http://votesmart.org/officials/NA/C/national-congressional#.WHK3vtw7XV0. Accessed 9 June 2016.

Ramirez, Mark D. 2009. "The Dynamics of Partisan Conflict on Congressional Approval." *American Journal of Political Science* 53(3): 681–94.

Riffkin, Rebecca. 2014. "2014 U.S. Approval of Congress Remains Near All-Time Low." *Gallup* 30 January 2014. Web. Accessed 23 March 2014.

Ripley, Randall B. 1967. *Party Leaders in the House of Representatives*. Washington, DC: Brookings Institution.

Roberts, Jason M. and Steven S. Smith. 2003. "Procedural Contexts, Party Strategy, and Conditional Party Voting in the U.S. House of Representatives, 1971–2000." *American Journal of Political Science* 47(2): 305–17.

Rodgers, Bethany. 2012. "Beverly Byron Watches a New Face Enter a Divided House." *The Frederick News-Post* 30 December 2012. http://www.fredericknewspost.com/news/beverly-byron-watches-a-new-face-enter-a-divided-house/article_468c1ed2-8c6b-5e81-bac4-d96fe5b5ef53.html. Accessed September 2015.

Rogowski, Jon C. and Stephanie Langella. 2014. "Primary Systems and Candidate Ideology: Evidence from Federal and State Legislative Elections." *American Politics Research* 43(5): 846–71.

Rohde, David W. 1979. "Risk-Bearing and Progressive Ambition: The Case of Members of the United States House of Representatives." *American Journal of Political Science* 23(1): 1–26.

Rohde, David W. 1991. *Parties and Leaders in the Postreform House.* Chicago: University of Chicago Press.

Rohde, David W. 2016. "Reflections on the Complex Causes and Probable Persistence of Political Polarization in the U.S." Presented at the Richard Lugar Symposium on Political Polarization, Denison University, Granville, OH.

Rohde, David and John Aldrich. 2010. "Consequences of Electoral and Institutional Change: The Evolution of Conditional Party Government in the U.S. House of Representatives." In *New Directions in American Political Parties,* ed. Jeffrey M. Stonecash. New York: Routledge.

Rohde, David W. and Kenneth A. Shepsle. 1973. "Democratic Committee Assignments in the House of Representatives: Strategic Aspects of a Social Choice Process." *American Political Science Review* 67(3): 889–905.

Rosin, Hanna and Noreen Malone. 2010. "The Mama Grizzlies You Don't Know." *Slate* 12 November 2010. http://www.slate.com/articles/double_x/doublex/2010/11/the_mama_grizzlies_you_dont_know.html. Accessed 23 March 2014.

Rubin, Ruth Bloch. 2013. "Organizing for Insurgency: Intraparty Organization and the Development of the House Insurgency, 1908–1910." *Studies in American Political Development* 27(2): 86–110.

Saad, Lydia. 2013. "Gridlock Is Top Reason Americans Are Critical of Congress." *Gallup* 12 June 2013. http://www.gallup.com/poll/163031/gridlock-top-reason-americans-critical-congress.aspx. Accessed 23 March 2014.

Sanbonmatsu, Kira. 2006. *Where Women Run: Gender and Party in the American States.* Ann Arbor, MI: University of Michigan Press.

Schattschneider, Elmer E. 1942. *Party Government.* New York: Holt, Rinehart and Winston.

Schlesinger, Joseph A. 1966. *Ambition and Politics: Political Careers in the United States.* Chicago: Rand McNally.

Schoeneman, Brian. 2014. "Why on Earth Would Anybody Ever Want to Run for Office Today?" *Bearing Drift: Virginia's Conservative Voice.* https://bearingdrift.com/2014/09/11/why-on-earth-would-anybody-ever-run-for-office-today/. Accessed September 2015.

Schreiber, Ronnee. 2012. "Mama Grizzlies Compete for Office." *New Political Science* 34(4): 549–63.

Schreiber, Ronnee. 2014. "Conservative Women Candidates." In *Women and Elective Office*, 3rd ed., eds. Sue Thomas and Clyde Wilcox. New York: Oxford University Press.

Seitz-Wald, Alex. 2015. "Keith Ellison Hands Bernie Sanders His Second Congressional Endorsement." *MSNBC* 12 October 2015. http://www.msnbc.com/msnbc/keith-ellison-hands-bernie-sanders-his-second-congressional-endorsment. Accessed 9 June 2016.

Seltzer, Richard A., Jody Newman, and Melissa Voorhees Leighton. 1997. *Sex as a Political Variable: Women as Candidates and Voters in U.S. Elections.* Boulder, CO: Lynne Reinner.

Shames, Shauna. 2017. *Out of the Running: Why Millennials Reject Political Careers and Why It Matters.* New York: New York University Press.

Sherman, Jake. 2012. "Candice Miller to Lead House Panel." *Politico* 30 November 2012. http://www.politico.com/story/2012/11/with-candice-miller-appointment-woman-will-lead-house-committee-after-all-084460. Accessed 9 June 2016.

Shor, Boris and Nolan McCarty. 2011. "The Ideological Mapping of American Legislatures." *American Political Science Review* 105(3): 530–51.

Sides, John and Lynn Vavreck. 2013. "On the Representativeness of Primary Electorates." Presented at the Conference on Political Representation: Fifty Years after Miller and Stokes, Vanderbilt University, Nashville, TN.

Sinclair, Barbara. 1995. *Legislators, Leaders, and Lawmaking: The U.S. House of Representatives in the Postreform Era.* Baltimore: Johns Hopkins University Press.

Sinclair, Barbara. 2006. *Party Wars: Polarization and the Politics of National Policy Making.* Norman, OK: University of Oklahoma Press.

Skocpol, Theda and Vanessa Williamson. 2011. *The Tea Party and the Remaking of Republican Conservatism.* New York: Oxford University Press

Smidt, Corwin D. Forthcoming. "Polarization and the Decline of the American Floating Voter." *American Journal of Political Science.*

Smith, Steven S. and Bruce A. Ray. 1983. "The Impact of Congressional Reform: House Democratic Committee Assignments." *Congress & The Presidency* 10(2): 219–40.

Sniderman, Paul M., and Edward H. Stiglitz. 2012. *The Reputational Premium: A Theory of Party Identification and Policy Reasoning.* Princeton, NJ: Princeton University Press.

Snyder, James M. and Michael M. Ting. 2002. "An Informational Rationale for Political Parties." *American Journal of Political Science* 46(1): 90–110.

Sorauf, Frank J. 1980. "Political Parties and Political Action Committees: Two Life Cycles." *Arizona Law Review* 22(2): 445–64.

Soss, Joe. 1999. "Lessons of Welfare: Policy Design, Political Learning, and Political Action." *American Political Science Review* 93(2): 363–80.

Stimson, James A., Michael B. MacKuen, and Robert S. Erikson. 1995. Dynamic Representation. *American Political Science Review* 89(3): 543–65.

Stone, Walter J., and L. Sandy Maisel. 2003. "The Not-So-Simple Calculus of Winning: Potential U.S. House Candidates' Nomination and General Election Chances." *Journal of Politics* 65(4): 951–977.

Stone, Walter J., L. Sandy Maisel, and Cherie D. Maestas. 2004. "Quality Counts: Extending the Strategic Politician Model of Incumbent Deterrence." *American Journal of Political Science* 48(3): 479–495.

Stone, Walter J. 2010. *2006 Congressional Election Study.* University of California, Davis, CA. (http://electionstudy.ucdavis.edu/)

Stonecash, Jeffrey M., Mark D. Brewer, and Mark D. Mariani. 2003. *Diverging Parties: Social Change, Realignment, and Party Polarization.* Boulder, CO: Westview Press.

Strong, Jonathan. 2013. "The Tuesday Group Still Lives." *National Review* 20 June 2013. Web. Accessed 9 June 2016.

Swers, Michele L. 2002. *The Difference Women Make: The Policy Impact of Women in Congress.* Chicago: The University of Chicago Press.

Swers, Michele L. 2013. *Women in the Club: Gender and Policy Making in the Senate*. Chicago: University of Chicago Press.

Swers, Michele L. and Carin Larson. 2005. "Women in Congress: Do They Act as Advocates for Women's Issues?" In *Women and Elective Office: Past, Present, and Future*, eds. Sue Thomas and Clyde Wilson. New York: Oxford University Press.

Tausanovitch, Chris and Christopher Warshaw. 2013. "Measuring Constituent Policy Preferences in Congress, State Legislatures, and Cities." *Journal of Politics* 75(2): 330–42.

Theriault, Sean M. 2006. "Party Polarization in the U.S. Congress: Member Replacement and Member Adaptation." *Party Politics* 12(4): 483–503.

Theriault, Sean M. 2008. *Party Polarization in Congress*. New York: Cambridge University Press.

Theriault, Sean M. 2013. *The Gingrich Senators: The Roots of Partisan Warfare in Congress*. New York: Oxford University Press.

Thomsen, Danielle M. 2014. "Ideological Moderates Won't Run: How Party Fit Matters for Partisan Polarization in Congress." *Journal of Politics* 76(3): 786–87.

Thomsen, Danielle M. 2015. "Why So Few (Republican) Women? Explaining the Partisan Imbalance of Women in the U.S. Congress." *Legislative Studies Quarterly* 40(2): 295–323.

Wasniewski, Matthew A. 2006. *Women in Congress, 1917–2006*. Office of History and Preservation, Office of the Clerk, U.S. House of Representatives. Prepared under the direction of the Committee on House Administration of the U.S. House of Representatives. House Document 108–223, Government Printing Office, Washington, DC.

Weiner, Rachel. 2016. "Why Emily's List is Spending Big to Defeat a Progressive Democrat." *Washington Post* 24 March 2016. Web. Accessed 9 June 2016.

Wolbrecht, Christina. 2000. *The Politics of Women's Rights: Parties, Positions, and Change*. Princeton, NJ: Princeton University Press.

Wolbrecht, Christina. 2002. "Female Legislators and the Women's Rights Agenda: From Feminine Mystique to Feminist Era." In *Women Transforming Congress*, ed. Cindy Simon Rosenthal. Norman, OK: University of Oklahoma Press.

Zwick, Jesse. 2011. "Tuesday Mourning." *New Republic* 29 January 2011. https://newrepublic.com/article/82420/tuesday-group-gop. Accessed 23 March 2014.

# Index